First World War
and Army of Occupation
War Diary
France, Belgium and Germany

51 DIVISION
Divisional Troops
400 Field Company Royal Engineers
21 April 1915 - 10 April 1919

WO95/2855/1b

The Naval & Military Press Ltd
www.nmarchive.com
Published in association with The National Archives

Published by

The Naval & Military Press Ltd

Unit 10 Ridgewood Industrial Park,

Uckfield, East Sussex,

TN22 5QE England

Tel: +44 (0) 1825 749494

www.naval-military-press.com

www.nmarchive.com

This diary has been reprinted in facsimile from the original. Any imperfections are inevitably reproduced and the quality may fall short of modern type and cartographic standards.

© Crown Copyright
Images reproduced by permission of The National Archives, London, England, 2015.

Contents

Document type	Place/Title	Date From	Date To
Heading	WO95/2855 Apr 1915-Apr 1919 400 Field Co Royal Engineers		
Heading	51st Division 400th (H' Land) Fld Coy Re. Apr 1915-Apr 1919		
Heading	51st Division 1/1 Highland Field Coy RE Vol I 21.4.15-31.7.15		
War Diary	Bedford	21/04/1915	02/05/1915
War Diary	Southampton	02/05/1915	02/05/1915
War Diary	Havre	03/05/1915	04/05/1915
War Diary	Buchy	04/05/1915	04/05/1915
War Diary	Merville	05/05/1915	05/05/1915
War Diary	Chat. Des Quesnoys	05/05/1915	06/05/1915
War Diary	Paradis	07/05/1915	14/05/1915
War Diary	Busnes	14/05/1915	14/05/1915
War Diary	Meteren	14/05/1915	17/05/1915
War Diary	Neuf Berquin	18/05/1915	19/05/1915
War Diary	La Gorgue	20/05/1915	20/05/1915
War Diary	La Coutre	20/05/1915	31/05/1915
War Diary	Le Touret	01/06/1915	26/06/1915
War Diary	Nouveau Monde	27/06/1915	25/07/1915
War Diary	La Gorgue	26/07/1915	26/07/1915
War Diary	La Houssoye	27/07/1915	31/07/1915
War Diary	Martinsart	31/07/1915	31/07/1915
Heading	War Diary 1/1st Highland Field Co. From 1st May 1915 To 31st August 1915		
Heading	51st Division 1/1 Highland Field Coy R.E Vol II August 15		
Heading	War Diary Of 1/1st Highland Field Co R.E. From 1st August 1915 To 31st August 1915 Volume II		
War Diary	Martinsart	01/08/1915	13/08/1915
War Diary	Bouzincourt	14/08/1915	31/08/1915
Heading	51st Division 1/1 Highland Field Coy. R.E Vol III Sept15		
War Diary	Bouzincourt	01/09/1915	30/09/1915
Heading	War Diary Of O.C 1/1st Highland Field Co. R.E. From 1st October 1915 To 31st October 1915 Vol IV		
War Diary	Bouzincourt	01/10/1915	31/10/1915
Heading	War Diary Of The 1/1st Highland Field Co. R.E. 51st Division 10th Corps IIIrd Army From 1st November 1915 To 30th November 1915 Vol V		
War Diary	Bouzincourt	01/11/1915	30/11/1915
Heading	51st Div 1/1st High F. Co, R.E. Dec Vol VI		
War Diary	Bouzincourt	01/12/1915	11/12/1915
War Diary	Fremont	26/12/1915	31/12/1915
War Diary	Bouzincourt	12/12/1915	22/12/1915
War Diary	St. Gratien	23/12/1915	23/12/1915
War Diary	Fremont	24/12/1915	25/12/1915
Heading	1/1 Highland Fd Coy R.E. Jan 1916 Vol VII		
War Diary	Fremont	01/01/1916	05/02/1916
War Diary	Corbie	06/02/1916	07/02/1916

War Diary	Sailly-Le-Sec.	08/02/1916	27/02/1916
War Diary	Daours	28/02/1916	28/02/1916
War Diary	Flesselles	29/02/1916	06/03/1916
War Diary	Autheux	07/03/1916	08/03/1916
War Diary	Hem	09/03/1916	09/03/1916
War Diary	Beudricourt	10/03/1916	11/03/1916
War Diary	Maroeuil	12/03/1916	30/06/1916
Heading	War Diary Of 1/1st High Field Co R.E. From 1st July 1916 To 31st July 1916		
War Diary	Maroeuil	01/07/1916	13/07/1916
War Diary	L' Albert De Neuville Due	14/07/1916	15/07/1916
War Diary	Bouquemaison	15/07/1916	16/07/1916
War Diary	Barlette	17/07/1916	19/07/1916
War Diary	Montonvillers	20/07/1916	20/07/1916
War Diary	Buire Sur L'Ancre	21/07/1916	21/07/1916
War Diary	F.2.c.5.0	22/07/1916	25/07/1916
War Diary	F.2.c.5.0 Sheet 62 D N.E	25/07/1916	31/07/1916
Heading	51st Divisional Engineers 1/1st Highland Field Company R.E August 1916		
War Diary	F.2.c.5.0 Sheet 62 D N.E	01/08/1916	06/08/1916
War Diary	D 12d22	06/08/1916	09/08/1916
War Diary	Poulainville	09/08/1916	09/08/1916
War Diary	Surel	10/08/1916	12/08/1916
War Diary	Racquinghem	12/08/1916	16/08/1916
War Diary	Armentiers	17/08/1916	31/08/1916
Heading	War Diary Of 1/1st High Field Co R.E. For September 1916		
War Diary	Armentieres	01/09/1916	22/09/1916
War Diary	Erquinghem	23/09/1916	24/09/1916
War Diary	Meteren	25/09/1916	30/09/1916
Heading	War Diary Of 1/1st Highland Field Co. R.E 51st Division From 1st Oct 1916 To 31st Oct 1916		
War Diary	Meteren	01/10/1916	01/10/1916
War Diary	Beauval	02/10/1916	02/10/1916
War Diary	Louvencourt	03/10/1916	04/10/1916
War Diary	Courcelles	04/10/1916	18/10/1916
War Diary	Forceville	18/10/1916	31/10/1916
Miscellaneous	H.Q 256	02/09/1916	02/09/1916
Heading	War Diary Of 1/1st High Field Co R.E. From November 1916 Vol 17		
War Diary	Forceville	01/11/1916	22/11/1916
War Diary	Puchvillers	22/11/1916	24/11/1916
War Diary	Varennes	24/11/1916	26/11/1916
War Diary	La Boiselle	26/11/1916	30/11/1916
Miscellaneous	C.R.A 51st (H) Div	02/12/1916	02/12/1916
Heading	War Diary Of 1/1st Highland Field Co. R.E (T) From 1st December 1916 To 31st December 1916		
War Diary	La Boiselle	01/12/1916	06/12/1916
War Diary	Wolfe Huts	07/12/1916	08/12/1916
War Diary	Wolseley Huts	09/12/1916	20/12/1916
War Diary	Wolfe Huts	21/12/1916	31/12/1916
Heading	War Diary Of 400th Field Co R.E From 1st Jany 1917 To 31st-Jany 1917		
War Diary	Wolfe Huts	01/01/1917	12/01/1917
War Diary	Beauquesne	13/01/1917	13/01/1917
War Diary	Outrebois	14/01/1917	15/01/1917

War Diary	Conteville	15/01/1917	25/01/1917
War Diary	In The Field	26/01/1917	29/01/1917
War Diary	Arras	30/01/1917	31/01/1917
Heading	War Diary Of 400th Field Co. R.E From 1st Feby 1917 To 28th Feby 1917		
War Diary	Ecoivres	01/02/1917	08/02/1917
War Diary	Arras-St-Pol Road	09/02/1917	25/02/1917
War Diary	ACQ	26/02/1917	28/02/1917
Heading	War Diary Of 400th Field Co R.E. From 1st To 31st March 1917 Vol 21		
War Diary	ACQ	01/03/1917	26/03/1917
War Diary	Maroeuil	27/03/1917	31/03/1917
Heading	War Diary Of 400th (High) Field Co. R.E. For April 1917 Vol 22		
War Diary	Maroeuil	01/04/1917	08/04/1917
War Diary	High St.	09/04/1917	11/04/1917
War Diary	ACQ	12/04/1917	15/04/1917
War Diary	St Nicolas	15/04/1917	16/04/1917
War Diary	L' Abbayette	17/04/1917	18/04/1917
War Diary	Ry. Embankment	19/04/1917	25/04/1917
War Diary	Bailleul Aux Corneilles	26/04/1917	13/05/1917
War Diary	St Laurent Blangy	13/05/1917	31/05/1917
Heading	War Diary Of 400th Field Co. R.E. From 1st To 30th June 1917 Vol 24		
War Diary	L' Abbaye De Neuville Fm	01/06/1917	04/06/1917
War Diary	Sains Les Pernes	04/06/1917	05/06/1917
War Diary	Grueppe	05/06/1917	07/06/1917
War Diary	St Martin Au Laert	07/06/1917	08/06/1917
War Diary	Hellebrouck	08/06/1917	14/06/1917
War Diary	Camp At A.29.b.3.1. Belgium 1/20,000	15/06/1917	16/06/1917
War Diary	Dugouts At C25.a.9.7. Belgium 1/20000	17/06/1917	30/06/1917
Heading	War Diary Of 400th (Highland) Field Company, R.E. T). From 1st July 1917 To 31st July 1917 Vol 25		
War Diary	Dugouts At C.29.a.9.7 Belgium 1/20,000	01/07/1917	06/07/1917
Diagram etc	Diagram		
War Diary	Dugouts At C.29.a.9.7. Belgium 1/20,000	07/07/1917	14/07/1917
War Diary	Chateau De Trois Tours B 28.a.6.2 Sheet 28 Belgium 1/40,000	15/07/1917	15/07/1917
War Diary	Vlamertinghe Chateau H.3.a.0.1 Belgium 1/40,000	16/07/1917	30/07/1917
War Diary	Dugouts At C.29.a.9.7. Belgium 1/20,000	31/07/1917	31/07/1917
War Diary	War Diary Of 400th (Highland) Field Company R.E. For August 1917		
War Diary	Dugouts At C.29.a.9.7. Belgium 1/20,000 Sheet 28 N.W.	01/08/1917	05/08/1917
Diagram etc	Diagram		
War Diary	Dugouts At C.29.a.9.7. Belgium 1/20,000 Sheet 28 N.W.	05/08/1917	06/08/1917
War Diary	Camp At B24d.25.70	07/08/1917	08/08/1917
War Diary	Camp At B24d.25.70. Belgium 1/20,000 Sheet 28.N.W.	09/08/1917	18/08/1917
War Diary	Rear H.Q A 27b 2.3	19/08/1917	29/08/1917
War Diary	Canal Bank	30/08/1917	31/08/1917
Miscellaneous	C.R.E 57th Div.	01/09/1917	01/09/1917
Heading	War Diary Of 400th (Highland) Field Coy. R.E. For September 1917 Vol 27		
War Diary	Ypres Canal Bank W.	01/09/1917	05/09/1917
War Diary	Ypres Canal Bank W. C.19.c.25.20 St Julian 1/10,000	07/09/1917	19/09/1917

War Diary	C 14.C.3.7	20/09/1917	24/09/1917
War Diary	Drookentak Fm A 21a. 9.3	24/09/1917	30/09/1917
Miscellaneous	O.C. 400 Fd Coy R.E		
Miscellaneous	C.R.E 51st Div.	15/09/1917	15/09/1917
Miscellaneous	Orders By O.C 400th (Highland) Field	18/09/1917	18/09/1917
Heading	War Diary Of 400th (Highland) Field Coy. R.E From 1st October 1917 To 31st October 1917 Vol 20		
War Diary	Gomiecourt	01/10/1917	02/10/1917
War Diary	Ref. Sheet France 51.B 1/40,000	02/10/1917	04/10/1917
War Diary	N26.d.68 Ref. Sheet 51b	05/10/1917	29/10/1917
War Diary	Beaulencourt Ref. Sheet Lens 1/100,000	30/10/1917	31/10/1917
Heading	War Diary Of 400th (Highland) Field Coy R.E. For Period 1st November 1917 To 30th November 1917 Vol 29		
War Diary	Beaulencourt Near Bapaume	01/11/1917	01/11/1917
War Diary	Ytres P 26.b.6.3 Sheet 5.7.c 1/40,000	02/11/1917	08/11/1917
War Diary	Ytres P.26.b.60.30	09/11/1917	16/11/1917
War Diary	Havrincourt Wood Q14c4.8 Sheet 57.c	17/11/1917	22/11/1917
War Diary	Hindenburg Line K 36a	22/11/1917	24/11/1917
War Diary	Pioneer Camp P 268.8.5	25/11/1917	26/11/1917
War Diary	Havrincourt Wood Q 14a6.4	27/11/1917	30/11/1917
Heading	War Diary Of 400th (Highland) Field Coy R.E For Period 1st December 1917 To 31st December 1917 Vol 30		
War Diary	Havrincourt Wood	01/12/1917	01/12/1917
War Diary	Q14.a.6.4 Sheet 57c	02/12/1917	02/12/1917
War Diary	Shelters Near Doignies J.16.b.70.80	03/12/1917	04/12/1917
War Diary	Beugny I.16.d.0.2 Sheet 57c	05/12/1917	09/12/1917
Diagram etc	Diagram		
War Diary	Beugny I 16.d.0.2 Sheet 57c	09/12/1917	31/12/1917
Heading	War Diary Of 400th (Highland) Field Coy. R.E For Period 1st January 1918 To 31st January 1918 Vol 31		
War Diary	Beugny I 16 D 0.2 Sheet 57c	01/01/1918	16/01/1918
War Diary	Achiet Le Petit G14a 53 Sheet 57 C	17/01/1918	20/01/1918
War Diary	G.9.d 4.1	21/01/1918	28/01/1918
War Diary	G.9.d 4.1 Sheet 57c	29/01/1918	31/01/1918
Heading	War Diary Of 400th (Highland) Field Coy. R.E For Period 1st February 1918 To 28th February 1918 Vol 32		
War Diary	G.9.d 4.1 Sheet 57c	01/02/1918	10/02/1918
War Diary	Beugny I.15.d.9.0 Sheet 57.c.	11/02/1918	28/02/1918
Miscellaneous	400th (Highland) Field Coy R.E	28/02/1918	28/02/1918
Heading	51st Divisional Engineers 400th Field Company R.E. March 1918		
Heading	War Diary Of 400th (Highland) Field Coy. R.E For Period 1st March 1918 To 31st March 1918 Vol 33		
War Diary	Beugny I.15.d.9.0 Sheet. 57.c	01/03/1918	21/03/1918
War Diary	Beugny I.15.d.9.0	21/03/1918	23/03/1918
War Diary	Beugny	23/03/1918	23/03/1918
War Diary	Grevillers	24/03/1918	24/03/1918
War Diary	Forceville	25/03/1918	25/03/1918
War Diary	Pas	26/03/1918	26/03/1918
War Diary	Barly	27/03/1918	29/03/1918
War Diary	Lapugnoy Sheet Hazebrouck 5 A	30/03/1918	31/03/1918
War Diary	Lapugnoy	31/03/1918	31/03/1918
Miscellaneous	Appendix G	02/03/1918	02/03/1918

Heading	War Diary 400th (Highland) Field Company R.E. April 1918		
Heading	War Diary Of 400th (Highland) Field Co. R.E For April 1918 Vol 34		
War Diary	Lapugnoy	01/04/1918	01/04/1918
War Diary	Hazebrouck 5 A	01/04/1918	03/04/1918
War Diary	Camblain	04/04/1918	04/04/1918
War Diary	Chatelain	05/04/1918	05/04/1918
War Diary	Hazebrouck 5 A	05/04/1918	05/04/1918
War Diary	Burbure	06/04/1918	06/04/1918
War Diary	Hazebrouck 5 A	06/04/1918	08/04/1918
War Diary	Robecq Sheet 36 A 1/40,000	09/04/1918	11/04/1918
War Diary	Robecq Ref 36a S.E	12/04/1918	12/04/1918
War Diary	Robecq	12/04/1918	12/04/1918
War Diary	Busnes P.26.C.3.4 Sheet 36A 1/40,000	13/04/1918	14/04/1918
War Diary	St Hilaire T.6.c.2.1. Sheet 36A 1/40,000	15/04/1918	21/04/1918
War Diary	Labiette Farm P27b.8.0	22/04/1918	23/04/1918
War Diary	Labiette Fm P27b.8.0 Sheet 36A 1/40,000	24/04/1918	26/04/1918
Diagram etc	Diagram		
War Diary	P27b.8.0. Sheet 36a 1/40,000	26/04/1918	30/04/1918
Miscellaneous	400th High Field Coy. R.E	30/04/1918	30/04/1918
Map	Map		
Heading	War Diary For May 1918 Of The 400th (Highland) Field Company, R.E		
War Diary	La Pierre P.19.a.5.5	01/05/1918	02/05/1918
War Diary	Bourecq U.1.C Sheet 36 B 1/40000	03/05/1918	04/05/1918
War Diary	Ecoivres F13.c 5.5 Sheet 51c 1/40,000	05/05/1918	05/05/1918
War Diary	Ecoivres F13 Central Sheet 1/20,000 Maroeuil	05/05/1918	08/05/1918
War Diary	Ecurie Sheet Maroeuil 1/20,000	08/05/1918	13/05/1918
War Diary	Maroeuil F.27.c.6.6	14/05/1918	18/05/1918
War Diary	Maroeuil	18/05/1918	18/05/1918
War Diary	Coy. H.Q A.27.C.6.6 Maroeuil 14 Sheet 1/20,000	19/05/1918	22/05/1918
War Diary	A 27.C.6.6 Maroeuil Sheet 1/20,000	22/05/1918	31/05/1918
Heading	400th (Highland) Field Coy. R.E. War Diary June 1918 Vol 36		
War Diary	A.27.c.6.6. Maroeuil Sheet 1/20,000	01/06/1918	19/06/1918
War Diary	H.1.c.7.5. Bailleul 1/20,000	20/06/1918	30/06/1918
Heading	Divisional Engineers 51st (Highland) Division 400th Field Co. R.E. July 1918		
Heading	400th (Highland) Field Coy. R.E. War Diary July 1918 Vol 37		
War Diary	H.1.C.75 Bailleul 1/10,000	01/07/1918	10/07/1918
War Diary	Beugin Lens II	11/07/1918	15/07/1918
War Diary	Tinques	15/07/1918	16/07/1918
War Diary	Nogent	16/07/1918	17/07/1918
War Diary	Pierry	17/07/1918	19/07/1918
War Diary	Cumieres Ref-"Chalons 50 Reims" 1/50,000	19/07/1918	20/07/1918
War Diary	N.E. Of Bellevue	20/07/1918	20/07/1918
War Diary	Woods West Of Nanteuil "Reims Chalons" 1/50,000	21/07/1918	24/07/1918
War Diary	B In Bois De Quentin	25/07/1918	27/07/1918
War Diary	Reims Chalon 1/50,000	27/07/1918	28/07/1918
War Diary	Chaumuzy	28/07/1918	30/07/1918
War Diary	St Imoges	31/07/1918	31/07/1918
Heading	War Diary Of 400th (Highland) Field Company R.E. From 1st To 31st August 1918 Vol 38		
War Diary	St. Imoges (Marne)	01/08/1918	01/08/1918

War Diary	Pierry	02/08/1918	03/08/1918
War Diary	Calonne-Ricouart Lens II	04/08/1918	04/08/1918
War Diary	Bowvigny	05/08/1918	18/08/1918
War Diary	G16b.77 (St Michaels)	18/08/1918	20/08/1918
War Diary	G16b.77	21/08/1918	26/08/1918
War Diary	H 1.C.65.35	27/08/1918	31/08/1918
Heading	War Diary Of 400th (Highland) Field Coy R.E. From 1st September To 30th September 1918 Vol 39		
War Diary	H 1 C 60 35	01/09/1918	13/09/1918
War Diary	Villers Au Bois X 19 Sheet 44 B	14/09/1918	14/09/1918
War Diary	Villers Au Bois	15/09/1918	24/09/1918
War Diary	Ecurie	25/09/1918	25/09/1918
War Diary	Pond Du Jour H 3 C 51 Sheet 57 B	26/09/1918	26/09/1918
War Diary	Pont Du Jour	27/09/1918	28/09/1918
War Diary	Fampoux H 23a.90.65	29/09/1918	30/09/1918
Heading	War Diary Of 400th (Highland) Field Coy. R.E. From 1st October 1918 To 31st October 1918		
War Diary	Fampoux (H 23a.90.65)	01/10/1918	02/10/1918
War Diary	Ecurie (A27 C7.2)	03/10/1918	07/10/1918
War Diary	Ecurie	08/10/1918	08/10/1918
War Diary	V 25 C.70	09/10/1918	10/10/1918
War Diary	E6 C21	11/10/1918	11/10/1918
War Diary	S 20C.15	12/10/1918	14/10/1918
War Diary	Thun St Martin	15/10/1918	19/10/1918
War Diary	Lieu St Amand	20/10/1918	21/10/1918
War Diary	Douchy	22/10/1918	31/10/1918
Heading	War Diary Of 400th (Highland) Field Coy From 1st November To 30th November 1918 Vol 41		
War Diary	Paillencourt N. 19.d.88 (Sheet 51.A)	01/11/1918	01/11/1918
War Diary	Neuville St Remy A.3.a.9.8 (Sheet 57B 1/40,000)	02/11/1918	12/11/1918
War Diary	Paillencourt N. 19c4.1 (Sheet 51A) 1/40,000)	13/11/1918	13/11/1918
War Diary	Paillencourt N.19c4.1	14/11/1918	25/11/1918
War Diary	Paillencourt N.19c4.1. (Sheet. 51a)1/40,000	26/11/1918	30/11/1918
Heading	War Diary Of 400th (Highland) Field Coy. R.E. For December 1918 Vol 42		
War Diary	Paillencourt N.19.C.H.I Sheet 51A 1/40,000	01/12/1918	31/12/1918
Heading	War Diary Of 400th (Highland) Field Coy. R.E. For January 1919 Vol 43		
War Diary	Paillencourt N.19.c4.1 Sheet 51a 1/40,000	01/01/1919	09/01/1919
War Diary	Manage I 1.C.5.2 Sheet 46 Belgium 1/40,000	10/01/1919	20/01/1919
War Diary	Manage I.1.C.5.2. Sheet 46 1/40,000	21/01/1919	31/01/1919
Heading	War Diary Of 400th (Highland) Field Coy. R.E. For February 1919 Vol 44		
War Diary	Manage I 1.C.5.2 Sheet 46 Belgium	01/02/1919	28/02/1919
Heading	War Diary Of 400th (Highland) Field Coy. R.E For March 1919 Vol 45		
War Diary	Manage I.1.C.5.2. Sheet 46 Belgium	01/03/1919	31/03/1919
Heading	War Diary Of 400th (Highland) Field Coy. R.E From 1/4/19 To 10/4/19 Inclusive		
War Diary	Manage I 1.C.5.2 (Sheet 46 Belgium)	01/04/1919	08/04/1919
War Diary	Dunkirk	08/04/1919	10/04/1919

① WO95/2855

Apr 1915 – Apr 1919

400 Field Co. Royal Engineers

51ST DIVISION

400TH (H'LAND) FLD COY RE.
APR 1915-APR 1919

121/6357

51st Division

1/1 Highland Field Coy RE

Vol I 21.4.15 — 31.7.15

WAR DIARY
or
INTELLIGENCE SUMMARY.
(Erase heading not required.)

Army Form C. 2118.

Instructions regarding War Diaries and Intelligence Summaries are contained in F. S. Regs., Part II. and the Staff Manual respectively. Title pages will be prepared in manuscript.

Place	Date	Hour	Summary of Events and Information	Remarks and references to Appendices
	1915			
BEDFORD	29/3/15		Receiving & packing stores for mobilization in fine weather	
	30/3/15		Capt. Barr sent ahead with advance party	
	1/4/15		Completed mobilization with small references	
	2 Sun		1/2 Coy entrained 2.15 A.M. 1/2 Coy 3.15 A.M. difficulty with horses — N.B. stored away with R.T.O. journey	
	"		1/2 Coy arrived 8 A.M. & 9 A.M.	
SOUTHAMPTON	"		Embarked 3 officers 92 O.R. 75 horses 10 wags. 34 bicycles on s/s MATHURAN - N° 8120	Base Details
	"		" 2 " 118 " " " " " " " on s/s GOLDEN EAGLE N° 1268	Left Corps. Inscine Stores
	"	5 p.m.	Left SOUTHAMPTON	Sgt. Arthurton - Clerk
HAVRE	3 Mon.	Noon	Arrived - disembarking all afternoon - Toured Company - very wet	
	"	6 p.m.	Went to Rest Camp N° 5 - Interpreter Soldat René Bordier - 90 Terr.l. Inf. reported	
	"	9.45	Left Rest Camp for Gare des Marchandises Point 4	
	4 Tues	1.30 AM	Completed entraining - 2.59 A.M. left HAVRE - 6.58 A.M. at DARNETAL detached truck 17:275 with 5 wags.	Ht. 8. y. te
BUCHY	"	8.30	Watered & fed horses - watered men - 2.40 p.m. ABANCLE - interned R.T.O. re wagon - Interested	
			via St OMER - HAZEBROUCK to	
MERVILLE	5 Wed	12.15 AM	Detrained - met Major Kerr of Signals	
		3.00 AM	Marched by road via BUSNES to billets at CHÂT" DES QUESNOYS - (Commune BUSNES)	S.M.

1577 Wt. W10791/1773 500,000 1/15 D.D. & L. A.D.S.S./Forms/C. 2118.

Army Form C. 2118.

WAR DIARY
or
INTELLIGENCE SUMMARY.
(Erase heading not required.)

Instructions regarding War Diaries and Intelligence Summaries are contained in F.S. Regs., Part II. and the Staff Manual respectively. Title pages will be prepared in manuscript.

Place	Date	Hour	Summary of Events and Information	Remarks and references to Appendices
CHAT. DES QUESNOYS	5 Wed	1.00 AM	Reached Billets after ditching & bringing behinds - Horses in Orchard - men & Officers in farm houses	
	6 Thur		Route March - very wet -	
		6.00 pm	Instructions received send billeting party PARADIS	
		7.25	Reached starting point in BUSNES with Company - joined 2nd Inf. Bng. - H.Q. wag: Mules	
PARADIS	7 Fri	3 AM	Reached Billets - Farm 1/2 mile Charlet - 1 mile S. PARADIS	
		8.30	Paraded Coy. Supply Wag; R.Q. Mag: both up.	
		8 p.m.	Orders to be ready next morning - 11 pm orders cancelled.	
	8 Sat		Packing up preparing for 1 hours notice	
	9 Sun	5 AM	Great bombardment commenced - shelling by all day.	
	10 Mon		Orders 2 hrs notice to 4pm afterwards 1 hrs. notice	
	11 Tues	f.m 11.30	Route marching morning - Bridging instruction afternoon	
			Received orders shift back with Brigade to QUESNOY'S in morning	
	12 Wed	8 AM 12.30	Proceeded to starting point - then via Mt BERNENCHON - ROBECQ - BUSNES. arrived at Billets Chat: DES QUESNOY	
	13 Thur	midnt	Received instructions prepare for move morning - later received word pass starting point BUSNES at 9.55 AM	
	14 Fri.			

1577 Wt.W10791/1773 500,000 1/15 D.D.&L. A.D.S.S./Forms/C. 2118.

Army Form C. 2118.

WAR DIARY
or
INTELLIGENCE SUMMARY.
(Erase heading not required.)

Instructions regarding War Diaries and Intelligence Summaries are contained in F. S. Regs., Part II and the Staff Manual respectively. Title pages will be prepared in manuscript.

(3)

Place	Date	Hour	Summary of Events and Information	Remarks and references to Appendices
BUSNES	Fri 14	10 AM	passed starting point - marched via St Venant - MARBECQUE - HAZEBROUCK - CAESTRE & FLETRE	
METEREN		6 p.m.	arrived billets - town 500 yds N.E. of in FLETRE - good billets	
	Sat: 15		Resting / preparing -	
	Sun 16		Route marching & exercising horses	
	Mon 17	3 p.m.	Moved to starting Point Rouge Croix - Joined up with 153rd Bde marched via STAZEELE	
			+ VIEUX BERQUIN to NEUF BERQUIN	
NEUFBERQUIN		8 p.m.	Billets on road in Farm de fond Bois - Commune - DOUZIEU - 200 yds E of Rue Pruvost	
	Tues: 18		Sent in for stores stay to Brig. H.Q. - Field cashier not available	
		6 p.m.	received orders likely to move in evening - 7 w.s.p. received orders starting point close	
			to G.S. MRS - 10.5 p. - 9.10 p.m. left billets - arrived via via road 9.30 p.m. had to wait	
			until 11th Bde passed - moved off 11.30 A.M.	
	Wed 19		Proceeded with 51st Div. via LA GORGUE - 3 p.m. met Field Officer Littlejohn at PETITE	
			FARRIE farm. Monsr. DUCROQUET TRAUNEZ - Comme LA GORGUE - 4 AM	
			Crossed in with field amb. 4 p.m. div. hy passes moving to LA COUTURE	
LA GORGUE	Thurs: 20		Haveguyan - 3.15 p.m. Received word proceed LA COUTURE - Confusion about billets -	
			Billets with 1/2 F.A.Co. Corner de St VAAST - met Maj. Wilson & F. Anglian field Co	

1577 Wt. W10791/1773 500,000 7/15 D.D.& L. A.D.S.S./Forms/C. 2118.

Army Form C. 2118.

WAR DIARY
or
INTELLIGENCE SUMMARY.
(Erase heading not required.)

Instructions regarding War Diaries and Intelligence Summaries are contained in F. S. Regs., Part II. and the Staff Manual respectively. Title pages will be prepared in manuscript.

Place	Date	Hour	Summary of Events and Information	Remarks and references to Appendices
LACOUTURE	MAY			
	Thur 20		2 Sections on night work repairing communications + receiving instructions	
	Fri 21		Whole Company out	
	Sat 22		Tried to push out line on right - failed for ditch	
	Sun 23		Pushed out from advanced post to right + left	
	Mon 24		Working at — D⁰	
	Tues 25		D⁰ — Delays owing Regiment changes & troops.	
	Wed 26		D⁰ New C.R.E. Major Weeks, vice Col. Spencer.	
	Thur 27		3rd Brigade up - Brig." Several Albert	
	Fri 28		Got on better with work - working parties better organized	
	Sat 29		Tracing out & working on new advanced lines - bridging ditches + joining with Canadians on left - Lieut Hamilton - 20th Coy Sappers & Miners assisting.	
	Sun 30		Transced to shifting to new line - Lt Russell taking over - Lt Cleghorn NCC on wiring communications	
	Mon 31		Aircraft one killed - said to have been signalling - billet shelled - advanced post sent out to new billet 9am	
	JUNE			
	Tues 1		Lieut Russell getting information from Canadian Div. Billeted in farm in RUE DE BOIS - farm on fire last night	
LE TOURET	Wed 2		Lieut Cleghorn lost last night on night wiring to Indian Village - looking in communications	
	Thur 3		attack further down line left in W Div. - heavy bombardment - little work done	
	Fri 4		Working party 1&2 men in Communications - men not yet accustomed but fair amount done Major Jackson wounded working 9.30p.m. to 1.45 A.M.	SAA

Army Form C. 2118.

WAR DIARY
or
INTELLIGENCE SUMMARY.
(Erase heading not required.)

Instructions regarding War Diaries and Intelligence Summaries are contained in F. S. Regs., Part II. and the Staff Manual respectively. Title pages will be prepared in manuscript.

Place	Date	Hour	Summary of Events and Information	Remarks and references to Appendices
LOOS	1915 June Sat 5		Capt. Barr - Lieut Laing, Lieut Day sketches - Working party 300 on Communications.	
	Sun 6		Lieut Russell - Lieut McCrone & Self recon'g Parties	
	Mon 7		Communications { that difficult	
	Tues 8		D° { with working parties - Lieut Russell doing very good work	
	Wed 9		Same work on Working Parties - confusion with infantry - Little work done	
	Thurs 10		Very wet - thunder & lightning - no work done - delays with wiring - Sap'r Bordyer hit earth wires -	
	Fri 11		1 Sect. Communications - 1 Sect. front line - Lieut Day doing good work	
	Sat 12		D°	
	Sun 13		D°	
	Mon 14		D° - 2 Lieut. McCrae & No II Sect. detailed for special work in assault	
	Tues 15		Assault took place - N° IV Sect. not called upon	
	Wed 16		Preparing for further movements - See a. m.	
	Thur 17		No further more.	
	Fri 18		Communication now improved.	
	Sat 19		D°	
	Sun 20		3 Sections working - Consolidating front line Communications	

1577 Wt. W10791/1773 500,000 1/15 D. D. & L. A.D.S.S./Forms/C. 2118.

Army Form C. 2118.

WAR DIARY
or
INTELLIGENCE SUMMARY.
(Erase heading not required.)

Instructions regarding War Diaries and Intelligence Summaries are contained in F. S. Regs., Part II. and the Staff Manual respectively. Title pages will be prepared in manuscript.

Place	Date	Hour	Summary of Events and Information	Remarks and references to Appendices
LE TOURET	June Mon 21		3 Sections moving - Communications Support lines	
	Tue 22		D⁰ - Sapper Robertson - W. N⁰ 8990 - Killed - Sapper Dignus. R - N⁰ 8901 wounded severely	
	Wed 23		D⁰ - Buried Sapper Robertson - Le Touret Country N⁰ 2 - Grave 14 - Row 3 -	
	Thu 24		D⁰ - Communication Trench - Support about finished	
	Fri 25		D⁰ D⁰	
	Sat 26		Packing up & Preparing to move - 7.30 p.m. moved via LE TOURET - LA COUTURE - RIFLE CHARGES to starting Point ZELOBES at 9.0 p.m. thence via LA GORGUE & ESTAIRES to farm near NOUVEAU MONDE, where billeted for night arriving 11.30 p.m.	
NOUVEAU MONDE	Sun 27		Shifted at noon to Chemical Works at NOUVEAU MONDE - Lieut. Milroy & Lieut. Williams taken to Hospital	
	Mon 28		3 Sections on night work - night & left of FAUQUISSART improving dug outs	
			D⁰ D⁰	
	Tues 29		D⁰ D⁰ Started new support line	
	Wed 30		D⁰ D⁰ D⁰	
	July Thu 1		D⁰ D⁰	
	Fri 2		D⁰ D⁰	
	Sat 3		D⁰ D⁰ Started new support line on left	

Army Form C. 2118.

WAR DIARY
or
INTELLIGENCE SUMMARY.
(Erase heading not required.)

Instructions regarding War Diaries and Intelligence Summaries are contained in F. S. Regs., Part II. and the Staff Manual respectively. Title pages will be prepared in manuscript.

Place	Date	Hour	Summary of Events and Information	Remarks and references to Appendices
NOUVEAU MONDE	July 1915 Sun 4		3 Sections on night work - Support Trench - Sapper Ivan wounded - not serious	
"	M. 5		2 D° D°	
"	Tu. 6		Lieut: Lewis transferred temporarily to 2/L It. F. Co. Lieut: McGuire the militiaman returned from Hospital 2 Sections on night work - Support Trench - 1 Sect. repairing Breastwork	
"	Wed 7		D° - 2 Sections bay work in Post 5	
"	Thu 8		D° D° Sapper Bell - N°5 Section wounded	
"	Fri. 9		D° D°	
"	Sat. 10		D° D° - went over works with Maj. Freeman	
"	Sun. 11		D° D°	
"	Mon. 12		D° D°	
"	Tues. 13		1 Section - Maj took Support Trench finishing - D° Commenced work on new lou to Reserve line	
"	Wed. 14		D° - 1 Section on D° night work - Commenced new com. N° 14 - Continued N° 16	
"	Thu. 15		D° D° (1 section) D° D°	
"	Fri. 16		D° Support continued to right of N° 13 - D° D°	
"	Sat. 17		D° D° D°	

1577 Wt. W10791/1773 500,000 1/15 D. D. & L. A.D.S.S./Forms/C. 2118.

Army Form C. 2118.

WAR DIARY
or
INTELLIGENCE SUMMARY.
(Erase heading not required.)

Instructions regarding War Diaries and Intelligence Summaries are contained in F. S. Regs., Part II. and the Staff Manual respectively. Title pages will be prepared in manuscript.

Place	Date	Hour	Summary of Events and Information	Remarks and references to Appendices
NOUVEAU MONDE	1915 July S. 18		1 Sect: Daywork Support #3, #4. 1 Sect: night #2, #1. 1 Sect: No 14 - No 16 - Cpl. Stewing sick / Sec wounded.	
"	M. 19		D° D° D° (completed)	
"	T. 20		D° D° D°	
"	W. 21		D° D° D° (complete except #10)	
"	Th. 22		Equipment shift inspection - drill - Baths - #/Cpl. Campbell wounded slightly	
"	Fri. 23		D° D° D°	
"	Sat. 24		D° D° D°	
"	Sun. 25		Practising up - Church Parade Raiding over. Sent wagons to LA GORGUE Station during the afternoon - entrained Company at 8.30 p.m.	
LA GORGUE	Mon. 26	4.30 AM	Left LA GORGUE with 1 Sect. transport, Sanitary Squad - 8.00 a.m. Stopped & drew at CASSIS - 1.30 p.m. Stopped & drew at ABAUMIE Sp.80 detraining (?) Nr. - Left at 3.30 p.m. Column of route for TAROUSSOY - arr. about at TAROU: 7) Bivens LOISON or W. side Church. Heavy rain.	
LA HOUSSOYE	Tues 27		Getting Billet arranged - Company + Section Drill - C°+ 8th Argylls arrives -	
"	WED 28		Called at H.Q. 154" Inf. Brig. at ABOUT MONTGOMERY at 11.00 AM + at Division HQ ARMEDY in afternoon. Company Drill - rajaw.	
"	THUR 29		3 Sections - 3 Bridging teh. + 1 tool cart out all day for bridging	

Army Form C. 2118.

WAR DIARY
or
INTELLIGENCE SUMMARY.
(Erase heading not required.)

Instructions regarding War Diaries and Intelligence Summaries are contained in F. S. Regs., Part II. and the Staff Manual respectively. Title pages will be prepared in manuscript.

Place	Date	Hour	Summary of Events and Information	Remarks and references to Appendices
LA HOUSSOYE	1915 Fri IX 30		Packing up vehicles preparing for further move - advance party sent to MARTINSART.	
	Sat IX 31	4.30 AM	Moved off at 4.30 AM via FRANVILLERS, BAIZIEUX, WARLOY, HENCOURT, FORCEVILLE, ENGLEBELMER	
MARTINSART	SUN	11.15 AM	Reached MARTINSART & took up temporary billets.	

J Allan Major R.A.M.C.
O.C. 1/1st/Highland F.A.

990

CONFIDENTIAL.

War Diary
1st Highland Field Co:

from 18th May 1915 to 31st August 1915.

51st Division

1/1 Highland Field Coy RE
Doll
August 15.

6089/9/

✓

Confidential

War Diary

of

1/1st HIGHLAND FIELD Co. R.E.

from 1st August 1915   to 31st August 1915.

Volume II.

Army Form C: 2118

WAR DIARY
or
INTELLIGENCE SUMMARY.
(Erase heading not required.)

Instructions regarding War Diaries and Intelligence Summaries are contained in F. S. Regs., Part II. and the Staff Manual respectively. Title pages will be prepared in manuscript.

Place	Date	Hour	Summary of Events and Information	Remarks and references to Appendices
MARTINSART	1915			
	Sun. 1 May		Taking over from French engineers line to East of AUTUOLA & AVELUY - New line previously occupied by French - Very good front line trenches. Capt. HUOT - 1st Coy in charge -	
	Mon. 2		Three sections out at work - Repairing & improving water supply. Taking over Water supply & engine in MARTINSART.	
	Tue. 3		Do	
	Wed. 4		Very wet - Shifting billets - prospecting for wood - Settled in CHATEAU MARTINSART	
	Thu. 5		Continued work on line from HAMEL to AVELUY - water supply. Communications	
	Fri. 6		Capt Parr sighting new communications in front ALBERT. Other work as before	
	Sat. 7		Assisting farmers at BOUZINCOURT - Cutting passages in defences for carts.	
	Sun. 8		Work as usual till noon - Church Parade 2.30 p.m.	
	Mon. 9		Instructions to look for billets at BOUZINCOURT - also place for stores. Sighting trenches for 2nd Line between ALBERT & BOUZINCOURT.	
	Tue. 10		Work as usual - Shifted some stores to BOUZINCOURT	
	Wed. 11		Do - Handing over to 2nd Field Squadron. Capt. Hill.	
	Thu. 12		Shifted billets to BOUZINCOURT - H.Q. at School House.	
	Fri. 13		Maj Green went on tracks leave. Coy. settling into billets which are scattered.	

WAR DIARY or INTELLIGENCE SUMMARY.

Army Form C. 2118.

(Erase heading not required.)

Instructions regarding War Diaries and Intelligence Summaries are contained in F. S. Regs., Part II. and the Staff Manual respectively. Title pages will be prepared in manuscript.

Place	Date	Hour	Summary of Events and Information	Remarks and references to Appendices
BOUZINCOURT	1915 Aug Sat 14		Commenced work BOUZINCOURT — ALBERT defences — Line of trenches running S.E. — Chalk in. no rubber.	
	Sun 15		1 Section selling trench S. of BOUZINCOURT — Inferior film mostly. Trenches filling trench as above continued	
	Mon 16		Do	
	Tues 17		Do Do	
	Wed 18		Do Do 1 Sect. commenced new communication trench on the road	
			Do Do 1 Sect. with Lieut. T. Russell about 1/2	
	Thur 19		AVELUY to carry on defences.	
			Work continued as on 18th	
	Fri 20		Do "weather wet" — sore water level — men & horses healthy.	
	Sat 21		Major Allen — Returned from leave — work continues as above	
	Sun 22		Do Do — working by day in C.T.	
	Mon 23		Do Do Do Do with 2 men & 2 wounds — unknown	
	Tues 24		Do Do — Night work in C.T.	
	Wed 25		Handed over BOUZINCOURT — ALBERT defences to 2nd & 3rd Squad. Shifted sect. 4 to AVELUY to work on village defences — Lieut: Laing with Sec. 3 on night work.	
	Thur 26		Secs: 1, 2, & 4 on AVELUY defences. Sec: 3 on night work in C.T.	

Army Form C.-2118.

WAR DIARY
or
INTELLIGENCE SUMMARY.

(12)

(Erase heading not required.)

Instructions regarding War Diaries and Intelligence Summaries are contained in F. S. Regs., Part II. and the Staff Manual respectively. Title pages will be prepared in manuscript.

Place	Date	Hour	Summary of Events and Information	Remarks and references to Appendices
	1915			
BOUZINCOURT	Fri: Aug: 27		Sect 2.3. r4 on AVELUY Defences - Sect:1 on C.T at night	
	Sat " 28		Do	
	Sun " 29		Do - Lt: Russell detailed for Front Line Water Scheme	
	Mon " 30		" " 1.4. r3 - Sect: 2 on Water Scheme - No night work	
	Tues " 31		Do Do - 2nd S: W. Sq: left here for MARTINSART	

J.G. Allan.
MAJOR, R.E. (T.)
O.C. 1/1st HIGHLAND FIELD CO. R.E.

699/14

51st Division

1/1 Highland Field Co, RE.

Vol III

Sept 15

Army Form C. 2118.

WAR DIARY
or
INTELLIGENCE SUMMARY.

(13)

(Erase heading not required.)

Instructions regarding War Diaries and Intelligence Summaries are contained in F. S. Regs., Part II and the Staff Manual respectively. Title pages will be prepared in manuscript.

Place	Date	Hour	Summary of Events and Information	Remarks and references to Appendices
	1915		1/1st HIGHLAND FIELD Co. R.E.	
BOUZINCOURT	Wed Sep 1		Sections 1.3.4 on AVELUY defences - 2/Lieut Lang Laudesers ct. to 2/3d.Co. - Capt Barr went on leave -	
	Thu " 2		Sect: 1.4 on AVELUY defences - Sect: 2 Water Scheme - Sec: 3. Horse Standings - 143 2d.Co. Rfg came into BOUZINCOURT.	
	Fri " 3		Work as above	
	Sat " 4		Do Started concrete emplacements at AVELUY	
	Sun " 5		Do No Church Parade - Fine weather	
	Mon " 6		Do Do	
	Tues " 7		Do Do	
	Wed " 8		Do Lieut: Doig reported for duty Do - Lieut: J. Russell went on leave	
	Thur " 9		Do Capt Barr returned from leave - visited AMIENS to purchase Stores - Saw 4 G Prisoners at AVELUY	
	Fri " 10		Do - German aeroplane brought down in our lines	
	Sat " 11		Do - Sighted new communication in AVELUY defences. Very fair weather - easterly wind.	

1577 Wt. W10791/1773 500,000 1/15 D. D. & L. A.D.S.S./Forms/C. 2118.

WAR DIARY or INTELLIGENCE SUMMARY.

Army Form C. 2118.

1/1st HIGHLAND FIELD CO. R.E.

Place	Date	Hour	Summary of Events and Information	Remarks and references to Appendices
BOUZINCOURT	Sun Sept 12	1915	Disposition Working parties as before. Gen. Bullock & CRE inspected AVELUY Defences. Had extra working party) 150 S.W.B. only 2 Officers - men seem stale.	
	Mon Sept 13		Working parties as above - no officers with S.W.B. Inspected front line for G. ALBERT supervising with defences -	
	Tues 14		Do - No S.W.B. - Went to front line - found delay in getting up stores S-Lieut. Emerson took Henock to Chateau	
	Wed 15		Do - CRE visited AVELUY Defences for a short hour - timber not arrived to recommence upon Keep - Jacobs try to reach Bastion.	
	Thu 16		Do - Lieut Russell returned from leave - further leave stopped meantime - Sent Capt. Barr to see AVELUY defences. Drill	
	Fri 17		Do - Working Parties - 2.50 AVELUY Defences. 100 trench columns - stores Lent Bridge Railway by Express in route to Trench line.	
	Sat 18		Do - No ash-making parties. Capt. Barr worked all night at HQ returning. CRE came over to office. Capt. Barr back over from	
			145 Co RE. - BOUZINCOURT - ALBERT defences. - No mails today - Bombs testified on MARTINSART - 9.30 AM.	
	Sun 19		Do - CRE called for lunch. Capt. Barr to assist Durhams up for a few days & thus hand over BOUZINCOURT. ASSARI-MARTINSART Defences to them - Capt. Ritson & Durham Engrs to come to me for a few days.	
	Mon 20		Do - Reconnaissance at AVELUY - Capt. Barr left for SCOTLAND - very full over there. Major Hall, Capt. Bilsen & 11/3 Durhams DO. Co. came over this morning -	
	Tues 21		Do - Capt. Bilsen attached for a few days - Conference at 10 AM CRE gave instructions in case of forward action - took Capt. Bilsen to see AVELUY - saw few distinct - details distributed - Lieut. Russell for trench - No further in front line - the latter read reconnaissance.	

WAR DIARY or INTELLIGENCE SUMMARY

Army Form C. 2118.

1/1st HIGHLAND FIELD Co., R.E.

Place	Date	Hour	Summary of Events and Information	Remarks and references to Appendices
BOUZINCOURT	1915 Wed. Sept 22		Sect. 2 strengthening & building left – Sec. 1 AVELUY Defences, Sec. 4 – Saps in F.2 Sector, Sec. 3 – at BOUZINCOURT – Genl. Capper & CRE visited AVELUY defences –	
	Thur 23		Work as above	
	Fri 24		D⁰ – See Details for night work with 2 Sections 1/5 Durhams & 50 Cyclists – making dummy trenches – Sapper Honohn wounded whilst this duty. Wet weather set in. General Allason left the Division	
	Sat 25		D⁰ – Sect. 1 in AVELUY defences.	
	Sun 26		D⁰ – Heavy bombardment by G. Guns – Reverse attack N & S of us.	
	Mon 27		D⁰ – News of success of French & in Champagne – CRE called at 3 pm.	
	Tues 28		D⁰ – Met O.C. 154th Brig. in trenches – Clearing up ground & bridging Equipment.	
	Wed 29		D⁰ – Sect. 1 took up Tunnel Saps & See 4 went out at Front Line Communications – New General General Harper & A.D.S.I toured AVELUY Defences – the CRE. Sect billeted at AVELUY.	
	Thur 30		D⁰ – CRE. in communication Sector F.1	

Allan
MAJOR. R.E (T.)
O.C. 1/1st HIGHLAND FIELD CO. R.E.

51st Division

121/7376

— CONFIDENTIAL —

WAR DIARY
of
O.C. 1/1st HIGHLAND FIELD Co. R.E.

From 1st October 1915 to 31st October 1915

Vol IV

J.G. Anan
MAJOR, R.E. (T.)
O.C. 1/1st HIGHLAND FIELD CO. R.E.

Army Form C. 2118.

WAR DIARY
or
INTELLIGENCE SUMMARY.

(Erase heading not required.)

Instructions regarding War Diaries and Intelligence
Summaries are contained in F. S. Regs., Part II.
and the Staff Manual respectively. Title pages
will be prepared in manuscript.

1/1st HIGHLAND FIELD Co. R.E.

Place	Date	Hour	Summary of Events and Information	Remarks and references to Appendices
BOUZINCOURT	October 1915 Fri: 1		Sec:1 - Tunnel saps - F2. Sec:2: Water supply G, 2+3., Sec:3. Inside - Bath Arras - Stables - Workshop 1st, Sec 4 - AVELUY Defences + Tauchus F1.	
	Sat 2		- went round AVELUY + C.T. 3rd F1.	
	Sun 3		Same as above - B2. - Westwound FrontLine F1 + F2 - Gen. Hibbert rounded - A2 - C.R.E. visited AVELUY defences - C.T., F1 - + OVILLERS Rd -	
	Mon 4		B2 - more twice to work to be devoted to FrontLine work - Thickening parapet, deepening, line stop, dry - into 1st F. - Visited ABBERT to try + get iron plates - no success.	
	Tues 5		B2 - visited C.T. + FrontLine - saw Major Barnes + Brig-Major to arrange work parties. Very wet.	
	Wed: 6		D2 - Half day - visited FrontLine - F1.	
	Thu. 7		D2 - C.R.E. came round wood - F1. - C.T.'s (met G.O.E.) AVELUY Defences.	
	Fri. 8		D2 - Visited F2 with Maj: Milnes -	
	Sat. 9		D2 - Sec. 1. returned to BOUZINCOURT - visited AVELUY defences -	
	Sun 10		D2 - 2nd FrontLine + C.T.	
	Mon 11		D2 - Started classifying dugouts in Front + Support Lines - did 20 in F1 - Lt Lang did 12.0 25 in F2. went round with Major Barnes.	
	Tues 12		D2 - Continued classification of dugouts - Totals - 200 in F1. 23 in F2.	
	Wed 13		D2 - Recced part Fonk C6 + C.R.E. Lt. McIvere went in Trays have - G.O.E. + Lt Jerks Capt. Barr + others	

WAR DIARY
or
INTELLIGENCE SUMMARY.

(Erase heading not required.)

Army Form C. 2118.

Place	Date	Hour	Summary of Events and Information	Remarks and references to Appendices
	1915 October			
BOUZINCOURT	Wed: 13		Used Bath House for first time - very satisfactory - 80/90 men in 2 hours. Lt. McCrum went on leave.	
	Thu: 14		G.O.C. decided not sufficient shelters in Firing Line - Started Survey of Shelters	
	Fri: 15		Survey of Shelters Continued - with Maj. Barnes & Lt. Doig in F.1 - Maj. Thilbusch & Lewis in F.2	
	Sat: 16		Interviewed S.O.1 on subject with CRE rank. Biscot - Mce. Received at 4 NCOs. 16 Sappers + 2 drivers	
	Sun: 17		Making further report deciding on positions for new shelters.	
	Mon: 18		Started work on 13 shelters in F.1 + 12 in F.2 with Infantry & Sappers.	
	Tues: 19		D° work accelerated - Inspected F.1 shelters	
	Wed: 20		Inspector - Sect: 1 - New Shelters F2. Sect: 2 Water scheme. Sect: 3 New Shelters F1. Lt Doig went on Leave	
			Sect: 4 - Inf & HV Defences + John O Gaunt St - we perto F2 shelters - St Doig transferred to High. Div RE.	
	Thu: 21		Work as above - Inspected F1 shelters - Lt. McCrum returned from leave.	
	Fri: 22		D° Captain Mitchell - Town Major left on miss -	
	Sat: 23		D° Refreshments in dug out with 100th Foot, Charges function - dugouts too cheerless	
	Sun: 24		D° Inspected F1 + F2 Shelters - also Watership. very wet + cold	
	Mon: 25		D°	
	Tues: 26		Tried unsuccessfully to force down to shelters with 6" earth Auger. Cold + dry	
	Wed: 27		D° Inspected F1, F2 Shelters.	

1/1st HIGHLAND FIELD Co. R.E.

Army Form C. 2118.

WAR DIARY
or
INTELLIGENCE SUMMARY.
(Erase heading not required.)

Instructions regarding War Diaries and Intelligence Summaries are contained in F. S. Regs., Part II. and the Staff Manual respectively. Title pages will be prepared in manuscript.

Place	Date	Hour	Summary of Events and Information	Remarks and references to Appendices
BOUZINCOURT	1915 October Thurs 28		Trenches - very wet weather - Lt: Doig returned from leave - Draft 1 Driver + 1 Sapper arrived -	
	Fri 29		D°. Trenches very muddy - considerable shelling in Fr Salient - weather dry - dull -	
	Sat. 30		D°. Lt: McCrone out on all night work at Fr Salient, repairing damage caused by shelling - CRE inspecting ARTHUR Defences - also General Allenby.	
	Sun. 31		D°. Lt: McCrone + Lt. Russell + 12 Sappers on night work - CRe. Lt: Laing went on leave - ARTHUR shelled during the night - no casualties. So effects damage trench with Col. Gemmell - 8th R.d Pioneers + O.C. Infantry - Arrangements made for repair.	

[Signed] St Allan.
MAJOR, R.E. (T.)
O.O. 1/1st HIGHLAND FIELD Co. R.E.

1/1st HIGHLAND FIELD Co. R.E.

CONFIDENTIAL.

WAR DIARY
of the
1/1st HIGHLAND FIELD Co. R.E.
51st Division
10th Corps
IIIrd Army

121/7694

From 1st November 1915   to   30th November 1915

J.D. Allan, MAJOR, R.E. (T.)
O.C. 1/1st HIGHLAND FIELD Co. R.E.

Vol V

Army Form C. 2118.

WAR DIARY
or
INTELLIGENCE SUMMARY.

(Erase heading not required.)

1/1st HIGHLAND FIELD Co. R.E.

51st Div'n – 1b Corps – 3rd Army
{ on our left 5th Div'n
  „ right 1st Div'n }

Instructions regarding War Diaries and Intelligence Summaries are contained in F. S. Regs., Part II. and the Staff Manual respectively. Title pages will be prepared in manuscript.

Place	Date	Hour	Summary of Events and Information	Remarks and references to Appendices
BOUZINCOURT	1915 November Mon. 1		No 1 Section - Shelters Front Line - Sub sector F2. - No 2 Section - Water Supply Scheme to Front line - No 3 Section - A Heavy Defences - stables - machine gun. Roads. - No 4 Section - Shelters Front Line Sub sector F2 - Inspected various French at Salient Subsector F2 - with O.C. Pioneers to adjust.	
	Tues 2		Same as above - very heavy rain.	
	Wed 3		D°. Trenches very wet – G.O.E. decided to put men in to clean out & deepen Squad's hut as to make trench boards.	
	Thur 4		D°. Took on Trenches also continued - We did some firing in afternoon - resuscitation to cover.	
	Fri 5		D°. Work in Communication trenches - deepening - widening - continued & Shelters continued.	
	Sat 6		D°.	
	Sun 7		Aviator, heavy rain during day. Trenches are very wet. Major Allan went on leave	
	Mon. 8		Widening & deepening of Communications. Drawing & Front line carried on. Ammunition in F2 revetted - Aviator.	
	Tues 9			
	Wed. 10		Aviator – No. 3 Section worked in day – half holiday. Workshops furnished.	
	Thur. 11		Very wet day. Trench work carried on - also Artillery defences.	
	Fri. 12		Front line Communication cleared & working parties at work. Bombardment Thiepval.	

1577 Wt. W10791/1773 500,000 1/15 D. D. & L. A.D.S.S./Forms/C. 2118.

Army Form C. 2118.

WAR DIARY
or
INTELLIGENCE SUMMARY.
(Erase heading not required.)

1/1st HIGHLAND FIELD Co. R.E.

Instructions regarding War Diaries and Intelligence Summaries are contained in F. S. Regs., Part II. and the Staff Manual respectively. Title pages will be prepared in manuscript.

Place	Date	Hour	Summary of Events and Information	Remarks and references to Appendices
Bouzancourt	1915 November			
Sat.	13.		No 1 Section F2 Subsector. Shelters. No 2 Watson Sheave & J. Subsector. No 3. Aveluy defences and work in billets. total up scores No 4 F, Subsector. Workshop stores -	
Sun.	14		Aveluy. Trenches very wet. Trenches shewing signs of suffering from continued bad weather. Very dry.	
Mon.	15		As above - Heavy snow - Major Allan returned from leave.	
Tues.	16		Do - Inspected Subsectors F1, F2.	
Wed.	17		Do - Inspected Aveluy -	
Thurs.	18		Do - Thick fog allowed considerable work to be done in clearing weight of earth from top of trenches, walked outside, open communication with several R.E.'s. Work stopped at 12.30pm to allow artillery to do some shooting -	
Fri.	19		Do - Inspected C.T.'s in F1 with C.R.E.	
Sat.	20		Do - Took round Capt. Morrell attached - also Aveluy	
Sun.	21		Do - Inspected Passed 11 new shelters. F1.	
Mon.	22		Do - Inspected Shelters F2 - also C.T.'s F1. Very misty - Capt. Morrell left.	
Tues.	23		Do - Went round works at Aveluy - Called at Brigade. Inspected C.T.'s in F1	

Army Form C. 2118.

WAR DIARY
or
INTELLIGENCE SUMMARY.

1/1st HIGHLAND FIELD Co. R.E.

(Erase heading not required.)

(21)

Instructions regarding War Diaries and Intelligence Summaries are contained in F. S. Regs., Part II. and the Staff Manual respectively. Title pages will be prepared in manuscript.

Place	Date	Hour	Summary of Events and Information	Remarks and references to Appendices
Bouzincourt	November 1915			
	Wed. 24.		Work parties as before - CRE. inspects - C.T.s & Front Line F1 Subsector - Testing earth drill for turning roofs. Attempts to take periscope. Bauds saw nipping timber.	
	Thu. 25		Do - Inspected Mr Shillers by 8th R.E. also C.T. in Bois D'Authuille partially dug - Work was stopped early on account of an Artillery programme.	
	Fri. 26		Do - Inspected Authuille with Col. Allan. Heavy snow - visited Bouzincourt - Authuille Line. Set about having for periscope thro' roof of Shelters - very cold night.	
	Sat. 27		Do - Severe frost during night - Capt Barr left to act adjutant - inspected Shelters in F2 - came back by Rivington St.	
	Sun. 28		Do - Severe frost - inspected Authuille defences with Lieut Campbell - heavy shelling from Rivington St to Front Line - CRE. called at H.Q. in afternoon.	
	Mon. 29		Do - CRE. at Authuille defences. Hard frost during night - very heavy rain during day - severe flooding - heavy shelling in front Lesser - 100' parapet blown.	
	Tues. 30		Do - Weather mild + dry - visited F2 with CRE. - Dugouts progressing slowly. Gave instructions re keep. Draft arrived mid-night + A.Co. 9 men for Searchlight.	
	December			
	Wed. 1		Do - More rain - CRE. visited F1 - arranging to make new support trenches. Front line very bad.	
	Thu. 2		Do - Fixed with 8th R.S. effort to work tonight on new trenches.	

JJAllan Major. R.E. (L.)
O.C. 1/1st HIGHLAND FIELD CO. R.E.

Army Form C. 2118.

WAR DIARY
or
INTELLIGENCE SUMMARY.
(Erase heading not required.)

1/1st HIGHLAND FIELD Do. R.E. - 51st Div: - 10 Corps: - III Army

Instructions regarding War Diaries and Intelligence Summaries are contained in F. S. Regs., Part II. and the Staff Manual respectively. Title pages will be prepared in manuscript.

Place	Date	Hour	Summary of Events and Information	Remarks and references to Appendices
	1915			
BOUZINCOURT	Dec. 1 Wed.		D.O. 1 Sec: new shelters F.1, No Sec: Shakescheme, No 3 Sec: Aveluy defences, No 4 Improvement of trenches. Bridging St John o'Gaunts St. - Joiners, workshop &c - more rain - CRE visited F.1 - Arranging to make new sub-post trenches. Draft Lieut. very bad. Searchlight draft arrived - Shapero, Driver, 20 Mar. 2 Spr.	
	2 Thu		Work as above - more rain - CRE revisited F.1. Draft post to RE Pk to work tonight on new trenches.	
	3 Fri		D° - heavy rain - food progress made with new sub post Lt. Don Crome with 1 Sec: 219th Field Co.	
	4 Sat		1 Sec.	3rd Durham R.E. working parties at Bruce T. & Lancaster A. D° - more rain - Thurs - Mitchells fell over - pumping the river all the day - 1 Sec: sapp. draining T³ - during rays + clearing out again - squad repairing river bank - Some shells in Aveluy - Draft of 1 Officer arrived - 2/Lt: B.D. Patterson.	
	5 Sun		D° - Capt. Barr went on leave -	
	6 Mon			
	7 Tues			
	8 Wed		See rev -	
	9 Thurs			
	10 Fri			
	11 Sat			

Army Form C. 2118.

WAR DIARY
or
INTELLIGENCE SUMMARY. 1/1st HIGHLAND FIELD Co. R.E.
(Erase heading not required.)

Instructions regarding War Diaries and Intelligence Summaries are contained in F. S. Regs., Part II. and the Staff Manual respectively. Title pages will be prepared in manuscript.

Place	Date	Hour	Summary of Events and Information	Remarks and references to Appendices
FREMONT	Sun. 26	Bce.	Capt Bain to 152nd Inf. Bde re loading & repairs in villages. 2 Sections employed clearing up FREMONT & repairing billets. Two hours drill.	
	Mon. 27		Capt Bain to Vaux & St Vast to see B.M. organising Officer. 2 Sections recony up	
	Tue. 28		Bed making commenced by No. 4 Section in Vaux. Great shortage of material. 1 Section in FREMONT drilling 1½ hours.	
	Wed. 29		Work at Vaux continued. Remaining 2 Sections arrived about midday.	
	Thur. 30		Work at Vaux continued. (W) Party to Poix amuses & to Tarday Etre. No material available in the villages. Little erection started. 2 hours drill.	
	Fri. 31st		Capt Bean to Amiens re trench Warfare. No further progress made in war no.	

H. Allan.
Major, R.E. (T.)
O.C. 1/1st HIGHLAND FIELD CO. R.E.

Army Form C. 2118.

WAR DIARY
or
INTELLIGENCE SUMMARY.
(Erase heading not required.)

(23)

Place	Date	Hour	Summary of Events and Information	Remarks and references to Appendices
BOUZINCOURT	December Sun.	12	(continued)	
	Mon.	13	Work very much the same from yesterday - Continuous fight against water + mud -	
	Tues.	14	bumping - riveting - floorboarding - Major Allan in Hospital 8th to 15th - Lt. Doig ill - 2/Lt. Laing ill -	
	Wed.	15	Capt. Bass returned from leave -	
	Thur.	16	- No change - weather mild + damp -	
	Fri.	17	- CRE calles with CRE. 32nd Div. - The Coy has given a day off. - Majors 2 horses for search light arrived.	
	Sat.	18	- Profos? as before -	
	Sun.	19	- Lt. Russell went on leave - work as before - CE. 18th Corps. Gen. Powell called with CRE.	
	Mon.	20	- Work as before - CRE went back to TRESSEXIT & took my interpreter	
	Tues.	21	- Handing over to 219th Field Co: - instructions to move Co. less 2 Sects. on 23rd to ST GRATIEN & m xy th to ST TAAST - remaining 2 Sects. to follow on 28th inst. -	
	Wed.	22	- Packing up + handing over -	
ST GRATIEN	Thur.	23	Coy less 2 Sections moved to St. GRATIEN arriving about 2.30 p.m.	
FREMONT	Fri.	24	Coy less 2 Sections moved to FREMONT arriving about 3.0 p.m.	
	Sat.	25	No work. CRE. visited FREMONT and detailed work to be done.	
	Sun.	26	Reconnoitered works connected with Softwa Survey	

51

1/1 Highland Fd Coy RE
Jan 1916
Vol VII

WAR DIARY
or
INTELLIGENCE SUMMARY

Army Form C. 2118.

1/1st HIGHLAND FIELD Co. R.E.

(Erase heading not required.)

Instructions regarding War Diaries and Intelligence Summaries are contained in F.S. Regs., Part II. and the Staff Manual respectively. Title pages will be prepared in manuscript.

Place	Date	Hour	Summary of Events and Information	Remarks and references to Appendices
FREMONT	Jan Sat. 1.		Holiday. Capt Bain to Argoures no bees for feeding.	RB
	Sun. 2.		Work started in Sgt's & Cpl's Pavillion. Preparations in Yard & Basement. Hens nice.	RB
	Mon. 3.		As above. Capt Bain with Interpreter to Amiens. Visited Pepin re (a harrow manager?)	RB
	Tues 4.		Bee feeding & sewing. Work in all villages continued.	RB
	Weds. 5.		As above. Major Allen returned from leave.	RB
	Thurs 6th		Bee feeding commenced as before — work in villages as above — 40 horses swallowed?	RB
	Fri. 7th		Work in villages as above — remainder of horses mastered.	RB
	Sat. 8th		Bee making continued in morning — removals in afternoon.	RB
	Sun. 9th		Holiday.	RB
	Mon. 10th		Removals in villages carried on.	RB
	Tues. 11th		as above. Capt Bain to Div. H.Q. re. show hund.	RB
	Wed. 12th		Major Allen to Hospital. Wet weather as above. Shew hund continues with 2 Corps Scottish Rifles.	RB
	Thurs 13th		Bee making continued. Work at Shew ground continued.	RB
	Fri. 14th		as above.	RB

1577 Wt. W10791/1773 500,000 1/15 D.D.& L. A.D.S.S./Forms/C. 2118.

Army Form C. 2118.

WAR DIARY
or
INTELLIGENCE SUMMARY.
(Erase heading not required.)

1/1st HIGHLAND FIELD Co. R.E.

(26)

Instructions regarding War Diaries and Intelligence Summaries are contained in F. S. Regs., Part II. and the Staff Manual respectively. Title pages will be prepared in manuscript.

Place	Date	Hour	Summary of Events and Information	Remarks and references to Appendices
FREMONT.	Jan			
	Sat. 15th		Bootmaking in over continued in morning. Holiday in afternoon.	
	Sun. 16th		Kit inspection forenoon. Church parade in afternoon.	
	Mon. 17th		Bootmaking carried on - Show ground - discing commenced in rear line -	
	Tues. 18th		as above -	
	Wed. 19th		another - Reg'l Orders.	
	Thurs. 20th		another	
	Fri. 21st		another	
	Sat. 22nd		another. Rifle firing.	
	Sun. 23rd		another. Capt Bain went with OR to 8th Vict Engineer Mounted. Armentieres in morning	
			Capt Phan with Musical & Ellis Ground - met OR with 6th¹ Command & 950¹.	
			Conference at at Col H.Q. Ars with Co. Commanders.	
	Mon. 24th		Bootmaking continued - L.Muralis took over Ars Evening.	
	Tues. 25th		hand to mend.	
	Wed. 26th		Bootmaking & Transground continued in forenoon. Co.firing heavily afternoon.	
	Thurs. 27th		Bootmaking & Transground continued	
	Fri. 28th		as above. Capt Bain & Bn 1st Ars Camp (Musical) OC OR to Fremont.	

1577 Wt.W10791/1773 500,000 1/15 D.D.& L. A.D.S.S./Forms/C. 2118.

Army Form C. 2118.

WAR DIARY
or
INTELLIGENCE SUMMARY.

1/1st HIGHLAND FIELD Co. R.E.

(Erase heading not required.)

(27)

Place	Date	Hour	Summary of Events and Information	Remarks and references to Appendices
FREMONT	Jun Sat. 29th		Bedmaking & Bivs Ground carried on. Capt. Bain with Lt. Patterson, & Lieut. hope Luis for water supply from Vaux & St-Vast.	SB
	Sun. 30th		Church Parade. Capt. Bain to 153rd R.de. re Stopping runs in villages. Mr. Guerin joins unit.	SB
	Mon. 31st		Company training commenced. 1 section on Stun Ground. Capt Bain with interpreter to auxiliary re billets etc.	SB

Army Form C. 2118.

WAR DIARY 1/1st HIGHLAND FIELD Co. R.E.
or
INTELLIGENCE SUMMARY.
(Erase heading not required.)

Instructions regarding War Diaries and Intelligence Summaries are contained in F. S. Regs., Part II. and the Staff Manual respectively. Title pages will be prepared in manuscript.

Place	Date	Hour	Summary of Events and Information	Remarks and references to Appendices
	FEB.			
FREMONT	Tue. 1st		Company training. 1 Section at Swarpans.	
	Wed 2nd		Company training. French Hospitaliers afternoon.	
	Thurs 3rd		Company training. R.E. Stores removed to new area. Hospitalier Bodies leave Company for new duties. 1 Section at Swarpans.	
	Fri. 4th		Company training. 1 Section at Swarpans. 1 hour Rest. Section taken from area. U.O.W Came with Staff Capt. Knowles to select Coy Boundaries as [illegible] as [illegible] as [illegible]	
	Sat. 5th		Company training. Party which [illegible] advance reserve.	
Cohie	Sun. 6th		Company moved to Cohie arriving about 3 p.m.	
	Mon. 7th		Cleaning up.	
Sailly-la	Tue. 8th		Company moved to Sailly-la-See arriving 1.0 pm.	
See.	Wed. 9th		Billets managed.	
	Thur. 10th		Work in hutments commences, but timber cleaning starts.	
	Fri. 11th		as above	
	Sat. 12th		as above.	
	Sun. 13th		Work as above in morning, the work in afternoon.	
	Mon. 14th		Bathhouse, hedmaking, cleaning streets continued.	

Army Form C. 2118.

WAR DIARY
or
INTELLIGENCE SUMMARY.
(Erase heading not required.)

1/1st HIGHLAND FIELD Co. R.E.

Place	Date	Hour	Summary of Events and Information	Remarks and references to Appendices
Sailly-le-Sec	Feb. Tues 15th		Work in Battn. lines & on tram standings carried on – Capt Barr and Lieut Pritchett to Amiens re purchase of wood.	
	Wed 16th		Road repairing, Battns work carried on. Stay fords in afternoon.	
	Thurs 17th		Work as above. Capt Barr to Bray to take over from 305 Div Engineers three men & orders received at 9.40 pm for relieving 305 Div Engineers	
	Friday 18th		Road repairing. Practising rapid wiring. Battalions horse standings. Company medically examined – 2 cases of Scabies. Company billets. Operation orders received for relieving 305 Div of 17th inst. Weather bad.	
	Sat. 19th		Cleaning and packing wagons. Road repairing. Battalion employed Company bath. Capt Barr returned from Bray in the afternoon. Weather improved.	
	Sun. 20th		Pontoon equipment sent to Bridging grounds for training. Mother went to afternoon C.R.E. carried midday. Company in new quarters in afternoon. Company pd.	
	Mon 21st		Road repairing carried on between Vaux-Sailly le Sec. L. Cumberose reported from 3/4th B 1st/1st Div Coy Works. Frosty weather.	
	Tues 22nd		Road repairing with 300 men less 1st 14th Warwicks.	

Army Form C. 2118.

WAR DIARY
or
INTELLIGENCE SUMMARY.

1/1st HIGHLAND FIELD Co. R.E.

(Erase heading not required.)

(30)

Instructions regarding War Diaries and Intelligence Summaries are contained in F. S. Regs., Part II. and the Staff Manual respectively. Title pages will be prepared in manuscript.

Place	Date	Hour	Summary of Events and Information	Remarks and references to Appendices
SAILLY L'E SEC.	Wed. 23rd Thurs 24th		Roadmaking J. Leave mn returned from trenches - CRE. exceed. Lt Musser to Bray	
	Fri 25th		Snow all day. CRE 13th Corps inspected new ultraviolet line. 1 or Section inspecting 3rd Section on roads. Snow all day. Battalion [?] for Bray returned. 3rd Section [?] 11/2 Sectn on roads	
	Sat. 26th		Frost - snowy thick snow. All sections in none Than cruddy	
	Sun 27th		No work. Inspection of Captain of timer [?] panniers. 1 Sect. arrived [?] new snow -	
DOURS	Mon. 28th	4pm	Operation order issued 8.0.11 pm or 27th ordered 1 and 2nd Cos [?] to move at 10 a.m. less roads. Extra transport required in D.A.C. 1 Section to join Company via 1 Section [?] Equipment arrived Stores at 1.0 p.m. began [?] Junior Equipment required 8.15 pm. 1 sect. rejoined 6.15 pm. orders received 11 pm. Guard Plaselles at 10 am on 29th	
FLASELLES	Tues 29th		Company marched to Flaselles arriving 3.15 pm -	

Davis Lyon
Captn & OC
1/1 H.F. Co

A.D.S.S./Forms/C. 2118.

Army Form C. 2118.

WAR DIARY
or
INTELLIGENCE SUMMARY.
(Erase heading not required.)

1/1st HIGHLAND FIELD Co. R.E.

(3)

Place	Date	Hour	Summary of Events and Information	Remarks and references to Appendices
March. Lessalles	Wed. 1st	10t	Company preparing to move. Orders received 9.15 a.m. Division not to move for another day. C.R.E. called. Arranged motor transport for D.A.E.	
	Thur. 2nd	3rd	Company clearing hutments near Fienvet. Capt. Barr training. V.O. orders in brief. C.R.E. & Adj. called.	
	Fri. 3rd	3rd	Company clearing hutments near Fienvet. 1 P.H. tube flushed - issued in place of 1 P. tube flushed.	
	Sat. 4th		Snow in morning. Sections working as above - withdrawn about own owing to weather. C.R.E. called.	
	Sun. 5th		Company preparing to move. Adjt D.A.R.E. called - Batt 1-3 Co. Corry reports to assist in move. Op. order received 7.30 p.m. to move to AUTHEUX at 9.0 a.m. on 6th.	
	Mon. 6th		Moved from Lessalles at 9.0 am unit P.L.R.S. & AUTHEUX. Arriving there 1.55 p.m. First team Hans Front. Message received 12.45 am fr Capt. Barr, that he came forward to line R&D	
AUTHEUX	Tues. 7th		by Grand near Fienvels St Vaast at 6.0 am. Two further return for company grounds. Officers return for lunches abt 11.15 p.m.	
	Wed. 8th		Snow front. Company northward in morning. Op order received 5.45 pm to move to HEM.	
HEM.	Thur. 9th		Company moved to HEM with No 3 Co A.S.C. arriving 11.35am. Op order received 4 pm to move to BEAUDRICOURT. Snow throughout.	

Army Form C. 2118.

WAR DIARY
or
INTELLIGENCE SUMMARY.

(Erase heading not required.) 1/1st HIGHLAND FIELD CO. R.E.

Instructions regarding War Diaries and Intelligence Summaries are contained in F. S. Regs., Part II. and the Staff Manual respectively. Title pages will be prepared in manuscript.

(32)

Place	Date	Hour	Summary of Events and Information	Remarks and references to Appendices
	MARCH			
BEUDRICOURT	Fri. 10th		Company march with 8/153 Brigade to BEAUDRICOURT. Arrive 3.50 p.m. of. Orders received at 7.15 p.m. No orders concerning Company. Brigade wagon not issued not flying forward mvnt.	
	Sat. 11th		Orders received 6.25 a.m. Company bivouac in present billets. Start march in morning. Of. orders received 6.25 p.m. to move to MAROEUIL tomorrow.	
MAROEUIL	Sun. 12th		Company move 11.0 a.m. Joined 2½ Battalions of 153 Bde. Arrive MAROEUIL 8.10 p.m. Village very full of troops. Capt Ban & CRE not work.	
	Mon. 13th		Company cleaning out billets vacated by French troops. Capt Ban + all officers except Capt Ban to trenches - dump for stores arranged.	
	Tue 14th		All officers inspect in the trenches. CRE cared re taking over line. Fine weather	
	Wed 15th		Tracing trench maps commenced. CRE cared. One Section of work at UPPER BLANCHE REDOUBT. 14 5.9" shells fell in village - about 6 china.	
	Thur. 16th		Work as above. C.R.E. comes. Capt Ban to From 153 Brigade in trenches.	
	Fri. 17th		Company pay. Work in trenches commenced by 2 Sections. Trenches in very bad order.	
	Sat. 18th		Work as above. Capt Ban to 153 Brigade. Scheme grant matereals.	
	Sun. 19th		Work in trenches as before.	

Army Form C. 2118.

WAR DIARY
or
INTELLIGENCE SUMMARY.
(Erase heading not required.) 1/1st HIGHLAND FIELD Co. R.E.

Instructions regarding War Diaries and Intelligence
Summaries are contained in F. S. Regs., Part II.
and the Staff Manual respectively. Title pages
will be prepared in manuscript.

(33)

Place	Date	Hour	Summary of Events and Information	Remarks and references to Appendices
	March			
MORBECQUE	Mon 20th		Men return to Coys for discharge – Company works in trenches – Arrangements made for 2 Sections from interior Coys.	
	Tues 21st		1st Section withdraws to Clarmarais nr into shelter near Brigade Headquarters in trenches. Work for one Section in trenches as usual & train Reserve Section.	
	Wed 22nd		French railway started from MORBECQUE THIENNES road to reserve line – Company Employees as usual.	
	Thurs 23rd		Work as usual –	
	Fri 24th		C.R.E. (Lt Col Rundall) Coy S. Egypt – Coy S. Company at work in line.	
	Sat 25th		Seven Sappers discharged for Munitions work in Scotland – Company work as usual –	
	Sun 26th		Work as usual –	
	Mon 27th		C.R.E. orders no work – work in trenches continued –	
	Tues 28th		Work as usual –	
	Wed 29th		C.R.E. Capt Beer and 453rd Coys Sects. Headquarters and workshop Morbecque Saturday Company at work in trenches.	
	Thurs 30th		Company pay. C.R.E. visits Marsh Blanche defences with its Divisional Protester – Coys at Company & Coy in way trench. Work in trenches as usual.	

Army Form C. 2118.

WAR DIARY
or
INTELLIGENCE SUMMARY.

(Erase heading not required.) 1/1st HIGHLAND FIELD Co. R.E.

Place	Date	Hour	Summary of Events and Information	Remarks and references to Appendices
	March			
Mareuil	Fri. 3rd		Work as usual in the day. Drivers line at Mareuil in advance to him for taking divisional trenches.	

Bear Lt-Col Coy R.E.
Carrt Hallison
OC

Army Form C. 2118.

WAR DIARY
or
INTELLIGENCE SUMMARY.
(Erase heading not required.)

Army Form C. 2118.

Place	Date	Hour	Summary of Events and Information	Remarks and references to Appendices
MORGEUIL	April			
	Sat. 1st		Company work as usual in him chies - revetting repairing kitchen	SB
			Adjt & Serg & accustmn -	
	Sun 2nd		Capt Bean & him chies rounds night Subsection (N1) visit Aiveley Communication OP.	SB
	Mon 3rd		Company work as above.	
			Capt Bean round N1 Subsection with Lt Borg - work in nature lines arranged.	SB
			Company work as above.	
	Tues 4th		Capt Bean to Brigade Headquarters. CRE called & manoeuvre & visited head	SB
			railway. Good progress made with tnr. Company work as usual.	
	Wed 5th		CRE called 9 o.a.m. Lieutenant 153rd Lieutenant Bulgaria (Captain) - defence	SB
			scheme being prepared for Division. Lunch work W. at end Company employed	
			as usual. 2nd Lt Carmichael & Lop Kins to trenches to start survey (accurate)	
			of General Front. Enemy exploded mine about 7.30 pm. Heavy British	
			bombardment continued about one hour.	
	Thur 6th		CRE called at 9 am and proceed to trenches with Capt Bean	SB
			Company work as above.	

Army Form C. 2118.

WAR DIARY
or
INTELLIGENCE SUMMARY.
(Erase heading not required.)

1/1st H/Sfd TE

Place	Date	Hour	Summary of Events and Information	Remarks and references to Appendices
NARDEUIL	April Friday 7th		Capt Barr & Capt Russell returned. Trenches two returning to afternoon. Company work as usual.	S3
	Sat 8th		Capt Barr on leave. Coy taken over by Capt Russell. Company work as usual. Section I Workshop. Section II Showground. La Maison Blanche. Section III Supports, tram shelters and quarters. Bertata Redoubt. OP.	S3
	Sunday 9th		Cutting. Section IV. O.P. Moulin T French tramway. Weather fine — good progress with work.	S3
	Monday 10th		Company work as above. Weather fine	S3
	Tuesday 11th		Lt Parry to Anti Gas Course. Company work as above. Weather fine — good progress with work.	S3
	Wednesday 12th		Company work as above. Weather dull + wet. Work delayed by weather. Gnr D Rhoose sick.	S3
			C.R.E. called in morning. 2nd Platoon returned from leave. Company work as above. Weather dull + wet.	S3
	Thursday 13th		Weather stormy + wet. Company work as usual. Work delayed owing to weather especially cement work and drummed fort Sunday. Coy paid. All hands to feet and men recalled except two on wattle leave.	S3
	Friday 14th		Weather stormy + wet. Company work as usual. Work delayed owing to weather. Section busy in trenches. Better during afternoon.	S3
	Sat 15th		Weather stormy with showers. C.R.E. and Adjutant called. C.R.E. visited trenches. Company	S3

Army Form C. 2118.

WAR DIARY
or
INTELLIGENCE SUMMARY.
(Erase heading not required.)

1/1st yr to G R E

Place	Date	Hour	Summary of Events and Information	Remarks and references to Appendices
	April			
	Sunday 16th		Work as usual. Light railway damaged slightly by shell fire. Glasgow Dump shelled. W. Leary returned from Lewis Gun Course.	D3
	Monday 17th		Weather fine. Heel wind at times. Capt Russell to trenches. Arrangements made to remove the half of stones at Glasgow Dump to forward dump in light railway. Much enemy shelling. Company work as usual. Good progress made.	
	Tuesday 18th		Weather wet and stormy. Adjutant called. Company work as usual.	D3
	Wednesday 19th		Weather wet and stormy. Company work as usual. Work delayed by weather.	D3
			Weather dull & wet. Capt Ross returned from leave. CRE and Adjutant called to see us. Home record for refilling past. Company work as usual.	D3
	Thursday 20th		Capt Ross to trenches 10 am, returning in afternoon. Company work as usual.	D3
	Friday 21st		Adjutant called 1 pm. Trench mar. 57.D N.W. 1. 1/2000 Edition 2.D received. Company work as usual.	D3
	Saturday 22nd		C.R.E called at 11 am. Capt Ross to trenches 10.15 returning in afternoon. Work as usual.	D3
	Sunday 23rd		Weather bright sunshine. 9/00 Whittiar to England for Commission. Company work as usual.	D3
	Monday 24th		Capt Ross to trenches 10 am, returning in afternoon. Company work as usual.	D3
	Tuesday 25th		C.R.E called 10/30 am. British bombardment at 6.30 pm lasting 10 minutes. Company work as usual.	D3

Army Form C. 2118.

WAR DIARY
or
INTELLIGENCE SUMMARY.
(Erase heading not required.)

11th Fd. Co. R.E. 28th

Place	Date	Hour	Summary of Events and Information	Remarks and references to Appendices
	April			
MAROEUIL	Wednesday 26th		Weather fine. Sgt Laing to Hospital 30 sprained ankle. Coy Rarr Appointments with Draughtsman. Company work as usual.	58
	Thursday 27th		Coy Rarr 1st Tranchee 10am. Morning in Aviator. Dust- arrived. S.O.R. work as usual.	58
	Friday 28th		Weather bright, warm. MAROEUIL shelled in the afternoon. Company work as usual.	58
	Saturday 29th		Weather warm. Coy Rarr arrived on leave. Dust arrived S.O.R. German aeroplane brought down over ANZIN village. Company work as usual.	58
	Sunday 30th		Weather warm. Company Raid in Antwerp British Rombencourt 6/1.30pm Company work as usual.	58

Beau 28
Capt. R.E. Co. R.E.
Pros. 11.5.04

Army Form C. 2118.

WAR DIARY
or
INTELLIGENCE SUMMARY.
(Erase heading not required.)

1/1st Highland Field Co. R.E.

Vol XI

Place	Date	Hour	Summary of Events and Information	Remarks and references to Appendices
MARDEUIL	1/5/16		Weather bright. Quiet. Continued test with Oxo-acetylene searchlight. Results rather disappointing.	S.S.
	2/5/16		Dull. Showery. C.O.E. called 11 a.m. Capt. Barr accompanied him to trenches and returned in evening.	S.S.
	3/5/16		Fine weather. 2nd Lieut. Rawles sent to Base to be held as reinforcement, they being surplus searchlight personnel. Sections carrying on usual work.	S.S.
	4/5/16		Weather bright. Man injured by horse.	S.S.
	5/5/16		Quiet day. Capt. Barr to trenches in evening.	S.S.
	6/5/16		Dry but windy. 2nd Lt. Carmichael alone at H.Q. of Coy.	S.S.
	7/5/16		5 men proceeded on short leave. Capt. Barr returned from trenches in evening. C.O.E. and Adjt called 11 a.m. One man returned hospital.	S.S.
	8/5/16		Fair weather. Work as usual.	S.S.
	9/5/16		Quiet. Dull. Wet stormy. MARDEUIL shelled 5.30 P.M. Lieut Day returned from the horse. Lieut. 3 & 4 Batties. Horse injured & destroyed. — Last case 4 months before. 3rd horse to be destroyed since enemy overseas	S.S.
	10/5/16		Dull. 2nd Lt. Carmichael on course experimenting in use of explosives for entrenching	S.S.

1577 Wt.W10791/1773 500,000 1/15 D. D. & L. A.D.S.S./Forms/C. 2118.

Army Form C. 2118.

WAR DIARY
or
INTELLIGENCE SUMMARY.
(Erase heading not required.)

1/1st HIGHLAND FIELD Co. R.E.

Instructions regarding War Diaries and Intelligence Summaries are contained in F. S. Regs., Part II. and the Staff Manual respectively. Title pages will be prepared in manuscript.

Place	Date	Hour	Summary of Events and Information	Remarks and references to Appendices
MARDEUIL	10/5/16		Capt. Barr to trenches afternoon returned 4 P.M. C.R.E and Adjt called 1 P.M. 3 men from leave.	63.
	11/5/16		Org. Adjt called noon. Money drawn and halfpay paid. Capt. Barr in trenches afternoon returned 9.30 P.M. Work as usual.	63.
	12/5/16		Blankets and waterproof capes returned. Weather fine. C.R.E and Adjt called 11 a.m. Remainder Coy paid. 2 men from short leave. 1 N.C.O. from one month's furlough.	63.
	13/5/16		Heavy rain overnight. Quiet. Capt. Barr to Brigade Hd.Qr. (153-1.B.) at 1.P.M. 5 men left on short leave. 1 man to Base. 1 man from hospital. C.R.E called afternoon. N°1 Section training in rapid wiring. Gunfire heavy about 9.0 P.M.	63.
	14/5/16		Dull day. C.R.E called 10.30 a.m. Few aeroplanes up, first for few days. Some rain during day. Capt. Barr to 153rd Inf Bde Hd.Qrs and trenches.	63.
	15/5/16		N°1 Section at rapid wiring practice. 1 N.C.O & 20 men 100x in 6 min 35 secs. Wet Day. C.R.E called & saw Capt Barr in afternoon. Heavy bombardment 8.30 - 9.30 P.M.	63.

Army Form C. 2118.

WAR DIARY
or
INTELLIGENCE SUMMARY.
(Erase heading not required.)

1/1st HIGHLAND FIELD Co. R.E.

Place	Date	Hour	Summary of Events and Information	Remarks and references to Appendices
MAROEUIL	16/5/16		Fine day, aircraft & kite balloons up. Adjt called afternoon. 1 Man from leave	
	17/5/16		1 Officer (2/Lt Carmichael) 3 N.C.Os & 18 Sappers to HERMAVILLE. Experimental work at BOMB SCHOOL there. Adjt called. Clear night, full moon. Enemy aircraft believed over village 9.30 – 10.00 P.M. Dropped bombs Chopfes	
	18/5/16		Fine day. 6 Additional Sappers to BOMB SCHOOL.	
	19/5/16		Capt. Rowell returned from leave. Heavy gunfire during night 18/19th & evening 19th. Adjt called forenoon.	
	20/5/16		Weather still dry. Capt Barr to HERMAVILLE – Demonstration at BOMB SCHOOL	
	21/5/16		Warm weather. Heavy bombardment direction of VIMY. Capt Barr at trenches. Gas from Gas shells detected in village about 9.30 P.M., warning received 10.30 P.M. 10 – 12 H.E. shells in MAROEUIL during night. Horses removed out of village. Some casualties in village – none in Company.	
	22/5/16		2/Lt Carmichael & party from BOMB SCHOOL.	
	23/5/16		Fine weather. Heavy artillery quiet.	
	24/5/16		Some rain. 1 Driver hospital shell shock. Took over work in M2 Sub Sector from 2/2nd H.F.Co	
	25/5/16		Fine weather. Work as before.	

WAR DIARY
or
INTELLIGENCE SUMMARY.

Army Form C. 2118.

1/1st HIGHLAND FIELD Co. R.E.

Place	Date	Hour	Summary of Events and Information	Remarks and references to Appendices
MARDEUIL	26/5/16		Good weather. 3 men from leave. Half company paid.	B.S.
	27/5/16		Weather fine. 1 Driver hospital, ankle broken. 2 Lieut Carmichael to Sa bourne. 1,2,3 & 4 sections paid and bathed. 3 men on leave.	B.S.
	28/5/16		Warm. Quiet. Capt Ban Trench's foremen returned 5.30 P.M.	B.S.
			1 N.C.O. & 6 Sappers BOMB SCHOOL for experimental work, tapping by explosives.	B.S.
			C.R.E. called afternoon. No 2 Section paid & bathed. Capt Russell to BOMB SCHOOL.	B.S.
	29/5/16		Good weather, enough active. Drivers reported from course of shoeing at BASE.	B.S.
			Capt Russell and Party from BOMB SCHOOL. Wet night 29/30.	B.S.
	30/5/16			B.S.
	31/5/16		Capt called foremen enough active weather good. 2 Lieut Askey from Hospital. Increasing difficulty in obtaining working parties owing to length of line held. Much necessary work making slow progress on that account.	B.S.

Army Form C. 2118.

WAR DIARY
or
INTELLIGENCE SUMMARY.
(Erase heading not required.)

1/1 HIGHLAND FIELD Co. R.E.

(43)

Place	Date	Hour	Summary of Events and Information	Remarks and references to Appendices
MAROEUIL	JUNE 1st		Adjutant ceased during forenoon. Three Divisions living in trenches - working in M.T., N.T. & T.O.1 subsectors. Owing to extent of Brigade front great difficulty in getting working parties. Good weather. Considerable aerial activity.	D.R.
	2nd		Good weather. Work as above. 4 Dvrs on leave.	D.R.
	3rd		C.R.E. ceased forenoon, repair in afternoon. Capt Barr to Trenches in evening. British aviators much in evidence.	D.R. D.R.
	4th		C.R.E. ceased in forenoon. Adjutant ceased about midday. Major Allan returned at 2.30 p.m.	D.R.
	5th		Quiet day. Work in trenches as usual.	D.R.
			Wet day. Adjt. ceased forenoon. Draft of 4 O.R. reported 7.45 p.m.	
	6th		Wet day. Major Allan & Capt Barr to trenches. C.R.E. adjt ceased 12.15 p.m. Work as usual.	D.R.
	7th		Showery day. Capt Rumsey adjt. to Cavan (Fabrication or Barrel) evening jct. Lt McCum returned from leave. Three of Farriers in hospital.	D.R. D.R.
	8th		Showery. Coy paid. Major Allan, Capt Barr to trenches. 1 man to B.S.a. for hunter. Enemy airplanes over our dugouts bombs which village	D.R.
	9th 10th		Captain Rumsey. Major Allan reported for trenches. Demonstration in bombing machine work - under 2 officers. Major Allan, Capt Rumsey attended	D.R. D.R.
	11th		wet day. Major Allan to trenches. Adjt. ceased. Major Allan Capt Barr to trenches & 10 p.m.	D.R.

Army Form C. 2118.

WAR DIARY
or
INTELLIGENCE SUMMARY.

1/1st HIGHLAND FIELD Co. R.E.

Place	Date	Hour	Summary of Events and Information	Remarks and references to Appendices
Maurieul	June 12th		Weather improving. Capt. Goldsmith attached to Coy. which under[took] for R.F.A. Major Allan to the chier — work in line as usual - also proper being made —	DR3
	13th		Very wet day. Little work done —	DR3
	14th		Windy. Lt. Brig returned from leave. Summer time adopted —	DR3
	15th		Work moving. Adjt. called forward from trenches. Capt. Bain to trenches	DR3
	16th		Adjt. called forward. Major Allan returned from trenches. Capt. Bain to trenches.	DR3
	17th		Major Allan Stannus inspection. Capt. Sharpe home for munition work. 2 R. draft reported.	DR3
	18th		Major Allan at trenches for day. Nine or ten enemy aeroplanes over - Building of Camma finished	DR3
			Major Allan to trenches to B[rigade]. H[ead]. Q[uarters]. Capt. Bain returned in evening. The enemy aeroplanes over at 3.15 pm and 4 at 6.15 pm —	DR
	19th		Rain in morning. Adjt + R.C. called. Demolition in work in trenches	DR3
	20th		Good day. Gibson blanched slightly Camma Obscura etc.	DR3
	21st		Good day. Adjt. called forward. Lieut. Bain on leave - Major Allan returned from trenches. Cowell, Blackcock places into arrest.	DR3
	22nd		Fine day — Capt. Bain to trenches re Camma Obscura - Machine gun fire with R.F.A. Experiments in photograph with Camma Obscura carried out.	DR3
	23rd		Adjt. called forward. R.C. called in Evening. Saw Collins. Heavy bombardment South. Captain for trenches. DR	

WAR DIARY or INTELLIGENCE SUMMARY

Army Form C. 2118.

1/1st HIGHLAND FIELD Co. R.E.

Place	Date	Hour	Summary of Events and Information	Remarks and references to Appendices
MARICOURT	June 24th		Good day. Work in trenches progressing. C.R.E. Adjt. called previous evening before O.C. evidence taken. Capt Bain to trenches.	D/3
	25th		This morning steam sheers heard from S. Lt Carmichael to trenches re Craters Consolidation. Two trenches in trenches.	D/3
	26th		Good day. Preparing accommodation for 60th Divn. Brigade who are expected to come tomorrow. Adjt called previous. 2/Lt Leudon died at 10.30 pm last evening.	D/3
	27th		Village shelled about 1.0 am. Major Allan to trenches 10 am. Adjt arrived 11 am. O.C. Hutchinson 26 Co. called re Craters.	D/3
	28th		C.R.E. & Adjt. called previous. Capt Bain to trenches. Working party with 1/1st D.F.Co. Sappers.	D/3
	29th		Dull morning. Lt Carmichael to R.E. Headquarters with 7 O.R. to undertake instruction of 60th Divn in Crater Consolidation. Capt Purnell took up duties as acting Adjt.	D/3
	30th		Dull day. Major Allan to trenches 9 am. Capt's hided Russock called 11.0 am.	D/3

Isaac Capt. R.E.
1/1st Highland F. Co. R.E.

Vol 13

CONFIDENTIAL
No 3092A
HIGHLAND
DIVISION.

Confidential
War Diary
of
1/1st High Field Co R.E.

From 1st July 1916 to 31st July 1916

WAR DIARY
INTELLIGENCE SUMMARY.
1/1st HIGHLAND FIELD Co. R.E.

Army Form C. 2118.

(46)

Place	Date	Hour	Summary of Events and Information	Remarks and references to Appendices
Mailleul	July 1916.			
	1st		Three Sections working in trenches with attachment of 2/1/5 London Field Cos. Heavy bombardment heard from South. Capt Rain billeted in forward trenches in the evening - weather good.	DB
	2nd		Major Allan billeted in moving returned in the evening. Capt Russell carried during if previous. Hostile aeroplane over village in evening. Bombardment South continued.	DB
	3rd		Work in trenches continues - training of new Company progressing. Capt Russell carried more.	DB
	4th		C.S.M 5ot (6ot) Div. carried (previous. 3 incendiary aeroplane bombs dropped outside Company H.Q. about 11.30pm	DB
	5th		ord, 1 officer, 1 unspecified. Major Allen to trenches in morning. Cpl WS Blackstock informed of Commercial nulities wanded.	DR
	6th		half-day. Capt Rain to trenches at 10am. Continued to 10am. lasted till 8.30pm - work in trenches as usual. Village shelled about 5.30pm with light shells.	DR
	7th		Drill morning. Major Allen to trenches 9.0am. Capt Russell carried 11.0am. "C" Company forced.	DR
	8th		Major Allen to trenches 9.0am returned 4.15pm. C.O. & Capt. Russell carried.	DR
	9th		~~(struck through line)~~	DR
	9th		Cpl Pope carried 11.30am. Sentence on Capt. Blackstock promulgated - found brauls.	DR

WAR DIARY
or
INTELLIGENCE SUMMARY.

(Erase heading not required.)

Army Form C. 2118.

1/1st HIGHLAND FIELD Co. R.E.

Place	Date	Hour	Summary of Events and Information	Remarks and references to Appendices
MAROEUIL	July 1916 10th		Major Allan & Lieut. 9.0am returned 3pm - Capt. Ross & Lieut. 1.30pm returned 10.0pm. L/Cpls & No 3 Section return to trenches for trenches. Main work handed over - Preparation made for possible move - All work in trenches being handed over to 97th Field Coy.	DB.
	11th		Capt. Ross & No 3 Section - Capt. Ross & Lieut. 9.30am - Army Commander Divisional Commander visited Coy while Sections dismissed. Capt. Ross - my Section day. Major Allan to ASNIERES began preparation for move. All men & Corpors with drawn from trenches - handed over L/Zang to new area - Abbaye de Newville, joined with Stores. 3 OR. reinforcements left. All waggons loaded ready for move. Operation orders received for 1st & 2nd day. Coys. left 11.15 & later.	DB.
	12th		Lt Carmichael returned from ASNIERES	DB.
	13th		Company arrived at 2.0am to L'Abbaye de Newville. Farm - marched in new C/1st Gordon.	DB.
L'Abbaye de Newville farm	14th		Cert day - Company arrived l'Abbaye de Newville from 4- 8.0pm. Bright day. CRE crossed lines 8.0pm - Inspected rubber nipes - Major Lovett Sappers let dumps.	DB.
"	15th		Improved news received M.8's am - 51st minutes after details line - Sappers marched next at 1 am to Rollecourt & found water troops. Arrived BOUQUEMAISON 4 am. Transport under Capt. Ross left	DB.
BOUQUEMAISON			Jam at 2.15 am arrived BOUQUEMAISON 9.50 am	DB.

Army Form C. 2118.

WAR DIARY
or
INTELLIGENCE SUMMARY.
(Erase heading not required.)

1/1st HIGHLAND FIELD Co. R.E.

Instructions regarding War Diaries and Intelligence Summaries are contained in F.S. Regs., Part II. and the Staff Manual respectively. Title pages will be prepared in manuscript.

48.

Place	Date	Hour	Summary of Events and Information	Remarks and references to Appendices
BUSQUEMESON	JULY 1916 16th		Orders to move to RIBEAUCOURT received at 5.30 a.m. Company paraded & moved off 7.15 a.m. alt. N. Calme left with billeting park 6.30. Company arrived RIBEAUCOURT 1.30 pm. Informed no billets available. Moved to BAIZIEUX arrived 1.50 pm. Very poor billets.	D.B.
BAIZIEUX	17th		Informed 9.0 a.m. Company will remain in present billets today. Wet day. Wagons overhauled & greased. It being too L. Mulcaster on an instruction for O.in C. H.Q. to arrange billets at St Leger-les-Domart at 5.30 pm. L. Mulcaster informed that company would remain at St Leger-les-Domart. No billets available as troops in occupation. L. Mulcaster returned about 7.30 pm. no billets available as troops in occupation. Wraps from morning. Adjutant called 8.30 pm. with orders cancelling the move. Wraps forward area believed between HEBUTERNE the SOMME required.	D.B.
"	18th		Fine misty morning. Company paraded. Training for feet in forenoon. Company preparing to move. Horses rested. Wagons greased. Good weather. Operation orders to move at 7.45 pm received 6.55 pm. Company moved off for MONTONVILLERS D.R. at 7.45 pm.	D.B.
"	19th		Company arrived 1.35 a.m. Horses watered & fed. Men issued with tea. At 3.15 a.m. orders to move at 6.0 a.m. received. Moved off 6.0 a.m. for BUIRE SUR L'ANCRE arriving there at 2.45 pm.	
MONTONVILLERS	20th			D.B.

Army Form C. 2118.

WAR DIARY
or
INTELLIGENCE SUMMARY.

(Erase heading not required.)

1/1ST HIGHLAND FIELD Co. R.E.

49

Instructions regarding War Diaries and Intelligence Summaries are contained in F. S. Regs., Part II. and the Staff Manual respectively. Title pages will be prepared in manuscript.

Place	Date	Hour	Summary of Events and Information	Remarks and references to Appendices
	July 1916.			
BUIRE SUR L'ANCRE	21st		Company resting in good billets. Operation Orders issued at 8.30 p.m. Moved with 152nd Inf. Bde to bivouac at F2.c.5.0. Just north of Méaulte.	OS
F.2.c.5.0	22nd		Arrived 12.35 a.m. 2 Sections proved to Fricourt at 8.0 a.m. to prepare shelter for Div. Hd. Section I & II detailed for work in trenches between S.9.a.4.0 + S.9.c.9.0. Very heavy shelling all the time. Casualties 1 Sapper killed 2 Sappers wounded. Sappers returned to Battn Quarters 10.30 p.m.	DB
"	23rd		Major Allan & Lt. McClune to trenches in forenoon. C.O.S. detailed work for Company. Sect IV to Section to la clue at 1.30 p.m. Deepening & improving existing front-line. Sects I & II detailed for work in deans trenches by night - very quiet night with little shelling. Good progress made.	DB
	24th		Majors Allen & Lt Doig to trenches at 3.0 a.m. Returned abt. 8.0 a.m. Sections III and IV to trenches at 7.30 p.m. Section I & IV 6 trenches in afternoon for day work. Returned at 7.30 p.m. Section I & IV 6 trenches at 8.0 p.m. for night work. Working party ordered to stand to in event of outpost coming under attack. No word of this attack coming off. Returned work day & heavy shelling.	DB
	25th		Major Allen & Lt McClune at 9.30 a.m. returned 1.0 p.m. Reports from Gurkha Range	DB

WAR DIARY
or
INTELLIGENCE SUMMARY
(Erase heading not required.)

Army Form C. 2118

1/1st HIGHLAND FIELD Co. R.E.

Place	Date	Hour	Summary of Events and Information	Remarks and references to Appendices
F.2.c.5.0. Sheet 62 D N.E.	July 25th (contd)		Alterations made in working party arrangements. No. IV Section to trenches at 6.30 a.m. No. III Section to trenches at 9.30 a.m. Forenoon fine, warm & dry. Sections I & II on nightwork. Heavily shelled a return fire trenches – no casualties. Section II to trenches in afternoon. Daily quiet. Remaining Sections out at night – little shelling in this but on the return trenches were heavily shelled with gas shells. Men per sick eddy but were otherwise all right.	DB
	26th		Very hot clear day. Dust from M.T. very bad. Intense bombardment from 5 a.m. to 9.30 a.m. Quiet during day. No Section out during day – all Sections up to trenches at night. Major Allan L. Entwisle in company before breakfast. Hostile aircraft seen about 7.15 p.m on our lines.	DB
	27th		Very hot day. Capt Ban to trenches before breakfast. Almost no hostile shelling on Divisional front. Three Sections return trenches at midday. No. III Section trenches 2.30 p.m – Pioneer exceed forenoon. Major Allan to trenches 6.0 p.m – 9.0 p.m. Very heavy bombardment Read from POZIERES Sects IV & II to trenches between 6.0 p.m – 9.0 p.m. Section IV returned to quarters at 10.0 p.m.	DB
	28th		Section II &III return alt midnight. Section IV return at early morning. Inspection of direction alt midnight. Section IV & I return in early morning. Major Allan L. & Co. came to very hot day. Section IV B & I ditto. St Lang to trenches in forenoon – reconnaissance out H.Qr. in afternoon re – work parties etc. St Lang to trenches alt Section I & II to trenches in afternoon – Gas shells falling in front. Wind north of Communication to Show Wood. Reported at Cats trees a return – Section I &II to trenches heavy bombardment at 8.30 p.m. Gas alarm at Company dugouts at 10.15 p.m – No casualties.	DB
	29th		Section I orders were to have carried down to sleep. No casualties.	DB
	30th		Rain & much rain. Cool & July. Saps I & III return about 4.0 a.m. Section I returned about 9.30 a.m. Heavy thunder shower. Sects II &III return about 2.30 a.m. Section I to trenches in morning. No seeing out during day. Sapper W. McClyne to C.C.S. in evening. Repair. Raining under very severe barrage fire – no casualties. Operations of 1/3 R.E. although troops in progress after 6.0 p.m – Major Allen W. McClyne to Show fire. Section II ordered into trenches near damage by shell fire.	DB
	31st		All Sections in billets. Sects II & III ordered to proceed to BAZENTIN-LE-GRAND. Very hot day.	DB

51st Divisional Engineers

1/1st HIGHLAND FIELD COMPANY R. E.::::

AUGUST 1 9 1 6

WAR DIARY or INTELLIGENCE SUMMARY

Army Form C. 2118

Place	Date	Hour	Summary of Events and Information	Remarks and references to Appendices
F.2.C.5.0 SHEET 62D N.E.	AUGUST 1916 1st		Section II & III under Lt. W. Clark, Doig Paterson, Cramb, Guerdon for BAZENTIN-LE-GRAND at 2.30 am. To relieve Section 2nd & 3rd 2/c Cy, working on hydraulic pipe spring fed. Major Allen G.R.E. in morning. Station instruction that Section I & IV will now to BAZENTIN LE GRAND. Sudden morning. Station I Cy on fatigues in Fricourt. 2nd Section ordered to proceed to BAZENTIN-LE-GRAND at 3.0 am on 2/8/16. Very hot all day. Quiet night. Enemy put m.g. fire for shells about 9.0 pm.	DB
	2nd		Section I & IV with Lts Laing, Carmichael leave for BAZENTIN at 3.0 am. Arrive about 4.30 am. Major Allen to inclus at 3.30 am. Returned 8.0 am. Very hot day. Section II & IV tubes overnow working with Pte Irving Jack — repairing when damaged.	DB
	3rd		Section I. II. III. IV at BAZENTIN-LE-GRAND. Sects II & III working in firing line from 1/2 mid night. 2/c Coy R.E. making two sections joining up deadheads & pipes on lime supply from S.4.d.0.3 to S.10.a.80.85. Remaining two sections joining up deadheads & pipes on lime supply from S.4.d.0.3 to S.10.a.80.85 Sheet 27 C. S.W. Little progress made during night 3/c Aug. owing to heavy shelling. Enemy bombardment heaviest F.2.5.5.0 pm. several officers of the water parties were wounded. Situation taken place to night of 3/4 Aug. Enemy dumps several in N Easter direction as night operation unknown.	DB
	4th 5th		a nadish in N Easter direction as night operation not known. Soldiers on detachment working as above. Very hot day.	DB
	6th		Soldiers on detachment working as above. Sect.	DB
			Section II & IV return from BAZENTIN-LE-GRAND about 4.0 am. Section I & III returned to quarters in BAZENTIN abt. 5.10 am. Company moves for F.E.C.S.O. Section I — Arrive new area to D12d.2.2. at 7.0 pm. Section at 4.30 pm. Arrive new area to D12d.2.2. at 7.0 pm.	DB
D12d 22	7th		Company resting. Good day — cool morning, got warmer about mid day. Rain transport road under the guns again with running till 9.15. Cookhouses eased about 8.0.N.12's at movement of transport. Received 9.0 pm.	DB

WAR DIARY or INTELLIGENCE SUMMARY

Army Form C. 2118

Place	Date	Hour	Summary of Events and Information	Remarks and references to Appendices
D.12.d.22.	AUGUST 1916. 8th		Company paid at noon. Looked for moorland (?) trappers records. Transport moves at 3.30 pm for POULAINVILLE. Marching unit 153rd Inf. Bde group. Ven Elt march. Transport parked at POULAINVILLE at 10.30 pm. O.O. No. 126 received & Coy. Std.to at 10.45 pm.	DB
"	9th		Dismounted Brand. Entraining Hm at POGETTIVE St. 3.0 pm. Water tels 10.0 pm before they could be entrained.	DR
POULAINVILLE	9th		Mounted Brand moves off for SOREL at 9.30 am unit 153rd Bde Transport. Ven Elt march. Horses watered & fed. Arrive again at 5.0 pm. Arriving by Plf. man D.	DR
SOREL.	10th		SOREL 10-30 pm. Dismounted Band left POGETHLE at 1.0 am. Arrive LONGPRE at 7.15 am & detrained. Marches to SOREL arrive Tue at 11.0 am. Men fur Tued. Transport nothing. Draft 10 ORs gone mids at 7.0 am 1st unit. O.O. 127. received 4.10 pm. Company to entrain at PONT REMY at 1.48 am.	DB
"	11th		Coy. Resting.	DR
"	12th		Coy. entrained at PONT REMY by 5.15 am. Very awkward loading arrangements for vehicles. Train routed 5.30 am. RENE via ABBEVILLE. CALAIS. ST OMER - to STEEN BECQUE. De-train via ABBEVILLE. CALAIS. ST OMER to RACQUINGHEM eff. arrived about 1.0 pm. Detrained 7.0 pm. Coy moved } had word for RACQUINGHEM off. billets (bed). Arrive about 7.30 pm. Luggage received probable arrival departure 1055.	DR
RACQUINGHEM	13th		Coy. Bathed in Wood. McCrow & 3 ORs proceed to new found area. title Erdwa will outgoing Fuld. Coy. O.O. per O.R.I. received in afternoon to move in 16th Aug.	DR

WAR DIARY or INTELLIGENCE SUMMARY

Army Form C. 2118

Instructions regarding War Diaries and Intelligence Summaries are contained in F.S. Regs., Part II. and the Staff Manual respectively. Title Pages will be prepared in manuscript.

HIGHLAND FIELD COMPANY, R.E.
1st — T.F.

(53)

(Erase heading not required.)

Place	Date	Hour	Summary of Events and Information	Remarks and references to Appendices
RACQUINGHEM	Aug. 1916 14th		Company resting. Church Service in afternoon.	
	15th		Company bathed in Mmm. Wagons loaded read'y N move @ 9.0 pm.	
	16th		Mounted section moved with 133rd Bde Transport at 5.0 am. Arrived ARMENTIERES 6.20 pm. Arrived ARMENTIERES 8.0 pm. 196 Inft. or dept.	
ARMENTIERES	17th		Sappers entrained at EBBLINGHAM at 6.0 pm. Arrived ARMENTIERES 8.0 pm. Men removed from billets taken in use organisations. Company employed cleaning up billets. 3rd J.Co. N.Z.E. 1 Officer reinforcement joined Company.	
	18th		Work in trenches commenced. Sappers shelling machine gun emplacements etc.	
	19th		Work as above. Sappers working continuous shifts @ 8 hrs. Working parties of infantry now from Sappers allotted to Division.	
	20th		Work as above.	
	21st		Work as above. Difficulty in keeping section supplied with materials owing to shortage of transport. Two R.E. wagons received from DAC.	
	22nd		Work as above. Four additional lumber wagons received from 133rd Iy Bde. "Gas Alert."	
			Message received at 8.0 pm.	
	23rd		Message "Gas Alert" taken off 4.0 pm. "Gas Alert" put on again at 11.0 pm.	
	24th		Work as above. Gas Alert taken off about 9 am report. Materials being got up. Working parties to Brick Kanapat.	
	25th		Work as above. Gas Alert still on. Gas alert cancelled 6.0 pm, with adjutant.	
	26th		Work continued as above. Ammunition shelled during afternoon.	
	27th		Work as above.	

WAR DIARY
or
INTELLIGENCE SUMMARY
(Erase heading not required.)

Army Form C. 2118

Place	Date	Hour	Summary of Events and Information	Remarks and references to Appendices
ARMENTIERES	Aug. 1916			
	28th		Enemy artillery intensity trebles in comparison with 18 & 19th - Quantity of practical available half days work. Enemy trench mortars fully employed.	
			Ours in tremendous duellos. Headquarters dugouts T.M. emplacements etc.	OB
	29th		Wrote as above. Station Staffs withdrawn at midnight. We has 2 men - necessity of winded Gas attack. Reinforcement of 3 O.R. reported.	OB
	30th		Works above. Staffs withdrawn in evening owing to shortage of materials. Windward Staff & working parties cancelled. Considerable flooding.	OB
	31st		Works above. Steam bombardment began at ARMENTIERES about 2.0 a.m. Fires morning.	OB

BauCap..OC.
1st OC. Highland Co RE.

Confidential.

War Diary

of

1/1st High. Field Co. R.E.

for

September. 1916

CONFIDENTIAL.
No 21/A
HIGHLAND DIVISION.

Vol 15

Army Form C. 2118

1/1st HIGHLAND FIELD Co. R.E.

WAR DIARY
or
INTELLIGENCE SUMMARY
(Erase heading not required.)

Place	Date	Hour	Summary of Events and Information	Remarks and references to Appendices
ARMENTIERES	Sept. 1916			
	1st		From Stations working on covered shelters & on continuing shafts & pipes for Experiments with Land Torpedoes carried on behind billets. Brig. Gen. Commanding 153rd Bde. R.F.A. present. 2" dia. water pipes with armoured heads & special driving heads about 12'0 in use. 1½" piping cutting in a distance of about 8 ft. P.C. 1½" pipe, 8 litre use.	S.3
	2nd		Water tractors carried on as above. Enemy torpedoes burst with hindrance during the night 1/2nd. Work stopped till dk.	S.3
	3rd		Wrote in trenches as above.	
	4th		As above	
	5th		As above	D.3
	6th		Work as above. Gas alert on 11.30 p.m.	S.3
	7th		As above	S.3
	8th		Work as above. 2 cuts & 8 pipe piercing jobs and up to trenches in various & prepared operations throughout signal	S.3
	9th		30 feet in 180 min reported (a cut as Sapper works from 154th Bn. 153rd Bde. relieved 153rd Bde. Work in trenches continued. Concrete dugouts, T.M. emplacements & pill &c. Experiments begun carried on with Bangalore torpedoes & putting spare. Iron - Magnolia ships dropped wire on & open.	S.3
	10th		Work resumed again at 6.0 am.	
	11th		Work as above	S.3
	12th		Work as above	S.3

WAR DIARY
or
INTELLIGENCE SUMMARY

Army Form C. 2118

1/1st HIGHLAND FIELD Co. R.E.

(56)

Place	Date	Hour	Summary of Events and Information	Remarks and references to Appendices
BOMBARTZEE	Sept 13th		Work in tunnels continued. All parties works Sapper withdrawn at midday. Howite in afternoon. All available men carrying up gas cylinders.	DRS
	14th		Work in tunnels stopped meanwhile. McClure talking with Thompson. 2 carries up to tunnels in forenoon. Sappers returns carrying up Japanese ahead. Lancernes Paris changes-pulsar Ephedor fields in night 13/14. While carrying up Thompson fell with it. Carried to premises in trench (by incident.) As Thompson opened jar - Iron spanned shewed coat was — Supts. Kirkwood and McTavish looked in 3 places and to speaks to auto — Supt. Symans brooks Epipheia sources Couvelier Bamburgan — printin. Lieut Symans timber breeder Epipheia sources in forenoon. Two torpedoes successfully fired.	DRS
	15th		McClure arranging filling up of Newsletter in forenoon. Dannying out completed.	DRS
	16th		Pipe Push-Pipe fired out in forenoon beyond our wire. During afternoon evening it was fired from Dressings wire and blown. Good gap cut - nearly fifty metres that the pushed cleanest out.	DRS
	17th		All men writing curtains during forenoon. Work in trenches clapped. Gas carried up at night.	DRS
	18th		During forenoon all available men worked in three dressings. Trenches carried at 2.40 p.m.	DRS
	19th		Two shifts Employers in Power trenches each day as night work was cancelled. Cleaning in trenches. Very wet day.	DRS
	20th		One shift - in Power trenches Day. Remainder in trench.	DRS

WAR DIARY or INTELLIGENCE SUMMARY

Army Form C. 2118

1/1st HIGHLAND FIELD Co. R.E.

Place	Date	Hour	Summary of Events and Information	Remarks and references to Appendices
Armentieres	Sept 20th (contd)		Handing over trench work to 8th Australian Engineers. O.O. No 574 received from HQ 51st Div. Company to move to ERQUINGHEM on 22nd to be there by 6.0 pm. Company preparing to move.	R3
	21st		O.O. No 83 received. Company was received in present billets. Issued at 10.15 am. O.O 83 attached. Call at 2.30 pm. Company to exchange billets with 209th F.Co. at Erquinghem on 23rd inst. Noted Espinoy road to Company at 6.30 pm. Loading troops continues.	R3
	22nd		Company paraded 9.30 am. Loading wagons in forenoon. Rifle inspection 12.30. Marching order parade 2.30 & wagons looked at for inspection.	R3
	23rd		Company moved to ERQUINGHEM arriving there at 11.10 am. Billets in factory.	R3
ERQUINGHEM	24th		Small boy respirators issued to Company in forenoon. Instruction in fitting them & care. Instruction in fitting respirators given to Company in forenoon. In afternoon the Company went to AIRMYN NEUFS river further than given chance to test respirators. Practical all respirators gave complete protection. O.O No 136 received attached.	R3 R3
	25th		Company moved independently of 153 Bde to METEREN left billets at 10.0 am and arrived METEREN at 4.30 pm.	R3
METEREN	26th		Sappers busy at billets. Squad drill N/C Excursions. 110 Sappers inoculated	R3
	27th		Section drill in forenoon. Men playing football in afternoon. Lt Berg to Reserve & train returning	R3
	28th		Section drill. N.C.O's communication and recruiting wagons. Men inoculated 19 July	R3
	29th		To new position battn. in BAILLEUL in forenoon. Remainder in afternoon. Instruction given to Infantry in construction of strong points	R3

1/1st HIGHLAND FIELD Co. R.E.

Army Form C. 2118

WAR DIARY
or
INTELLIGENCE SUMMARY
(Erase heading not required.)

5-8

Place	Date	Hour	Summary of Events and Information	Remarks and references to Appendices
METEREN	Sept. 1916. 3rd.		Company preparing to move by rail to Matzen. Baggage loaded.	S.B.

[signature], MAJOR, R.E.
O.C. 1/1st HIGHLAND FIELD CO. R.E.

3/10/16.

Secret

Oct 16

War Diary
of.
1/1st Highland Field Co R.E.
51st Division.

from 1st Oct. 1916 to 31st Oct. 1916

Army Form C. 2118

WAR DIARY
or
INTELLIGENCE SUMMARY
(Erase heading not required.)

1/1st HIGHLAND FIELD Co. R.E.

Place	Date	Hour	Summary of Events and Information	Remarks and references to Appendices
METEREN	Oct. 1916	1st	Company entrained at BAILLEUL at 7.0 am. left 9.0 am. detrained at DOULLENS and marched to BEAUVAL arriving there at 6.35 pm. O.O. N°. 138 issued at 6.35 pm.	A.3.
BEAUVAL		2nd	Company left BEAUVAL 10.0 am arrived LOUVENCOURT 3.0 pm.	A.3.
		3rd	Company resting. Very wet.	A.3.
LOUVENCOURT		4th	Company left for COURCELLES - AU BOIS at 9.0 am arriving there 11.0 am. Billets taken over from 1/1st East Anglian been billeted in huts. Very hot dinner given. Billets taken over from 1/1st East Anglian Div R.E Co H.Q. Very wet + wind - N° 3 Sec. All officers called to Div. Headquarters.	A.3.
COURCELLES		5th	3 parties work repairing watering points in town. Stellar Officer reconnoitre listening Posn taped off by listening Posn.	A.3.
		6th	Company work erecting wireless [?] in frenvar. Section own unit top Infantry parties carrying down to trench. Sappers wiring [?] Hamelt [?] returned to base.	A.3.
		7th	Company out in afternoon + taught a lineh. Practised Complete Bugle Cy. Company in afternoon + night. Finishing [?] + laying line to trench.	A.3.
		8th	All Sections go out in afternoon + night. Finishing [?] + laying line to trench. Ration water dump.	A.3.
		9th	Work in line as above. Making trench ones R.E. dumps, Ration water dump.	A.3.
		10th	Work as above.	A.3.

Army Form C. 2118

WAR DIARY
or
INTELLIGENCE SUMMARY

(Erase heading not required.)

1/1st HIGHLAND FIELD Co. R.E.

Instructions regarding War Diaries and Intelligence Summaries are contained in F. S. Regs., Part II. and the Staff Manual respectively. Title Pages will be prepared in manuscript.

Place	Date	Hour	Summary of Events and Information	Remarks and references to Appendices
Contreuve	Oct. 1916			
	11th		All Sections working in line. Construction of R.E. Advanced Dumps, Brushstairs, Ration dumps etc.	B
	12th		As above	B
	13th		As above	B
	14th		As above	B
	15th		As above	B
	16th		As above	B
	17th		As above — Work in line practically finished. 4 Sections withdrawn to prepare to move.	B
	18th		G.O. No. 99 received at 8.30 pm. Co. to move to Forceville. Company left Contreuve at 11.15 am. O.C. ½ staying to watch to the take over new line party about 2 Loyds in front of Auchonvillers. Co. arrived Forceville at 1.30 pm.	B
Forceville	19th		Horses received rations 9.30 am. O.C. returned 2.0 am. Men resting. Infantry billets. General instructions regarding work received by O.C. Work allotted to Section Officers. Arrangements made with Camp Commandant at Mailly wood for 3 Sections to bivouac there following day. Three Sections going to timber standpoint. Repairing communications leading to R.E. dumps etc.	B
	20th		[three] Sections working in timber return to bivouac at 1.0 pm. Going to shelling bivouac wood and Company settling down. Bivouacs used again at 5.0 pm. Instructions for C.R.E. take over increase of 1/2 Dh. F.E. R.E. Company's Value Sections asked for their Section in increase. Section on workshops at Forceville. Details of three Sections leave Forceville 10.0 am for Vines. Sections continue work in trenches.	B
	21st		Work in trenches continued. Instructions regarding Offensive received. Orders not accepted.	B
	22nd		Work as above. Heated country in materials attempted. Daily offensive postponed owing to weather.	B
	23rd			B
	24th		Operating postponed further 24 hours owing to weather.	B

Army Form C. 2118

WAR DIARY
or
INTELLIGENCE SUMMARY

1/1st HIGHLAND FIELD Co. R.E.

(Erase heading not required.)

Place	Date	Hour	Summary of Events and Information	Remarks and references to Appendices
FORCEVILLE	Oct 25	1916.	O.C. to Detachmt. 153 Brigit Trenches. Rain all morning & half of afternoon - Little Artillery fire. Left instructions regarding relations with our Officers. Sent draining fishing parties & working parties. Received instructions to send Capture form to Flying Corps - N.C.O. & 2 men from Sec. II sent to Sunk Detacht.	M
	26		Daily conference at 11 A.M. with C.R.E. S.R.G (ag. 153)- 1st 153 D.C.R. Brigat hours parade. Orders to this Unit - Captn Bain left at 3 p.m. for 4 fort to Flying Corps - When off thereof.	M
	27		Working in Trenches. Preparing for operations. More rain - O.C. to Brigade Detachmt & Brigade in morning & to Detachmt in afternoon.	M
	28		O.C. to Detachmt. Hencourt working in Trenches in morning - Big Arms / Sonic Race. Instructions received from Corps Commander as to arrangements to single from Mailly Wood Pox. & 57. to Mailly Wood East at P.18 Central. Arrangements made for the Subaltern & Cpl Bain H.Q. is going to explain position tonight in Trenches. Lt G.B. Paterson returns from leave at 11 a.m.	M
	29		Wagons left at 8.30 a.m. to assist in sifting Detachment. - Rain - duel - Sections I, II & III now located at P.18. Central. In huts. No wagons or horses with them. At 11 a.m. Conference C.R.E. gave instructions as to employment of Coy in operations viz: Repair of BEAUMONT-HAMEL ROAD from AUCHONVILLERS through BEAUMONT on lengths to BEAUCOURT as circumstances permit.	M
	30		2/Lt. G.B. Paterson rejoined section on Detachment & Lt. Grant visited Detachment. O.C. to Detachmt. Brigade & Trenches. Very wet from 5 p.m. with high wind. - Mr taken at a standstill. Detachment digging in. In evening receives motor engine. Decided saw to set up there.	M

1875 W: W593/826 1,000,000 4/15 J.B.C. & A. A.D.S.S./Forms/C. 2118.

Army Form C. 2118

WAR DIARY
or
INTELLIGENCE SUMMARY

1/1st HIGHLAND FIELD Co. R.E.

(62)

(Erase heading not required.)

Place	Date	Hour	Summary of Events and Information	Remarks and references to Appendices
FORCEVILLE	Oct. 31	1906	Fine day - Strong N.W. wind - Getting saw Pingies set up - Trench Boards ↑↓ - Brig: Towers failed to turn up - Wagons to Detachment to dig in & with Trench Boards ↑↓ - Brig: Towers turned up later. Received word from C.R.E. that Corps Commander has awarded military medal to one of my men viz :- No 8627. Corporal David Kerr Mackie for bravery & coolness on 22 & 23 Oct: 1915 whilst in charge of making parties under heavy shell fire. (authority E.C.G.L. M9M.M.103 of 29/10/15 - 51st (H.) D. No 6 (A) Detachment digging themselves shelters.	JBL

J.B. Lewean. MAJOR. R.E.
0.C. 1/1st HIGHLAND FIELD Co. R.E.

H.R. 256

CRE 39th Div.

Herewith War Diary for August.

A Bain
Capt RE
for CO 1/2nd H'd'd S'G RE

2/9/16.

51/
Vol 17

War Diary
1/2 High Field 66 R?
fm
November 1916

Confidential

WAR DIARY
or
INTELLIGENCE SUMMARY
(Erase heading not required.)

Army Form C. 2118

1/1st HIGHLAND FIELD Co. R.E.

Instructions regarding War Diaries and Intelligence Summaries are contained in F.S. Regs., Part II. and the Staff Manual respectively. Title Pages will be prepared in manuscript.

(63)

Place	Date	Hour	Summary of Events and Information	Remarks and references to Appendices
FORCEVILLE	Nov. 1916			
	1		O.C. to Trenches - hour day. Called for Mail Fact'y - Mr all Sections. Pieces Run - Water to Brew - Called Detachment - Called Lt. Reeves at Regiment. Party the excoming out of Hastings Passage. Seen Bay. is to carry + see Huts at 4 S. 2½ Party here above as well. O.C. inspected Works at 5.30 Returned from drys. O.C. Deliberation from general. Detached at Mmart from Brig. at Sq. Hudy sent. up 5.30 p.m. to Queens - Dry Day	Ast
	2		Dry morning. Met Maty with Sutt Lewis R.E. Discussed interviews G.R.A. re ammunition. He considered if more detaches DiControls Despy's 7 2 Mags. here: Said re fix at light Orchard Maty system was not... at Light Orchard Maty system	Ast
	3		Dump returning Showns here about 10 feet. Called Detachment - Fine morning - Fog late. To Trenches - Inspected work on Serve - Springwood - Poopys - Inages at -- - Wrote -- and took a note - over Brig. General.	Ast
	4		Dry morning. No news of interest - Irying to make siege bridge to Mary Jack in duckwalks - Metro - Saw Mr. Baines making satisfactorily. Visited Detachment - 153 Brig. Rifled T at Rees work - Heavy fire from 0.8. between 4 + 5. Dry Day - Mail came in this morning - letters sent to Depict from Scotland.	Ast
	5		Dry morning - very strong Mr. wind. To Trenches with M. Laurchert - Lt. E. Lcey - M. Harre. Warned Burvelations Bucket at 112 MAJRY - Called on 154 Brigade Just in to Capt. Jordan - Martry. Their Mess for his purpose - R.E. Buy. send 4 Lieut. Toad to Baincentre. 153 Brig. to Conselt Rev at Trench Centre. Relief hard at niht Surface Ice. Artinto alt force between F 3 pm. - were not at night.	Ast
	6		Continuing dry - a few showers. Detaching Officers at O.P. Springs - To Detachment from Trenches - Brung at + from O.B. at 4.30 a.m. With all three of good issues in Rue Tree Lane. A moment after some gift was Rue S. Squat Intellects a Duehus Trench	Ast

WAR DIARY or INTELLIGENCE SUMMARY

Army Form C. 2118

1/1st HIGHLAND FIELD Co. R.E.

Place	Date	Hour	Summary of Events and Information	Remarks and references to Appendices
FERFAY	Nov 7 1916	7 ᵃᵐ	Some heavy explosions during night said to have been German dumps near Tincques blown up. Going over to Givenchy dug out moving — Yesterday instructions received — Instructions to Sect Medical Officer — Bathing room in Treuvelu's. To Brig: 15ᵗʰ in afternoon. Very bad report. Trenches, especially Saint Luce — Decided leave work for a day. Very bad in writing Rpt. Precautions tried to effect — Sects working night shift continuous rain.	
	8		Very heavy rain during night — Trenches getting into a very bad condition. Division Brigadier all issuing instructions as to covering with the sandbags — Much wet and much in the Forge at the tour to betachment Brigade on afternoon. Sent in my Report. Shelters & dug outs need to be more shelved. Some leave till 24ᵗʰ from some kind of German — 1st Scots Down at Light road past 15ᵗʰ the unit also affected. Any action being taken please inform when known probably.	
	9		To Treuvelus — TIPPERARY — STPATRICK — NEW ROAD — DINNER ST — PICCADILLY — Very bad — General Gough cleaning a Brick Mansions — Waterland St. All Brigadiers & Divy Commands officers. Were there. S.E. making me Coy tour of new dugouts 15ᵗʰ — new dugouts in use 1568.	
	10		In July every morning drew to the Somme, Weather was over 4 hours very damp. It has been dropping & Haigh in V.B. I. — Section reliving Robson Rye Tipperary C.T. — Waiting Shelters — weather very bad — reinforcement Roads getting very bad, at 15ᵗʰ Brig. in afternoon.	
	11		Section took ration G.T.'s during day.— Inspect TIPPERARY & DIMMER — new 15ᵗʰ Bgde working day full deft working at an entanglement in front of 15ᵗʰ Bgde. Woking day full deft working at an entanglement in front.	

Army Form C. 2118

1/1st HIGHLAND FIELD Co. R.E.

WAR DIARY
or
INTELLIGENCE SUMMARY
(Erase heading not required.)

Place	Date	Hour	Summary of Events and Information	Remarks and references to Appendices
FORCEVILLE	Nov 12th	1916	To TREUX — C.T.S sprang to SnowLus — Saw Germans working N of 107 away — no firing. Took over post. (65) Instructed to get AUCHONVILLERS — BEAUMONT Rd as far as No 4 Section sent up to join Detachment at P.18. Central — H.Q. at WHICHTROU=VITRE F	JM
	13		Zero at 5.45 P.M. — Very heavy bomb'ment — Weather dry but burst in morning. Clearing about 9 am, but we could not see smoke if possible — Reports coming in that Regts. were successful — BEAUMONT taken — but final objective not reached. Along R rd. Germans retaking ground to 153 Bde H.Q with 3 Sections 15 Feb. to R.E. Recon'd situation & instructions received to billet through heavy barrage to O.C. D 7 Black watch & O.C. 16 Gave what assistance I could. Either through lack of knowledge — linked Rgts. Fellows ? heavy bomb'd positions. Capt by Lions + German Cavalry — United Regts. into 4 — sent Lt. Boys to see O.C. 6th Black Watch + O.C.C.L.C.G. Durh British pouring in from SW ratials & wire. So we were occupied with two Thin Coas Leftn. Barth 3 A.M. O.C.C.L.M. until 5 A.M. Dull mist night but no alert — Sect. II worked all yesterday repairing MAILLY — AUCHONVILLERS ROAD. Sect. II Yesterday through FORCEVILLE — about 1000 fbs incoming. Section IV task (commenced) this morning to take final objective — Means another hour's light in & ground work	JM
	14		OURSELVES & NoM — Very good advance in (possible?) Beauly was taken early. No 4 Section continued repair rd at 9 P.M. Sects 1,2,3 + 1 platoon 1/6 Royal Scots Infantry AUCHONVILLERS — Nth BAUMONT HAMEL NEW ROAD — finished work at 10 P.M. Five mon - now carried on up to OLD British front line — much shelling + stray bullets - SGS Dugouts + 24 shelter bowies bringing materials	JM

WAR DIARY or INTELLIGENCE SUMMARY

Army Form C. 2118

1/1st HIGHLAND FIELD Co. R.E.

Place	Date	Hour	Summary of Events and Information	Remarks and references to Appendices
FORCEVILLE	1916 Nov.	15	Sect. 4 to work on BEAUMONT ROAD up to OLD GERMAN Line - Killed work 3h.m. - 1 driver wounded, 1 horse killed, (?) horse to Fd. Hosp. - Fine day cold N.E. wind - Cool clouds - fresh attack at 6.51 A.M. by 152 Brig: to take FRANKFORT T. appeared did not materd. Secs: 1,2,+ 3. making up to OLD GERMAN Front Line, at night this was turned for traffic - 154 Taking over whole Front at Munich TRENCH.	B.R.
		16	Frost at night - Fine clear day - No 4 Sec: in Roads during day - Sunken Rd - H. Paterson taking up Italian Road - New BEAUMONT ROAD under process of main to OLD GERMAN 2nd Line - H.Q. ground Bourage behind the Left - I	B.R.
			BEAUMONT HAMEL - 1 Batt. 154 Brig: Holding New MUNICH - Strong Point on PEARS Avenue & BEAUMONT - TB - Sect: 1,2,+3 taken over road at MUNICH	B.R.
		17	Sharp frost - Dull Cloudy weather - O.C. Fd. Co. 154 Batt: to Confirm round of Co's Bath: Front - Instructed to report at Head Qrs. Mun. HAMEL Road and report to BEAUMONT HAMEL. To Detachment - Work during day & night as before - Roads at 2nd Div: - Instructed to report at Head Qrs. Mun. HAMEL Road and report to BEAUMONT HAMEL.	B.R.
		18	BEAUMONT Road very difficult to clean. Cold night inclined to cloud - Strong N.E. wind Very cold - Snow during night - turned to rain - 32nd Div attacking at dawn from New Munich Tr to FRANKFORT - not successful - 153 Brig: moving back to RAINCHEVAL. Instructions received to send out No IV Sect: assist 1/2 H.F. Co. in construction Strong Point immediately behind Wagon Road at 5 A.M. tomorrow. Sect. I will go on with Roads during day & Sect: II in Reserve -	B.R.

WAR DIARY or INTELLIGENCE SUMMARY

Army Form C. 2118

1/1st HIGHLAND FIELD Co. R.E.

Place	Date	Hour	Summary of Events and Information	Remarks and references to Appendices
FORCEVILLE	Nov 19	19.16	To BEAUMONT HAMEL ard am – met It. Gordon I/1st G. AUCTONIETERS who informed me of casualties to No IV Sect. On arrival BEAUMONT found killed 2/Lt: T.F. W. KUMSTON, 9448 a/Cpl J. McLEAN, 92.11, a/o/Cpl P. MCPHAIL, unprasted 9435. Sapper J. WALKER – wounded No 977 Sapper J. WILBIE, & 9750 Sapper Thos. HOBBINS – Sect IV had just left work & about 8.45 AM in WAGON ROAD a shell caused right in front of head of column. Found bodies already had been taken off by parties unknown – officers revolver & infected took (Sect: I & III) – 154 Bry: party relieved today hotel fire 1E – Infected iss & lectures at night for Sect. I & II to go out at in support by 1 SD – Sect: IV to be continued with Sect: III & remain in A/Capt. J. Road tomorrow. McLEAN was one of the finest specimens of manhood I have known. He is a great loss. His officer too who has only been with me a short time has proved an able Engineer & a conscientious Officer.	[signature]
	20		Above members of Coy killed yesterday were buried at British Military Cemetery MAILLY at 10 A.M. All formalities attended to as to location & recovery belongings to be sealed up & returned to Base – Sect: I & II on road. Orders in afternoon to send I Section to BOYNETIRE on 21st – later orders cancelled – clear, mild.	[signature]

WAR DIARY or INTELLIGENCE SUMMARY

1/1st HIGHLAND FIELD Co. R.E. Army Form C. 2118

Place	Date	Hour	Summary of Events and Information	Remarks and references to Appendices
FORCEVILLE	Nov. 21	1916	To BEAUMONT – Sect: III r/v on Road – Orders received to move on 22nd to PUCHVILLERS – ISSUED instructions to Detachmt: to cease work & pack up –	JM
	22		Begans at 7.15 AM to move Detmt: who left MAINLY WOOD EAST at 8 A.M. – H.Q. left FORCEVILLE at 8.30 A.M. – Route via YARENNES – HARPONVILLE – TOUTENCOURT – Roads heavy & bad hills –	JM
PUCHVILLERS	23		Pontoons stuck twice, pulled out by M.T. Before entering TOUTENCOURT Detmt: joined H.Q. Met Advance Party under Lt. Lacey & billeted PUCHVILLERS at 1.30 P.M. men in Barns – Resting – inspecting equipment, repairs – fine weather – halted Cars in afternoon – 4 D.A.C. magazine attached – Transferred 22nd to 2/3 Coy: – Received 183 Brigade O.O. 162 at 9.30 p.m. to shift on 24th to YARENNES.	JM
	24		Lt Lacey & advance party to YARENNES at 7 A.M. to take over ½ H.Q. to billets. Moved out of PUCHVILLERS at 9.30 A.M. Route via TOUTENCOURT & HARPONVILLE – Passed 154 Brig: moving back – Some rain – heavy roads – Reached YARENNES & billeted at 1 p.m. Transport one side village in mud. Billets at the side village – Issued instructions for Detachmt: Proceed on 25th to LA BOISSELLE – take over from 11th Coy: R.E. – 4th for Canadian Div: – Received instructions re future 2 G.S. wagons to D.A.C. We are taking over (left 6) Line M.15.a.b.5. to R.17.b.2.6. (about 2700x) extreme right of III Corps (4th Army) Joining left flank of the III Corps.	JM
YARENNES				

WAR DIARY or INTELLIGENCE SUMMARY

Army Form C. 2118

1/1st HIGHLAND FIELD Co. R.E.

(69)

Place	Date	Hour	Summary of Events and Information	Remarks and references to Appendices
VARENNES	Nov. 25	1916	Very heavy Rain - Lt. Doig & Lt. Lainy - 2 batmen & 20 men to LA BOISELLE at 11 a.m. with 1 G.S. & 3 Technical vehicles, to be unloaded & returned. Cpl. Craig & 19 Sappers to take over Dumps in vicinity LA BOISELLE - rpt. to C.R.E. 4th Canadian Div. Operation Orders received to proceed with 153 Brig: to VARENNES tomorrow - Capt. Donald sent on Special leave 27th Nov: to 7th Dec:	SSS
	26		Very heavy rain - cold - Passed VARENNES CHURCH at 8.30 A.M. - Starting Point at HED- AUVILLE at 9.15 A.M. - No. 4 Sect: Forage Cart broke down before BOUZINCOURT. Had to be left. Went via AVELUY & ALBERT to Junction BAPAUME - LA BOISELLE Rd. - Transport arrived 12.45 p.m. Sappers & Officers dug into LA BOISELLE Rd. X.13.d.5.3. - Transport & horses to N. BAPAUME Rd. - no standing in Crew - 2 Officers 11th Can. Field Co. received & what information has about Trenches, no Stores - 153 Brig. H.Q. at X.13.a.7.5. C.R.E.: Div: H.Q. 20th W.H. Lt: Doig to Trenches -	SSS
LA BOISELLE	27		To 153 Brig. H.Q. - Lt. Doig with Lt. Lainy Carmichael to Trenches. Rec'd 4 D.A.C. wagons -	SSS
	28		To Trenches - 10th St - REGINA - DESIRE FRONT LINE & down MIRAUMONT Rd WEST - TO 153 Brig: H.Q. Advance - arranged parties for tonight. No 3 Sect: on 10th St. & Nos. 1 & 2 on Watson Av: - very dark & foggy - little work done -	SSS

WAR DIARY
or
INTELLIGENCE SUMMARY

(Erase heading not required.)

Army Form C. 2118

1/1st HIGHLAND FIELD Co. R.E.

(70)

Place	Date	Hour	Summary of Events and Information	Remarks and references to Appendices
La Boisselle	Nov 29	19/16	Received allocations & dressed huts near POZIERES – fractional request to shift Hars – To trenches in morning. 10th St & WATSON Av. – To 153 Brig. H.Q. Avenue – arranges parties for night – No 3 on 10th St & No1 in WATSON Av. – No 3 got started near hand shelter No 9276 – A. DA COSTA, Sapper, killed – No 9267 – Sapper DUFF, J. missing, believed killed – Little work done – No 1 Sect: got into a heavy barrage – were dispersed & returned without doing any work –	[signature]
	30		Change of Batts: in line – No 4 Sec. shifted to new billets – Sappers on Stables & new billets – Lt. Paterson confined to billets, injured knee –	[signature]
	Dec 1		Spiers & Sappers worked at Pop. Fr.: No 3 & 4 Sappers staying at billets. Officer Corporal & Lance Cpl. went on leave – Lt. B.J. MacIntyre joined on the 1st inst. To 153 Brig: took C/Ed. Lt. Rainey confined to billets sick –	

[signature]

MAJOR R.E.
O.C. 1/1st HIGHLAND FIELD Co. R.E.

CONFIDENTIAL.

H.E. 758.

C.R.E. 51st (H) Divⁿ

Herewith War Diary for the month of November 1916.

JB Allan MAJOR, R.E.
O.C. 1/1st HIGHLAND FIELD CO. R.E.

2.12.16.

CONFIDENTIAL.
No 91(A)
HIGHLAND
DIVISION.

Vol 18

War Diary
of
1/1st Highland Field Co., R.E.(T.)
From 1st December 1916
to 31st December 1916

Army Form C. 2118

WAR DIARY
or
INTELLIGENCE SUMMARY

(Erase heading not required.)

(71)

Place	Date	Hour	Summary of Events and Information	Remarks and references to Appendices
LA BOISELLE	Dec. 1	1916	Buried Sappers A. DaCosta & J. Duff at POZIERES at X.H.C. — Sappers Stubbs billets. Officers to Trenches — St: Brant went on leave — Lt: G.J. Akin joined on loan from 2/2 H.F.Co: — St. Laing confined to billets sick. — To 153 Brig (Adv.) with C.R.E.	SGA
	2		Shifted billets to WOLFE Huts — X.6.d. — 8 Niessen huts close to N side BAPAUME Rd. St: Paken sent to hospital — Sect: IV — moving in DESIRE SUPPORT — 2nd Lieut: P.G. Clark reports for duty. To 153 Brig: — Advance — St: Laing in Light hut — Lt/Cpl. Hatchwell & Sapr. Milam on leave —	SGA
	3		To Trenches in morning inspecting work — called 153 Brig: — Change over of Brigades at Advance — saw 164 Brig: there in evening. Sects: II & IV in work as on previous night — Sergt: McNeil. A.J. sent away as instructor at IV Corps school.	SGA
	4		C.R.E. called about noon — To Trenches in afternoon — inspected IRONSIDE Ay DESIRE SUPPORT to FRONT LINE — at ADVANCE Brigade — Sect: II on IRONSIDE (Lt. Carmichael) — Sect: III — (Lt Clement) on 10th ST	SGA
	5		2/Lieut: A.M. Telford joined me on loan from 2/2 H.F.Co: — 2/Lieut: I.C. Blakey reports for duty. Attended conference at 154 Brig: Adv: — Sect: I (Lt Telford) took over from Lt. Carmichael) on IRONSIDE. Sect: III (Lt Clark) on 10th ST. — Lt. Allan laying new support on right.	SGA
	6		C.R.E. called — 2/Lt. A.M. Telford confined by M.O. to billets — Bath: Change over — no work trenches — made reconnaissance for new support line fr 10th ST — Gilbed at Brig: H.Q. Adv: & reported results.	SGA

Army Form C. 2118

WAR DIARY
or
INTELLIGENCE SUMMARY
(Erase heading not required.)

(72)

Place	Date	Hour	Summary of Events and Information	Remarks and references to Appendices
WOLFE HUTS	Dec 1916 7		2/Lt Carmichael confined to billets – To Brig: H.Q. Aorange – Took at night as before Lt: Quan making further reconnaissance of Support line – To C.R.E. to be instructed for leave tomorrow.	S.M.
"	8		Major Allan proceeded on leave. Lieut King left on command of Company. Returns II + IV on night work. Arrangement made to hand over work on line to 1/2nd H.F. Co. R.E. & take over from 2/2nd H.F.Co.R.E. at Sawmill, POZIERES Dump, C.T. Pulling & pump. Change over with 2/2nd H.F.Co. completed. Counter-attack at WOLSELEY HUTS. 2/Lt King reports Company 2/Lieuts: Account supplied.	1875
WOLSELEY HUTS	9		Lieut King taken charge of sawmills. Him report 2/2nd H.F.Co. R.E. 2/Lt Heal laying trunks on ALBERT + CRUCIFIX CORNER. supplied to relieve men at Sawmills, * woodcutting & C.I. rolling on progress. Inspected pumping station. Lieut Carmichael visits pumping station.	L.K.
	10		Work as above. Lieut Bladey visits pumping stations. W. Carmichael turns its charge afternoon. Inspect pumps at CRUCIFIX CORNER, woodcutting + C.T. rolling.	L.K.
	11		Work as above. Lieut Carmichael having been commanded employed by Lieut Sawmill. Conference at C.R.E.'s. 9th Army reports for duty. G.O.C. calls.	L.K.
	12		Woodcutting + C.T. Saw Capt Annie at Aveler + proceeded by car	J.K.
	13		to LEALVILLERS for stones.	L.K.

1875 Wt. W593/826 1,000,000 4/15 J.B.C. & A. A.D.S.S./Forms/C. 2118.

WAR DIARY or INTELLIGENCE SUMMARY

Army Form C. 2118

Place	Date	Hour	Summary of Events and Information	Remarks and references to Appendices
WOLSELEY HUTS.	Dec. 1916 14		Work as above. Hunts Carnival & Tanks continued to Hilsh. POZIERES DUMP during afternoon. Heavy Barge disposp forwards at D.A.C. dump.	
"	15		Work as above. Lt. Grant returns from leave. Hunts Carnival & Tanks continued to Hilsh.	
"	16		Work continued as above. Lieut Bank takes over from Lieut Day. Lieut Day went to Amiens for the purpose of purchasing R.E. Stores. 2 Lieut Carmichael & Clarke continued to Hilsh. Heavy Barges to Aveluy town during forenoon & afternoon & teleported home of making Pollard road.	
"	17		Work was continued as above. Lieut Pumps, Pumping Station, Making F. tanks &c. 1/C Payne Lieut take over POZIERES Dump. Lieut Kin Leyhoffer returned from leave to Coy H.Q. & be left in charge here for 2 days for purpose of handing over. 2 Lieut Clarke on duty. 2 Lieut Carmichael doing up to study. Went to Pozieres. Dumps during forenoon.	

Army Form C. 2118

WAR DIARY
or
INTELLIGENCE SUMMARY
(Erase heading not required.)

(74)

Place	Date	Hour	Summary of Events and Information	Remarks and references to Appendices
WOLFF HUTS	Dec 1916. 18.		Took no slaves. Went to OVILLERS HUTS with A.D.M.S. and went on site for hospital — to be composed of 12 NISSEN HUTS and went barricaded to hospital. 2nd Lieut Blakey made report re ledger supply from ALBERT to BOUZINCOURT	J.P.W.
"	19		Work continues on works. Took up commission on building of NISSEN HUTS for A.D.M.S. Foundation & were laid. 2nd Lieut Blakey enquired to BELLE VUE to RESERVE.	J.P.W.
"	20		Work on Sawmill, Aveluy Wood. Lieut Huth Pumps as who carried on. Went to 1/2 Highland Field Coy R.E. re taking over of BELLES at WOLFF Huts — to 2/2 Highland Field Coy R.E. about taking on Intermediate work in tunnels. Capt. Stops 1/2 Highland Field Coy R.E. who when over work at Sawmill re an carried on by this unit.	J.P.W.
WOLFF HUTS	21		Coy. went to BELLES occupied by 1/2 Highland Field Coy R.E. and took over Intermediate line work from 2/2 Highland Field Coy R.E. 1/2 Highland Field Coy R.E. took over our BELLES & work in OVILLERS POST Dump. Road cutting in Aveluy Wood, Pumps in ALBERT and Aveluy, Erection of NISSEN HUTS &c. Commenced work on Intermediate Line	

WAR DIARY or INTELLIGENCE SUMMARY

Army Form C. 2118

Place	Date	Hour	Summary of Events and Information	Remarks and references to Appendices
WOLFF HUTS	Nov 21	1916	Bright, fine. Work - gun huts, Lairs and Boyd on work of laying by on Overland Routes. 2nd Lieut. Clarke i/c in charge of work on IRONSIDE AVENUE. 2/Lt Allan returned from leave and took over command of Coy. from Lieut. Grant.	
"	22		Heavy rain in morning - very clear later - Lt. Blakey confined to billets by M.O. - Sect. III in absence dressing station, key work on IRONSIDE AV. - Lt. Cooper unable to work - G.O.C. + G.S.O. called about men - to trenches in afternoon c/o Brig. Maj. 15th Brig: at advance H.Q. - Sect. I - overland Route laying out - Sect: II IRONSIDE AV. - Sect: III overland Route laying out.	
"	23		Seeking III day work as above - Sec. I - on IRONSIDE AV: with cavalry Pioneers + 30 sappers makes - Sec. II + III continuing overland Routes to "B" Dump + New Dump - work continued on 7 Nissen huts.	
"	24		To Trenches in morning c/o Brig: to Same as above	
"	25		No work except on Nissen huts. Lts: Boyd + Blakey reported fit for work. Drs: Clark 2a Dumps A. + B.	
"	26		Work continues as above - Lairs placed at Dumps A. + B.	
"	27		Work as above but no working parties for overland routes. Lt. Blakey again unfit for duty.	

Army Form C. 2118

WAR DIARY
or
INTELLIGENCE SUMMARY
(Erase heading not required.)

(76)

Place	Date	Hour	Summary of Events and Information	Remarks and references to Appendices
NO 1FF HQTS	Dec 28 1916		Hard frost at night - thaw during day Fog - Sect: 3 in bg work on IRONSIDE AV: - motor pump taken up working - Sect 1 - working - Sect: I - in IRONSIDE at night - Sect: 2 & 4 on Overland Routes - O.C. to Trenches -	Sgd.
	29		Foggy Wet night - O.C. to Trenches - work as usual - IRONSIDE AV much damaged by weather Brig 152 dissatisfied with making of overland routes - aughe-in-pickets to be used tracks to be put up - G.O.C. called in afternoon -	Sgd.
	30		To Trenches - very much surface water - IRONSIDE very bad - called 152 Brig: H.Q. - C.Rb. Hue - Weather dry - atmosphere very clear - shelling in COURCELETTE RD overland Routes fair - "A" 100 men cut out tonight - draft of 4 arrived - 1 driver & 3 sappers -	Sgd.
	31		Dry Day - To Trenches - work as above - hot water extra in to IRONSIDE AV: - Park, cooking there heavy shelled - left - Innes to Base for dentistry -	Sgd.

J.J.Mann, MAJOR, R.E.
O.C. 1/1st HIGHLAND FIELD CO. R.E.

Designation of 1/1 Highland Field
Coy changed to 400th Field Coy
1st February 1917

CONFIDENTIAL.
No 1(A)
HIGHLAND
DIVISION.

Vol 19

Confidential

War Diary
of
400th Field Coy R.E.

From 1st Jany 1917 to 31st Jany 1917

ho 77.

Army Form C. 2118

WAR DIARY
or
INTELLIGENCE SUMMARY
(Erase heading not required.)

CONFIDENTIAL
No. 2102
HIGHLAND DIVISION

(77)

Instructions regarding War Diaries and Intelligence Summaries are contained in F.S. Regs., Part II. and the Staff Manual respectively. Title Pages will be prepared in manuscript.

Place	Date	Hour	Summary of Events and Information	Remarks and references to Appendices
WOLFE HUTS	Jan 1917 1		To Trenches - Work continued on IRONSIDE Av. - Conference at 4.30 P.M. at "G" -	JfA
	2		To Horse Lines - relief shifted to mine Crater at LA BOISELLE - Called on Brig" 153 at ARMLY to arrange about works - Lt. I.C.R. GRANT returned to unit 2/2 H.F.Co. - Lt. R.W. McCrime returned to rejoined this unit from sick leave -	JfA
	3		To Trenches & 153 Brig. HQ. Absence - Dry day - Shored Lt. McCrime round - Shifted this day to front line work - Sect. I - making shelter at Post 14 - Sec: 4 Firestepping Posts 13 & 16 - Sappers mates on IRONSIDE Av. all night work - food night - To Trenches at night - materials like hacering & Rain at C. Dump -	JfA
	4		To Brig. H.Q. - Lt: McGregor returns for work from 1/2 H.F.Co. - Sec II Finishing Firestepping - Sect. III in IRONSIDE Av. - DESIRE SUPPORT - Sec. I on Firestepping at Post 14. Very bright moon.	JfA
	5		To Brig. H.Q. - Very clear day - Considerable shelling - A.R.S. Doig went on 10 days leave - Work at night - sappers mates carrying - very good work done - extra shelter made at Post 16 - 24 firestepping put in at (13) & (14) Post - Sapper McGinniall stripes two legs -	JfA

Army Form C. 2118

WAR DIARY
or
INTELLIGENCE SUMMARY
(Erase heading not required.)

Instructions regarding War Diaries and Intelligence Summaries are contained in F.S. Regs., Part II. and the Staff Manual respectively. Title Pages will be prepared in manuscript.

(78)

Place	Date	Hour	Summary of Events and Information	Remarks and references to Appendices
WOLFE HUTS	Jany 1917 6		To Brig H.Q. - Clear morning - Shelly Railway Corner & ETTER Rd - Brig-Gen Hamilton called - visited stables - Sgt. Hows makes carrying for Sec III - Priester & Spring at Post 10.	RW
	7		O.C. to Brig. H.Q. - Frosty morning - to Kenny, Boyd, & back to trenches at night. I not stopping & making shelter at Post 10 - Firestepping support induction huts - Clearing & leave support trench rain fell all night - great hindrance to work. O.C. at conference at "G" - in Return turned in sick -	RW CAO
	8		Brig: Change in Line - No carrying parties - Sec II - With Lt. Blakey on Left Subsector supporting Post - Work continued at Post 10.	RW CAO
	9		Heavy Bombardment commenced 8 A.M. No working parties. Lt Weekes called to see O.C. during afternoon - 12 sappers held in readiness for 154 Brig. in case of emergency - sappers not called out	RW CAO
	10		Heavy Bombardment still continues. Major Allen gone to 29 C.C.S. sick. Col Weekes Moved up at 6 PM to say O.O.126. was cancelled for us - we are to be attached to another Div. for work behind the lines. Lefroy Challis & Brigade joiners regen their units.	RW CAO

WAR DIARY or INTELLIGENCE SUMMARY

Army Form C. 2118

Place	Date	Hour	Summary of Events and Information	Remarks and references to Appendices
Wolfe Huts	Jan 1917. 11.		G.O.C. Division calls to inspect camp – Weather very cold some snow falls. New operation orders received – to be attached to 11th Division for work behind the lines – Sappers employed all day cleaning wagons & billets. Officers from 226 Field Coy reports at 4 o'clock.	Purche
do	12.		Morning very wet – Heavy showers all day. Heavy bombardment goes on all day on our left. Lt Boyd takes Officers from 226 Coy round the work – Sappers continue work on wagons, all wagons packed by 5. PM ready to move. Permission obtained to go through ALBERT.	Purche
Beauquesne	13.		Move off from Wolfe Huts 7.30. Route taken. ALBERT – BOUZINCOURT – HEDAUVILLE – VARENNES – LEALVILLERS – ARQUEVES – BEAUQUESNE. Company arrived 3.30. Billets good – horse standings very poor.	Purche
Outrebois	14.		Move with 152 Infy Brigade – Starting point West end of BEAUQUESNE. Route F.M.E. DE ROSEL CROSS ROADS – CANDAS – FIENVILLERS – OUTREBOIS. Heavy snow fall overnight – roads very bad. Company arrived 4.45. Billets all very poor – Town Major had not been warned by 152 Infy Brigade	Purche
	15.		Hard frost overnight – roads very slippery – Move with 152 Infy Brigade South with transport on OUTRE BOIS – BERNAVILLE ROAD.	Purche

WAR DIARY
or
INTELLIGENCE SUMMARY
(Erase heading not required.)

Army Form C. 2118

Instructions regarding War Diaries and Intelligence Summaries are contained in F. S. Regs., Part II. and the Staff Manual respectively. Title Pages will be prepared in manuscript.

(79)

Place	Date	Hour	Summary of Events and Information	Remarks and references to Appendices
CONTEVILLE	15th Jan 1917		Starting point Western end of BEAUMETZ. Route BEAUMETZ – LONGVILLERS – DOMLEGER – CONTEVILLE – Company arrived in billets at 2 P.M. Billets fairly good.	Buche
	16th		Two pontoon wagons sent to HIERMONT for stores for improvement of billets. Thorough inspection of 5th Coy 9.30 - One hours drill rest of day gave for repair of billets.	Buche
	17th		Hard frost over night - roads very bad for horses - two hours French drill one hour close order drill. More work done on billets.	Buche
	18th		Major Allen DAA+QMG calls at 12.30 P.M. - We have to clear out of our present billets to allow Ordnance 11th Div to occupy them. Major Allen takes me down + allots new billets to one at ABBAYE FARM. I kilometre from CONTEVILLE. Col WEEKES calls at 4.30 P.M. says we are to start training, not much work to be done by us for 11th Div.	Buche
	19th		Coy removes to new billets at ABBAYE FARM. Major Allen calls at 8.30 P.M. + says we are to return to other billets in CONTEVILLE. LEAVE WARRANTS for four men fail to arrive. I phoned C.R.E. at 9.30 + got authority to extend their leave. Two sections return to CONTEVILLE.	Buche

WAR DIARY
or
INTELLIGENCE SUMMARY

(Erase heading not required.)

Army Form C. 2118

Place	Date	Hour	Summary of Events and Information	Remarks and references to Appendices
CONTEVILLE	20.1.17.		Lieut Doig reports often ordinary leave. Lt. Doig, truck & others horsed to chine - He & taken on the afternoon very hard frost nets in with a slight fall of snow - I note of 5 sapper report from base	Rische
do.	21		No work done by Coy - food supper horsed or ordinary leave - one driver to hospital	Roche
do.	22		Course of instruction was laid down by C.R.E. commenced. C.R.E. & Capt GOODSMITH call at 11.15 AM inspect billets & the Coy on parade. C.R.E. tells me Sergt ROBERTSON is going to rejoin the Coy.	Roche
do.	23		Coy left Billet therm at 9.15 for C.R.Es H.Q. Sergt ROBERTSON reports for duty at 9.15. Made arrangements for a field for riding drill with afternoon to march. Coy employed all day on trotting & leading & posturing.	Roche
do.	24		Very hard frost overnight - horses had to be shifted out of stableness on account of the cold - We started giving the drivers extra drill. Coy never work as yesterday.	Roche
do.	25		Still very hard frost - Very large rich hands this morning - 5 men to hospital - 3 return from hospital. Town Major calls to get list of billets. attacks & others - to & return for Coy money.	Roche

WAR DIARY
or
INTELLIGENCE SUMMARY

(Erase heading not required.)

Army Form C. 2118

Place	Date	Hour	Summary of Events and Information	Remarks and references to Appendices
Authuille	26.1.17		Coy training – Pay parade of Coy at 4.30 PM. Padre from 11th Div calls & arranges about a service for Sunday 28th at ABBEY FARM.	RWO/C
do	27.1.17		Frost not just so hard, strong wind blowing from N.E. Four sappers return from leave. I went to YVRENCH during afternoon to see work done by Coll Shreite, Capt Ferguson from III "ARMY SCHOOL" calls & spends the evening. Four men on leave to ABBEVILLE.	RWO/C
do	28.1.17		Church parade at 10.15 – Receive letter or word to church saying body of RE two then near HANCHY found. NCO to identify the body – D McCook used for exposure. Proceed to HANCHY during afternoon to get particulars – has fallen from cycle – Body left with 1/6th Lincolns. Orders received that we were to move on the 30th to VI Corps.	RWO/C
do	29.1.17		Full particulars about the move received. Dismounted going by motor wagon – mounted going by road. C.R.E. calls 11.15. Three two men for being absent from parade orders harness not very well pleased. Four sappers attached to Divns to make up for sick men.	RWO/C
ARRAS	30.1.17		Dismounted leave CONTEVILLE at 9.30 am. Mounted at 10 am. Dismounted spend two hours at AVESNES-LE-COMTE for lunch – arrive ARRAS at 4.45 – Billets fairly good – my cold journey.	RWO/C
do	31.1.17		Were received from VI Corps saying one Field Coy is to go to ANZAC – I go to Signals & ask Corps which one is to go – 1/2 is fixed. 12.30 PM another wire received saying we are to go to ECOIVRE & transport to MAROEUIL. I get permission from Four Major to move	RWO/C

1875 Wt. W593/826 1,000,000 4/15 J.B.C. & A. A.D.S.S./Forms/C.2118.

WAR DIARY
or
INTELLIGENCE SUMMARY

(Erase heading not required.)

Army Form C. 2118

Place	Date	Hour	Summary of Events and Information	Remarks and references to Appendices
ARRAS.	31.1.17		Out of ARRAS in daylight	Rifle

Hutchison Lt
for O.C. 1/1st HIGHLAND FIELD CO. R.E.

Confidential

War Diary

of

400th Field Co RE

From 1st Feby 1917 to 28th Feby 1917

Army Form C. 2118

WAR DIARY
or
INTELLIGENCE SUMMARY
(Erase heading not required.)

409 Holland Field Coy R.E.

(81)

Place	Date	Hour	Summary of Events and Information	Remarks and references to Appendices
ECOIVRES	1.2.17		Company leave ARRAS at 10 P.M. Motor lorries promised by the XVII Corps to report at 9 A.M. fails to arrive. Dismounted arrive at Mouss hut near ECOIVRE at 1 P.M. Motor lorries turn up at ARRAS at 3 P.M. Dismounted leave ST QUENTIN at 11 A.M. Entrainnue MAROEUIL at 2 P.M. Designation of Coy changed to 400th (Highland) Field Coy R.E. Orders received for two parties to report at XVII Corps H.Q.	Res. Ap.
do	2.2.17		Very cold night-frost much hindered Coy. Started work on erection of Nissen hut & blacks to Ridge MAROEUIL at 10 A.M. Nine huts nearly completed. Motor lorries to have lories at 2.30 P.M. for stores & making arrangements about huts for Coy. & Melvone to have lines at 2.30 P.M. & arranges about getting cover for horses. Camping ground with O.B.'s of the Companies.	Ridge —
do.	3.2.17		& McCrue continues Khan.	K.A.S. T.L.S. W.F.
do	4.2.17		"	Cpt. Bowen
do	5.2.17		arrives & takes over command of Company.	

Army Form C. 2118

WAR DIARY
or
INTELLIGENCE SUMMARY
(Erase heading not required.)

1/1st Highland Field Coy RE

(83)

Place	Date	Hour	Summary of Events and Information	Remarks and references to Appendices
ECOIVRES	6.2.17		Carry on with erection of Nissen huts made necessary by shortage of floor joists and funiture. McCRONE sick and furnished man shortly after midday. Inspection of Lines and Kennel.	febs.
	7.2.17			febs.
	8.2.17		Visited by AA + QMG, HD, Kilbirnie. Carry on with huts 28 into completed	febs.
	9.2.17		Receive orders at 8 a.m. from CE XVII Corps to move to on ARRAS - ST POL Road where MAROEUIL Road Branches off; and start work there. Promoted must during day. Arrived Maroeuil at MAROEUIL.	febs.
ARRAS-ST- POL ROAD	10.2.17		Erection of Nissen huts commenced. Lt McCRONE returned ditter.	febs.
	11.2.17		To advance Expenses for clothing & stores from HD. CRE visits the Company in the early afternoon. 2/Lt L.C. BLAKEY reports for duty from the Base; Capt HUNTER from No 2 Reinforcements by OE.	febs.
	12.2.17		Carry on with huts. 2DR ventilated.	febs.
	13.2.17		Reinforcement with huts and appearance of 3 Officers and 19 cases of infantry equipment despatched to Infantry (Culflin + Sinne) after shipping.	febs. febs. febs.
	14.2.17		Carry on with huts, etc	febs.
	15.2.17		Ordered to return 2/Lt HUNTER & 401 st Coy	febs.
	16.2.17		2/Lt Hunter returns to 401 # Coy. FREVILLERS with GPO 3 ft reasonable huts & 2/Lt BLAKEY sent G.P.O. 3 ft reasonable huts to Anti training. Same febs.	QH

WAR DIARY
or
INTELLIGENCE SUMMARY

(Erase heading not required.)

Army Form C. 2118

4th Highland Field Coy

Place	Date	Hour	Summary of Events and Information	Remarks and references to Appendices
MERCA- TEL	18.2.17		Hangs [?] in their Respective sites from 7 a.m. to 9 a.m. Company on Rests etc.	Yes.
	19.2.17		2/Lt BLAKEY and 3 O.R. PREVILLERS by car to commence Engineering Training Ground.	Yes.
	20.2.17		Cutting materials present, motor transport being prohibited.	Yes.
	21.2.17		Company one truck of material — Loading Point of Barrackow Tentis Capt. WARREN to R.E. Hd. Qrs. and Barry + Capt. RUSSELL has been appointed Adjutant to 1st Army RE dated from 27/1/17. Authority Third Army Letter AMS/4999 dated 14/2/17. "Road restrictions" on road from 7 a.m. to 9 a.m. on 24th Suit of hutting material received. 2 huttings at Camp — now called Y Hutment CAPT WARREN with	Yes.
	22.2.17		OC 288 AT. Coy. to visit Col. WAGHORN C.O. C.E. VII + see sites of new Camp HQ — B Camp. 2 huttings commenced work in B Camp, Lorries arriving with huts about 11 a.m. Camp on with huts at Y Hutment — 1 lee — and B Camp — 3 free.	Yes.
	23.2.17		"Road Restriction", 3 huts at B Camp m 26th. Y Hutments, 3 huts at B Camp m 26th. 1 Latrine work at	Yes.
	24.2.17		Arrange to move Company to B Camp m 26th Monkstown.	Yes. Yes.
	25.2.17		Remains of B Camp in morning. 2 Latrines in Billets.	Yes.
ACQ	26.2.17		Simmonds [?] with [?] both of Billets — No.1 Camp Whereon Coy.	Yes.

Army Form C. 2118

WAR DIARY
or
INTELLIGENCE SUMMARY
(Erase heading not required.)

407 Highland Fd My RE

Place	Date	Hour	Summary of Events and Information	Remarks and references to Appendices
ACQ	27/2/17		All lectures in No 1 Coy	Sket.
	28/2/17		All lectures in No 1 Coy. Lee. WAGHORN calls on afternoon 1 and nothing that functions well the best to o/c 221 A.T. Coy for transport of water pipes	

J Brown Capt.

Vol 21

War Diary
for
400th Field Co R.E.
from 1st to 31st March, 1917

WAR DIARY
or
INTELLIGENCE SUMMARY

(Erase heading not required.)

Army Form C. 2118

407 N. Field Coy RE

Place	Date	Hour	Summary of Events and Information	Remarks and references to Appendices
ACQ	1/3/17		All return on No.1 Camp. Cookhouses and Latrines commenced. Huts everything occupied by 1 Battery R.A. in evening. Draft received 8 O.R. - 3 Drivers & 5 Sappers	
	2 and 3		Carry on with No.1 Camp	
	4/3/17		1st half of No.1 Camp (31 Huts) completed - 2nd half to finish with flor. BISCUIT 404 Coy. No work for Coy afternoon	
	5/3/17		Carry on with 2nd Coy of No.1 Camp - Within O.P.E. at Caux - man killed by falling tree - allowance of 4 sandbags for each man sufficient to make walls with. Capping material from base	
	6/3/17		Major ALLAN returns from leave. McCRONE and 2/Lt BOYD	
MARCH 1917	7		Inspecting billets & going new work. Taking over from Capt. WARREN - other Officers with Coy Lt McCRONE, Lt DOIG, Lt CLARK, Lt BOYD - Capt. GREEN R.A.M.C. attached - Lt BLAKEY detached for special work - work on No.1 Camp -	
	8		with Capt WARREN & Lt McCRONE to Trenches - Inspected Stables at MARDEUIL on return.	
	9		Heavy snow & very cold wind - work continued No.1 Camp - work continued No.1 Camp -	
	10		No.1 Camp - 60 Huts, with Cookhouses, Latrines - mess & Officers, destructors, Urinals Completed - Stores material arrived at 7.15 p.m. for No.2 Camp -	
	11		No.2 Camp - Commenced hutting - Did some demolition work for Coy CB: near Billets - Lt McCRONE sent to billet at MARDEUIL to look after horses - weather milder -	

WAR DIARY or INTELLIGENCE SUMMARY

Army Form C. 2118

(Erase heading not required.)

Place	Date	Hour	Summary of Events and Information	Remarks and references to Appendices
ACQ	March 1917 12		Work continued in O2 camp - 4 huts finished - Lt. Rice went round horses Hos: crits Capt. WARREN - ADR.S. Capt. TAYLOR went round Hrmr. with O.C. later - 40 horses classified as H.D.	JJA
	13		Work continued in camp 2 - 9 huts completed - Cookhouses - latrines - incinerators started - D.D.V.S. went round horses with CRE. decided 22 horses sick to Kearn scale of feeds Rau I.D. Capt. WARREN & Lieut. Doig to trenches	JJA JJA JJA
	14		17 Huts completed Camp 2. Waiting materials -	JJA
	15		19 Huts completed - waiting further materials -	JJA
	16		Do Do - Major ALLAN to MARŒUIL - Sections	JJA
	17		Party at Strong Point 5 - Inspections of Do -	JJA
	18		Huts completed. Capt. WARREN + Lieut. McCRONE to trenches to trenches at night Reconnoitering transport routes.	JJA
	19		20 Huts completed - Cpl. called at billets in forenoon - Major Hern + Capt. WARREN inspecting work Playing out permanent trench by Lieut: BLAREY.	JJA
	20		23 Huts completed No Camp -	JJA
	21		30 Huts completed - No Camp "B" front completed - C.S.M. JJA Engineers went home to Cadet School with a view to a Commission.	JJA

Army Form C. 2118

WAR DIARY
or
INTELLIGENCE SUMMARY

(Erase heading not required.)

Instructions regarding War Diaries and Intelligence Summaries are contained in F.S. Regs., Part II. and the Staff Manual respectively. Title Pages will be prepared in manuscript.

Place	Date	Hour	Summary of Events and Information	Remarks and references to Appendices
HQ	Mar 22	1917	No 3 Coy. Course commenced - Conference with CO's, NCO's at MAROEUIL - Col Ingham called at Billets where he took - continued exam. good work - ordered the return of the Coy to Div. at an early date - CC on Dist. Rail. lecturing to Cos on various	Sgt
	23		Material for huts to start - Capt Ivoneou to Recruits for aboard a time - concentration in Edyn.VE for operations - Squad Drill & lectures - clearing ground at No 3 Coy. Course - erecting Cook house.	Sgt
	24		Squad Ma; drill - Capt Ivoneou Best MrGeer & Seargt Mackie to FRENILER'S Bretteire mebal tribute from Corps Commander.	Sgt
	25		Coy drill and Rapid Wiring in morning. Capt Ivoneou + Sgt Boyd to Warnonte with NCO + 3 officer examinee an drawing with Sapper by R.E. NCO & Orr. to lecture of ORE. hospital & Capt Ivoneou + Lewis trained footwear to the Div in afternoon orders to mysts from Capt Ivoneou + Lewis tent to chagrin. 3 more officers received to Coy to Agnie Lt Boyd + Instructor taken to Warnonte	
	26		to MAROEUIL on 24th Company orders near AGNIERES to warnonte	Sgt J.R. Shawm Capt

Army Form C. 2118.

WAR DIARY
or
INTELLIGENCE SUMMARY.
(Erase heading not required.)

Instructions regarding War Diaries and Intelligence Summaries are contained in F.S. Regs., Part II. and the Staff Manual respectively. Title pages will be prepared in manuscript.

Place	Date	Hour	Summary of Events and Information	Remarks and references to Appendices
MARŒUIL	Mar 27	1917	Company moved to billets in Church St. Maroeuil. Mounted Chateau at Maroeuil.	Apps.
	28		Work commenced on improvement of billets — contents — ladrs. Installed footrest casks. Erection of 2 Nissen huts commenced to accommodate Sappers meantime	Apps.
	29		Carried on with Nissen huts. Commenced improving billets in Aubigny and St Laurent, also erecting shelters in shelters Bernaville. Capt. WARREN Lt. DOIG mounted to Maroeuil to Chevaliér Bernaville. No 4 Section from Blanchard C.T. and to billets in Aubigny. Lt Boy D to work on Blanchard C.T. from H.Q. Gy. Capt. WARREN and Capt Fauthorne now H.Q. at Lt. BOYD. work commenced there them billets at Nissen hut 1/2 with 6 Sapprs bones was relieved by Capt CRAIG with	Apps.
	30		Lt. DOIG with has 3 sections. Construction of 2nd 2 Nissen + shelter parties Nissen huts (completed); chalk & spacing; started; done donkey; studs up chalking to sheet Major ALLAN	Apps.
	31		To Trenches inspecting Trenchwork Roclincourt Ronville-Capt Warren to Trenches with Major Haslam - Sec I - erecting shelters ECURIE - Sec 2 Overland Route to Arras Overland Route to MADAGASCAR from BRAY HUTS - Sec 4 in Trenches working	Apps.

1577 Wt. W10791/1773 500,000 1/15 D. D. & L. A.D.S.S./Forms/C. 2118.

Army Form C. 2118.

WAR DIARY
or
INTELLIGENCE SUMMARY.
(Erase heading not required.)

Place	Date	Hour	Summary of Events and Information	Remarks and references to Appendices
MARŒUIL	MAY 1917 31		On PHANTOM + BLANCHARD - other small work - MARŒUIL heavily shelled in afternoon with H.E. shells. Heavy rain fell in afternoon.	Nil.

400TH
(HIGHLAND)
FIELD COMPANY, R.E.
No. ....
Date. 31.3.17

J.J. Allan
Major R.E. (T)
O.C. 400th (H'ld) Field Co., R.E.

WAR DIARY
of
400th (High) Field Co. R.E.
for April 1917

Army Form C. 2118.

WAR DIARY
or
INTELLIGENCE SUMMARY.
(Erase heading not required.)

Place	Date	Hour	Summary of Events and Information	Remarks and references to Appendices
MAROEUIL	April 1	1917	Lieut Kelly with 41 Sappers makes reported billets to Township - took 2 & 3 horses. Billet area heavily shelled or bombed - a good many casualties - none this with - several horses destroyed - no guns hit.	App.
	2		Work continued as before - Lieut. BLAKEY - Sec I to billets nr HAY ST - ECURIE. Capt. WARREN to Trecules.	App.
	3		Major MINN to Trecules - work as before - conference at Bde - Maroeuil cleared of troops preliminary for shelling - bad work delayed - 4 shells near in afternoon - one through harness room - a dud - no damage - horse lines shifted to jeer -	App.
	4		Major ALAN to trenches with Capt - very wet - inspecting Cp's about Barricade - infantry RE's & Pioneer billeting area about ECURIE. A few shells near MAROEUIL. One in horse lines between 2 horses - a dud - no damage - work being carried out in Chalk tunnel at MAROEUIL.	App.
	5		Work was carried on in BLANCHARDS, FANTOME, T. NIGHT., also on overhead routes & tunnel near MAROEUIL.	App.
	6		Work as before. Howitzers were moved to the outskirts of MAROEUIL besides the ETRUN ROAD - completion of move began on the 10th.	App.

Army Form C. 2118.

WAR DIARY
or
INTELLIGENCE SUMMARY.
(Erase heading not required.)

(92)

Instructions regarding War Diaries and Intelligence Summaries are contained in F. S. Regs., Part II. and the Staff Manual respectively. Title pages will be prepared in manuscript.

Place	Date	Hour	Summary of Events and Information	Remarks and references to Appendices
MAROEUIL	APRIL 7	1917	Lt DOIG with his batman goes to his work in HIGH ST — Little grandson MAJOR FLEMING C.R.E. Hospital — slightly wounded — Major ALLAN's R.E. Hd Qrs. To No 201 MOUTON and HIGH ST to row 4 & 1 to adjust they looked + ditches had many wires by Little Cabin	
	8		Lt CLARK with his batmen and details of all other sections to Little granted in HIGH ST. Later to also move to HIGH ST. To HIGH ST in evening. Lt KELLY with 37 other ranks also to HIGH ST. Remainder handed over to 401 Coy. R.E.	R.E.
HIGH ST.	9	5:30 a.m.	Highland Division attacks in front of ROCLINCOURT and FEUCHY — 34th Division on Right, Canadians on left. Lost all day for orders. Reported that Division has taken all their objectives. Canadians seen entering THELUS. 34th Division also reported firmly established. Lt DOIG numbering captured ground with party of Pioneer who are making strong point.	R.E.
	10		Lt DOIG detailed to mark out an overland route from the LILLE ROAD to a point on the road to the COMMANDANTS HOUSE on the R. of the famous objective.	R.E.

1577 Wt. W10791/1773 500,000 1/15 D. D. & L. A.D.S.S./Forms/C. 2118.

Army Form C. 2118.

WAR DIARY
or
INTELLIGENCE SUMMARY.
(Erase heading not required.)

(93)

Place	Date	Hour	Summary of Events and Information	Remarks and references to Appendices
HIGH ST	APRIL 10	1917	Patrolling 3 sections detailed to make a Strong Point on evening stormy front CAPT WARDEN & LT BOYD to reconnoitre. Constructed in REGIMENTS WEG by day 1/2 and 6 with rifles marks	Sk.
	11		Relieved by 2nd Division. Handed over to 226 Fld Coy. Company moved to MAROEUIL, & there after holding details tonight and Regt move to HQ	Sk.
HQ	12		Company billeted and inspected. Major ALLAN visits Coy. LT BOYD to HIGH ST. to ascertain whether reinforcements of O.R. up or not	Sk.
	13		Closing & repairing wagons and trayeks	
	14		Had arrived late at night that 51st Division will relieve 9th Division opposite ARRAS. Orders received to move to ST NICOLAS in 15th	Re.
	15		LT BOYD to billet in ST NICOLAS. At 3 p.m. a runner returns from LT BOYD and the Company moves to ST NICOLAS, which is very crowded Cy billets and cellars & old ammunition pits. Arrange for observational features to move forward area	See.
ST NICOLAS				

Army Form C. 2118.

Instructions regarding War Diaries and Intelligence Summaries are contained in F. S. Regs., Part II. and the Staff Manual respectively. Title pages will be prepared in manuscript.

WAR DIARY
or
INTELLIGENCE SUMMARY.
(Erase heading not required.)

(94)

Place	Date	Hour	Summary of Events and Information	Remarks and references to Appendices
	APRIL	1917		
ST. NICOLAS	16		Beaurepaire. Capt WARREN & Lt BLAKEY to forward area to billet with 5 N.C.O.s. Nothing available but shallow trenches near L'ABBAYETTE. Mounted N.C.O. sent with orders for sappers to move up & to bring shelter material. Billeting officers to reported here & meet B.G.C. 153rd Bgde with whom 2 tractors with work, and find that work so required on HOPEFUL TRENCH, a C.T., has suffered & found this on left of point. Boot & Robinson ad R.E. H.Q. and got final instructions from C.R.E. as to work on enemy. CAPT WARREN took Fletcher and Lack forward and billets about 5 p.m. Company shifting itself in and making shelter with a little corrugated iron. CAPT. WARREN and 2 N.C.O.s forward to reconnoitre HOPEFUL TR. both hands down badly. Lts BLAKEY & BOYD followed with Parties 1 & 4 and meet 100 Infantry at L. Bn. H.Q. Night very wet & dark and ally 36 infantry arrive at work with sappers. Little work done owing to weather. Letters back to billets to find dugouts flooded.	Rs.
L'ABBAYETTE	17		Weather continued bad during day. No 3 travel in with no	As.

1577 Wt. W10791/1773 500,000 1/15 D. D. & L. A.D.S.S./Forms/C. 2118.

WAR DIARY OF INTELLIGENCE SUMMARY

Army Form C. 2118.

Place	Date	Hour	Summary of Events and Information	Remarks and references to Appendices
L'ABBAYETTE	APRIL 17 1917		ATHIES and neighbourhood. Lectn-2 on Overland Routes from CAM TR. to L. BATT. H.Q. via Support Line. Reconnoissance to improve Billets. Men instructing got of Lts BLAKLEY & BOYD to ST NICOLAS in afternoon. Billets at L'ABBAYETTE shelled. Arrangements made to send S. Officers for testing nightly to war HA. to clean & rest. Lt. BOYD and party to go on HOPEFUL with 100 infantry who arrive without tools. Only 35 old short tools; weather still bad; no suffers.	Apx.
	18		CAPT. WARREN & HOPEFUL in morning. Finds Overland Routes unable to be used for motor Lorries and Field Bridges. Lectn. 2 carried on with This. Billets shelled. New 6oz. Commenced Little Railway Embankment at H.13.b.8.5. 20 found lines attended. CAPT WARREN & LT DOIG to C.R.E. Bridges required on SCARPE Canal at met in front of Railway Ridge at H.24.a.4.7. Weather improves. CAPT. WARREN & LT. DOIG with Lectn-3 to attempt Bridges. Dug down canal on a front to site. Back to FAMPOUX to meet Lectn-4 carrying party.	Apx.

Place	Date	Hour	Summary of Events and Information	Remarks and references to Appendices
LABOYETTE	APRIL 18	1917	and bring up stores. Lower level foot-bridge put across canal close beside Railway Bridge - span 20'. Owing to bridge attempting 200 x double traverse any length of kilt by a tartle. There turn out to be too long - reconnaissance not having been possible except from above - and cannot be shortened on spot. Jail to bridge live. 2/Lt BOYD to ST NICOLAS to night.	Sks.
RY. EMBANK- MENT	19		Move to new camp near by. Embankment at H.12.b.8.5. 2 tents obtained. Conditions very much more comfortable. CAPT. WARREN to ST NICOLAS to see van Riblets. Material prepared for wood trestle bridge in H.24.a. and carried up at night by Sectn. 1. Lt. DOIG to ST NICOLAS to night.	Sks.
	20		trestle finr + fitted though cold. Lt BOYD trestle sectn 4 to reconnoitre canal and bank between ATHIES + point two to prepare of foreshore; and also place up of Canning group about 500 x Kent of FAMPOUX - 2 8" and 3 5.9". Sectns 2 with 100 Infantry	Sks.

WAR DIARY or INTELLIGENCE SUMMARY

Army Form C. 2118.

Place	Date	Hour	Summary of Events and Information	Remarks and references to Appendices
RY EMBANKMENT	APRIL 20 1917		To make infantry shelters in tunnels and shell holes near RY. EMBKT. Hitchin at Div. H.Q. Sec: 3 inch footbridge at H.24.a.4.7. to. 6" to take fuel minerals. Route for fuel minerals is along R. bank of SCARPE to FAMPOUX, across Railway at H.23.6.7.3. and across SCARPE by footbridge. Sec: No. 1 Coy up moving stores for tunnels bridge.	Ref:
	21		Sec: No. 2 Coy on with tunnel shelters — hot kitchen completed. Refs to main rifle canal to pontoons & improve tow-path and works for pontoon wagons. 4 pontoons stones in river. Taking to FAMPOUX by 209th Coy (attached 51st Div) and taken over by 400 th Coy. Sec: No. 3 repairing & strengthening footbridge across SCARPE. Sec. 1 Pnt truss and road bearers now carried (60') at H.24.a.7.3. Roadway not completed on account of visibility. S.O.S. also taken over Sec: No. 2 Coy on Ry. Bridge. 2 more pontoons floated in river at FAMPOUX by 209 th Coy & taken over by 400 th Coy. 6 pontoons in all at Pakewn & 2 above Ferry at FAMPOUX.	Ref:
	22		Sec: 4 making wood horses for carrying structures on pontoons and repairing an ramp to enable bridgy vehicles to leave river.	RR.

Army Form C. 2118.

WAR DIARY
or
INTELLIGENCE SUMMARY.
(Erase heading not required.)

Place	Date	Hour	Summary of Events and Information	Remarks and references to Appendices
APRIL				
P.EMBARKMENT	22	1917	Scout out. Stood down by camp. Turtle bridge passed & passed by Lt BLAKEY who I used for use by 11 p.m. Capt WARREN & men H.Q. & turned to see Lt BLAKEY at Turtle Place.	
	23		The Highland Division advance in front of FAMPOUX out to 4.45 a.m. 37th Div on right & 17th Bde on right. Previous plans went on 37 H Drs engd & 17 D on reported not doing well. Hghd Divn reported to be hung up by M.G. fire on Rgt. Report out 7.10 Gtts Divn on ROEUX and Chemical works but unable to get further. 17 Bde road to have pushed their forward. Later reports seem to confirm. Enemy reported counterattacked repeatedly without success. About midday positions are called on to keep trenches across from FAMPOUX to ATHIES by Comd. road through FAMPOUX impossible owing to barrage. Lt BOYD leaves with Co. 4 to Canal, taking a wagon with timber & frames to trenches. Lt CLARK sent out with the 1 section Coy OPs with work. Remainder men arrive from C.R.E. for one additional escort. Section 2 under orders Lt CLARK running 2 lates held in reserve by C.R.E. Lt BOYD comes back and puts Parker to Two	

Army Form C. 2118.

WAR DIARY
or
INTELLIGENCE SUMMARY.
(Erase heading not required.)

(99)

Place	Date	Hour	Summary of Events and Information	Remarks and references to Appendices
AYENBANK HENT	APRIL 22	1/17	Platoons. At 6.30 p.m. running parties were sent out. No 3 to relieve Cos 4 and No 1 to work on repair of footpath. Meanwhile Lt BOYD has been called on by 154 Regt to repair Turtle Bridge at H.24.a.7.3 which, before being hit by a shell, had become the only available means of getting near the front. The footbridge under Turtle Ridge was completely wrecked and the hi Ridge itself heavily damaged. Lt BOYD gets to work with party of his native orderlies & carrying material to Turtle Bridge. Repairs is completed about 8.30 p.m. and about 250 reinforcements immediately cross towards front line. Cos to be relieved. Cos No 1 & 2 withdrawn about midnight. Carry Sectors 3 & carry on with evacuation of wounded. Maintenance of Turtle Bridge handed over about midnight to 209 & Fd. Cy. R.E.	J.B.
	24		Cos Nos 4 relieves Cos No 3 about 6 a.m. Cos Nos 2 relieves Cos No 4 about 9 a.m. but work on evacuation of wounded went on about midday. It is learnt that the Highland Div.	J.B.

WAR DIARY
or
INTELLIGENCE SUMMARY.

(Erase heading not required.)

Army Form C. 2118.

Place	Date	Hour	Summary of Events and Information	Remarks and references to Appendices
	APRIL	1917		
ANZIN ST AUBIN ENCAMPMENT	24		Coy had to give up ROEUX owing to want of support on the Right & to also fallen tanks from the Chemical Works, but had field of heavy enemy counter-attacks. Reserve Coy rch for relief of Coy on 25th.	J.A.
	25		Capt WARREN & Lt BLAKEY to ST NICOLAS at night for Indus reserved for dumbed features to Pressed by trench mortars. HORAS & LIEUT. ST. NICHEL, returned by road to BAILLEUL AUX COR- NAILLES overtan by mill Killes 11th with 153rd Bde front. Coy arrive at ST. NICOLAS about 10.30 a.m. & entrain at ARRAS running to BAILLEUL about 9 p.m. Transport Coy already arrived. Major ALLAN reporting Company.	J.A.
BAILLEUL AUX CORNEILLES	26		Company employed improving billets & getting a note of deficiencies. O.C. Relieves	J.A.
	27		to O.C. Troops in village to Brigadier 153.	do
	28		Inspecting kits & equipment - O.C to C.R.E. drawing stores. Whole Company kit Kurd- Improving roads & horselines very fine weather	do
	29		Divine Service - Rev Capt. Hunter Chaplain to 1st Black Watch	do
	30		Physical drill - Squad drill - Rifle Exercise - Pontoon & trestle bridge on dry land	do

J.A. Allan, MAJOR, R.E.
O.C. 400 HIGHLAND FIELD CO. R.E.

400th Field Co. R.E.

WAR DIARY
or
INTELLIGENCE SUMMARY.

Army Form C. 2118.

(101)

Place	Date	Hour	Summary of Events and Information	Remarks and references to Appendices
BAILLEUL aux CORNEILLES	1917 May 1		Working in wagons - fitting new gear on technical vehicles for motor traction -	
	2		Care of horses - long distance to go for watering - Passfectory - vehicles interiors -	
	3		for hot weather - Painting out rifles - baths for all ranks - clean clothing -	
	4		Inspection of horses & men by D.A.D. - Training continued -	
	5		Training continued. Warning instructions received to prepare to relieve 404 Co. at ST. NICHOLAS	
	6		Transport left BAILLEUL at 9am & Sappers at 9.30 am. Former for MARŒUIL, latter for SAN NICHOLAS - Took over Transport lines from 404 Co. at MARŒUIL & tents & 404 Co. at SAN NICHOLAS.	
	7		Commenced working on road numbers C.E. XVII Corps	
	8		Do	
	9		Do	
	10		Do	
	11		Do	
	12		Do Repairing m'adam - bare & drainage -	
	13		Came under orders again 1/51st Div" -	

WAR DIARY
OF
INTELLIGENCE SUMMARY
(Erase heading not required.)

Army Form C. 2118.

Place	Date	Hour	Summary of Events and Information	Remarks and references to Appendices
ST LAURENT BLANGY	1917 May 13		Sections moved during day to ST LAURENT BLANGY. Dug outs in old German front line about ½ Sheet 51B N.W. G. 18. a. 7. 1. Transport & Qu. moved in to SAN RICCOLAB.	AM
	14		Troops had & found evacuated, Sappers at SAN RICCOLAB. Infantry Billets	AM
	15		Sect. 1 Repairing Bridges in SCARPE. Sec: 2 mending pontoons - Sect. 3. Clearing heavy rain - So truly pontoons - Lt. Clark to Trenches with working party in CAMEL CT - Heavy shelled - German Counter attack - no work - Lieut. Bagh came on able. Reconnaissance of Bridge & SCARPE at ROEUX -	AM
	16		Sect. 1 (Lieut. BLANEY) went out early to repair bridges - Heavy bombing of Germans - no work - Sect. 3 - Clearing river - Sect: 2 very working parties with wounded from TAMPOOX to ATHIES.	AM
	17		Section 1 Repairing Infantry Bridges - Section 2 - mending pontoons - Section 3 Clearing Tourfell - Sec. 4 working at night clearing CAMEL CT with 125 infantry -	AM
	18		Work of 17th Continued - 2/Lieut. P.G. CLARK sent on Special Leave - 10 days	AM
	19		Section 1 +4 Constructing piers - Section 3. heavy down 3 pontoons below TAMPOOX also 2 poster across track - Section 2. mending pontoons below TAMPOOX - Service & pontoons started from Ry Bridge.	AM

Army Form C. 2118

WAR DIARY
or
INTELLIGENCE SUMMARY
(Erase heading not required.)

Place	Date	Hour	Summary of Events and Information	Remarks and references to Appendices
ST LAURENT BLANGY	1917 May 20 } 21 }		1 Sapper & 1 driver went on leave in U.K. - Work continued in clearing Tourlette - making Officers' quarters to Fermur Bridge - small railway commenced at Tampoux Lock for Establishment of Stores - 1 Section 16th (A.) drawing pontoons from Roclincourt TAMPOUX & ATHIES -	AA1
	22		Weather very wet - O.C. to see Sapper with C.R.E. & C.E. re bridge in Canal - Sappers working as before. Sapper Aust. slightly wounded by shell splinter -	AA1
	23		Sectional work carried on - Made small reconnaissance Survey for bridge work with Lt. BLAKEY - Lt. BLAKEY slightly wounded by shell fire - Sapper STEPHEN killed -	AA1
	24		Sectional work continued - (C) bridge damaged by shell fire	AA1
	25		Do - Repairs to bridge much interfered with by heavy shell fire -	AA1
	26		Do - Damage to trees & towpath along Canal Boulincourt & Athies.	AA1
	27		Do - (C) Bridge has broken by shell fire - a trench shelter laid.	AA1
	28		Do - (C) Bridge men had to make a dummy bridge - O.C. & 54 A.G. to came out to inspect	AA1
	29		Do - Work continued on River SCARPE.	AA1
	30		Do - owing to shelling we were to keep close in the night. A Section went out to camp at ROEUX - No work done	AA1
	31		Do - Preparing to move out of line.	AA1

S.S. DIXON, MAJOR R.E.
O.C. 400 (HIGHLAND) COY R.E.

400TH (HIGHLAND) FIELD COMPANY, R.E.

WO 24

— Confidential —

— War Diary —
of
400th Field Co. R.E.

From 1st to 30th June. 1917.

CONFIDENTIAL
No 21 (A)
HQCRT
ND Division
400th Highland of Field Brigade

Army Form C. 2118

WAR DIARY
or
INTELLIGENCE SUMMARY
(Erase heading not required.)

(104.)

Instructions regarding War Diaries and Intelligence Summaries are contained in F.S. Regs., Part II. and the Staff Manual respectively. Title Pages will be prepared in manuscript.

Place	Date	Hour	Summary of Events and Information	Remarks and references to Appendices
	1917			
L'ABBAYE de NEUVILLE FM	June 1		Moved away from BLANGY ST LAURENT - Transport by road at 9am. Soldiers by rail ARRAS to LIGNY at 2.35 P.M. - Whole Coy Billeted for night at L'ABBAYE de NEUVILLE FARM. Sorry our equipment of wells - water for watering horses a long way off - Coy Mess run up to 6th Div'l Co. Rd - 9th Div'n attached.	
	2		Resting & preparing for marching north by road. Received O.O. from 153 Eng. Bgde.	
	3			
	4		Moved off & billet at 6.30 am. Passed starting point at 6.40 am - marched to R Vesnel 10 min - halt for Env. Superior Halfmoon Brigadier 153 Inft Brig. met us & said we were late that Coin was very bouzy. Passed through HALLENCOURT-TINCQUET. Arrived destination at SAINS LES PERNES at 9.45 a.m. Billets in houses Horses wagons in back inter for horses 1/2 mile away - fine day weather. All went well. Brigadier 153 Inft Brig. called at 11 am to say we had come 10 miles route reverse up to time.	
SAINS LES PERNES	5		Moves out of billets at 5.00 am. Used starting point at 5.15am. Fine dry weather. Other starting point not no other troops. Passed thro' TIERS-PILFART- BEAMETZ LES AIRES arrived destination at PUSCUM. Billeted GRUEPPE in houses Horses & transport in field. Div water in burn beside field - One Saffer fell out en march - Sore heel - boots too small -	
GRUEPPE				

1875 Wt. W593/826 1,000,000 4/16 T.R.C. & A. A.D.S.S./Forms/C. 2118.

Army Form C. 2118

WAR DIARY
or
INTELLIGENCE SUMMARY
(Erase heading not required.)

(105)   400 Highland Field Coy RE

Place	Date	Hour	Summary of Events and Information	Remarks and references to Appendices
GRUEPPE	1917 June 6		Resting - attending to men's feet - wagons & horses - Brigadier 153 Bde called at	Rhodes
		11.30 am	Unseen in afternoon. Some heavy rain at night.	
		7	Moved out of billets at 6.50am - passed starting point 8.15am - Marched past Brigadier 153 at starting point - Weather very warm - little dust - passed thro' THEROUANNE - INGHAM + WIZERNES about 12.30 pm. Halted Rausson for 1 hour to water, feed - saddlers + WIZERNES. Halted 2 an hour. Proceeded Rausson following - skirted W. of ST OMER - arrived destination ST MARTIN au LAERT 2.30pm. Good billets - horses in stables - bygones in road.	Rhodes
ST MARTIN au LAERT		8	Moved out of billets at 5.40am - passed starting point 6.15 am - march - dry weather - route thro' TILQUES - MOULLE - HOULLE to HELLEBROUCK where arrived billets at 8.30 am - scattered billets but good - horses & wagons in good field - washing about in stream on SCARPE for CRE.	Rhodes
HELLEBROUCK		9	OC to see CRE Brigadier 153 - Started washing Bath horses at HOULLE - OC bringing RE stores to EPERLECQUES, arranging to supply Brigade - Men bathing, washing -	Rhodes

1875 Wt. W593/826 1,000,000 4/15 T.R.C.&A. A.D.S.S./Forms/C. 2118.

Army Form C. 2118

WAR DIARY
or
INTELLIGENCE SUMMARY
(Erase heading not required.)

409 of Highland Field Amb

Instructions regarding War Diaries and Intelligence Summaries are contained in F. S. Regs., Part II. and the Staff Manual respectively. Title Pages will be prepared in manuscript.

Place	Date	Hour	Summary of Events and Information	Remarks and references to Appendices
HELLEBROCK	June 1917	10	Took entries in Bath House at HOOGE – arranging stores for Brigade – drawing Kits & preparing Baths – Section of Sedan Drill – musketry – bombers & trophies.	AA
do		11	Same as above	AA
do		12	do	AA
do		13	do	AA
do		14	Orders received that we should probably move the following day – Dismounted sections, cooks cart, & spare cart to move by train, remainder of transport to move by road. – Wagons packed ready for move.	AA
Camp at A.29.6.3.1 BELGIUM 1/20,000		15	Definite orders for move received at 3.30 A.M. Detachment sent at A.29.C Central. Dismounted march off from billets at 10 A.M. & train at WATTEN leaving there shortly after noon. Detrain at POPERINGHE about 5 P.M. & march to camp at A.29.6.3.1. arriving there about 6 p.m. Mounted Move by road – route WATTEN – BROXEELE – RUBROUCK – WORMHOUDT – HERZEEL. Billets for the night in farm 1 kilometre S.W. of HERZEEL. Billets & watering arrangements very good.	AA

Army Form C. 2118

WAR DIARY
or
INTELLIGENCE SUMMARY
(Erase heading not required.)

400 Highland Field Coy [?]

Instructions regarding War Diaries and Intelligence Summaries are contained in F.S. Regs., Part II. and the Staff Manual respectively. Title Pages will be prepared in manuscript.

Place	Date	Hour	Summary of Events and Information	Remarks and references to Appendices
CAMP AT A.29.b.3.1. BELGIUM. 1/20,000	1917 June	15.	The horses were very tired on arrival at HERZEELE owing to the above heat & the heavy state of the roads were very bad.	SM.
		16.	Sappers engaged improving Bivouacs & camping area. Received report to be prepared to move up. 3 sections left at night & drew N.G. YPRES-OR CANAL de L'YSER. Transport left HERZEELE at 8AM. and joined up at Camp at A.29.b.3.1. ROUTE – HOUT KERQUE – WATOU – ST TWISTER – BIEZEN – POPERINGHE – CAMP A.29.b.3.1. Transport arrived shortly before noon & was billeted in a field about 300 yds from Sappers. Changed with 225th Coy for guides for sections 2, 3 & 4. also for rations, water, & blanket wagons at night. 6.6. and advanced party left for trenches at 4 P.M. took over dug-outs from 151 field Coy & wrote from 225th Field Coy. Sappers arrived and relieved two sections one E side of canal & one on W. side about 11 P.M. Transport arrived & discharged & returned to Rear H.Q. Roads exceedingly difficult to obtain, rate for trucking and passing very difficult to obtain.	SM.
DUG-OUTS AT C.25.a.9.7. BELGIUM. 1/20,000		17.	Section officers to trenches to take over work. Sects 3 & 4 relieving TURCO FRONT LINE only at present held by posts posts 2 & dig new C.T. connecting BOAR GAME with FRONT LINE.	SM.

1875. Wt. W593/826 1,000,000 4/15 J.B.C. & A. A.D.S.S./Forms/C. 2118.

WAR DIARY or INTELLIGENCE SUMMARY

Army Form C. 2118

407 Highland Field Coy RE

Place	Date	Hour	Summary of Events and Information	Remarks and references to Appendices
DUG OUTS AT C.29.a.9.7. BELGIUM 1/20,000	July 1917 17th		Sect I at REAR H.Q. employed making horse lines and doing general camp fatigues.	JM
	18th		Commenced work taken over on the 17th. 100 Infantry working party from 13th ROYAL SUSSEX on FRONT LINE — no working party for men 27 – storm very short – heavy thunder storm and heavy rain — Sect I carry on with work started on 17th. 50 trench board piers made and put into position.	JM
	19th		Work in trenches continued — 10 o trench board trestles sent to D work at STATION COTTAGE. Sapper MATHE wounded – work slow owing to want of carrying parties to bring up materials – Heavy rain delays work too.	JM
	20		Same work. O.E. & CRE in forward area – more rain – Established a Company RE Stores Dump at MARFORD HOUSE.	JM
	21		O.C. to War H.Q. — 2/Lieut. J. Boys awarded Military Cross —	JM
	22		153 Inf Brigade took over line with 1/5th Gordons & 1/7th Blackwatch on our Bank. They did not get in until late at night — Work continued on BOAR WIRE & FRONT LINE. REAR H.Q. shifted at 10.30 P.M. to new camp at A.9.9.2.9. about 500yds S.W. of old camp. New camp fairly good but crowded — 40.24 40.4 Zillebeke	JM

Army Form C. 2118

WAR DIARY
or
INTELLIGENCE SUMMARY
(Erase heading not required.)

400 Highland Field Coy RE

(109)

Place	Date	Hour	Summary of Events and Information	Remarks and references to Appendices
DUGOUTS AT C29.a.9.7. BELGIUM 20,000	June 1917 22nd		in Dave Hill.	JM
do	23rd		Arranged with 153rd Inf Brigade for working parties & carrying parties - 192 in all. Considerable damage to trenches by enemy shelling, especially HALIFAX, WILLOWS & CONTHORPE - work continued as before - 4 ORs to ESMS H.Q. before going on leave	JM
do	24th		Round trenches with Brigadier 153rd Inf Brigade - chiefly WASH [unreadable]. Early morning - All working parties not employed holes put in and Banks heavily shelled. Traffic & Stoke Mortars dismantled - 4 BOJO you on leave - 2/L BLAKEY returns from leave - 2/L BLAKEY posted Coy HQ to DIV. HQ. to Coy and training around	JM
do	25th		Round trenches including dug in front line with O.C. 400 Field Coy R.E. on route - in duck boarding a Lightening rehearsal in front Line. New work on BOAR LANE - LANCASHIRE FM & WILLOWS heavily shelled - camp 8:20 P.M. GERMAN Aeroplane flew very low over CPE 42. 40 in heavily fired on by ANTI AIRCRAFT & LEWIS GUNS but turned successful	JM
do	26th		Inspected trench work & progress of new - WILLOWS & CORTHORPE. LIEUT PW MORRIS to be taken on heavily shelled - Also CONTHORPE. Carry the duties of that rank.	JM

t875   Wt. W 593/826   1,000,000   4/15   J.B.C. & A.   A.D.S.S./Forms/C. 2118.

Army Form C. 2118

WAR DIARY
or
INTELLIGENCE SUMMARY
(Erase heading not required.)

4/5 Highland Field Co. RE

Place	Date	Hour	Summary of Events and Information	Remarks and references to Appendices
DUGOUTS AT CEGA 97 BELGIUM 1/20,000	June 27		Very little trench work - CONTHORPE very heavily shelled - returned to spend a 2nd Lieut PATERSON temporarily to 404th Field Coy R.E. Bridge & C. Canal heavily shelled. GERMAN aeroplane over REAR. H.Q. at 5.30 P.M. - One of our OBSERVATION BALLOONS near REAR H.Q. at A.29.d.29. brought down in flames. Observer left safely.	JH
	28th		Very heavy rain with thunder storm - night work further cancelled - Canal heavily shelled - several casualties - 6th Black Watch & 7th Gordons took over line from 7th Black Watch & 5th Gordons respectively. Enemy aeroplane over REAR H.Q. at 4 P.M. very heavy shelled. Transport heavily shelled going to line at night with stores & rations.	JH
	29th		O.S. visits Coy. REAR. H.Q. - Little work until too ah day	JH
	30th		BOMRLANE cut through mud work collecting & trenches Heavy remonstrately. Mind. Sect III go back to REAR H.Q. - Sect IV comp at to CMPH BANK CMPH BANK in vicinity of billets Continuously shelled with 4.2 from 5 - 7 P.M.	JH

Hammer Major R.E.(+)
O.C. 4/5 (Highland) Field Co. R.E.

CONFIDENTIAL.

WAR DIARY

OF

400th (HIGHLAND) FIELD COMPANY, R.E.(T).

from 1st JULY 1917   to   31st JULY 1917.

WAR DIARY or INTELLIGENCE SUMMARY

Army Form C. 2118

Place	Date	Hour	Summary of Events and Information	Remarks and references to Appendices
DUG OUTS AT C.29.a.9.7 BELGIUM 1/20,000	July 1917	1	O.C. visited trenches - Heavy rain - Work retarded - Work parties reduced by 100. Reptr H.Q. Shelled at 7.15 p.m. - one shell falls on horse lines - another cuts light rail'way running past end of lines. Horses removed from lines at 9.30 p.m. to a place of safety at A.23.C.2.11.	
		2	Horses returned to lines at 3.30 am all quiet - O.C. inspected working trenches - Still much wind but drying - some progress.	
		3	Canal Bank heavily shelled in vicinity of billets - a number of casualties amongst infantry - Work parties further reduced - Small raid undertaken by 7th Gordons up PILKEM RD TRENCH opposite found to be unoccupied.	
		4	No morning shift - all work closed down in previous night as 153 Brig being relieved by 152 Brig - no work after 10 h.m. Officer D.H/S Black Watch brought up as suspected spy - released on identification. Capt McCrone came up + went over trenches -	
		5	Work parties continued after 12 noon - OC visited Brig: 152 - Capt McCrone came up + took over from OC. BOARLANE Trench handed through at night. Capt McCrone + Lt Donald rom of FRONT LINE at 2 P.M from ROUTE POWEY - GIBSON	
		6	ST - CAWTHORPE - FRONT LINE - BOARLANE - CONEY ST. CAWTHORPE TRENCH very badly destroyed by shell fire - Impossible to work at parts - CANAL BANK heavily shelled with GAS SHELLS between 11 pm + 12 midnight	

A. ORIGINAL. (12)

X. P.M. Gabion

Borrow Pit.

Duckwalk.
Trestle

←12'→ ←12'1"→
  ←4'-0"→
←9'6"→ ←2'-6"→

— Approx Scale 1/48. —

Has the trace
cut-up.

For B.S. type trestle needed for ppl.

Army Form C. 2118

WAR DIARY
or
INTELLIGENCE SUMMARY
(Erase heading not required.)

(112)

Place	Date	Hour	Summary of Events and Information	Remarks and references to Appendices
DUGOUTS AT C.29.a.9.7. BELGIUM 70,000	7th July 1917		Work continued on BOAR LINE & FRONT LINE – no night working parties available on account of relief of Battalion in the line. H Boyd from line.	RWMc
	8th	do	Very wet morning – Major Allen good on leave – Lt CLARKE take over the transport lines, a fork of REMARK 9. – Cpl Cellio at R.Q. Comm BANK at 3 P.M. – Work & to start on TURCO FRONT LINE by LY COWTHORPE RD. Lt TELFER, BOYD & Capt McCRONE to harden night. – Lt BOYD & sect on TURCO FRONT LINE NEAR POST 8. heightening & thickening parapet & parados. Lt TELFER revetting in BOAR LANE. Lt Lyle & party of men (not an above) on absent – above sketch A	RWMc
	9th	do	Sandie mail line – small party of sect I on FRONT LINE in daylight work knocked on account of hostile fire. BOAR LANE hostile military – men + above located in BOAR LANE.	RWMc
	10th	do	Capt McCRONE to conference at C.R.E. at 11 P.M. – three of the cony	RWMc

WAR DIARY
or
INTELLIGENCE SUMMARY.
(Erase heading not required.)

Army Form C. 2118.

Place	Date 1917	Hour	Summary of Events and Information	Remarks and references to Appendices
DUGOUTS NR C.29.a.94 BELGIUM.	10th July		Major Burton partially explained to Trench Mortar Officers with C.R.E. & LIEUT. COL. FEMMEL 1/2nd K.R. the account of survey at 15.24 of July 15 154th Inf. Bde.	Pushe
	11th	do	Lt BOYD & CAPT McCRONE to trenches at 5 P.M. Observers were with 154th Inf Brigade. Lets red lights on to kill an enemy party but no. of might wondering party CAPT McCRONE back in vicinity of FULLERS FARM & killed at 3.30 P.M. whilst in the East trench of CANAL about 40 yds short — no damage done. Lt BLAKEY reports for duty at 8 P.M. Lt D. BLAKEY, DONALD, TEMPLER & CAPT McCRONE to trenches at night they lost half about 10% - excellent night but work - good they were made up.	Pushe
	12th		CAPTAIN HOPKINS 1/5 EAST YORKS calls at 9 A.M. — POOR LANE & Lt DONALD accompany him over informal OVERLAY D.T.R.M.C.R.	Pushe

Army Form C. 2118.

WAR DIARY
or
INTELLIGENCE SUMMARY.
(Erase heading not required.)

(114)

Place	Date	Hour	Summary of Events and Information	Remarks and references to Appendices
DUGOUTS A.T.C.29.9.97.	12th July		From BRIDGE 4 to TURCO FRONT LINE at LT. C.H.Q. 33. STIRLING LANE fairly heavily shelled all morning. LT DONALD was too put [out of line?] of the track in the afternoon. LT STARKE & TEMPER to trenches at night.	Rwche
BELGIUM 1/20,000			TURCO FRONT LINE & BOMB. LANE suffered much on account of constant shelling with 6H5 shells - not very much [?]ce.	
	13th	do	1 NCO & 4 men sent to CHATEAU DE TROIS TOURS & that work of Location of new camp for two sections G.H.E. Cole. About 100th LT BOYD reconnoitred tunnel at LANCESTER FARM FOR & FORTH point. LT DONALD & BLAKEY to the shed at Regimental work or FRONT LINE & BOMB. LANE. Causeway at BRIDGE 4 heavily shelled about 11PM. C.Q.M.S. to ENGLAND FOR COMMISSION.	Rwche
	14th	do	LT BOYD on day work in FRONT LINE. CAPT MCCRONE LTS BLAKEY & CLARKE to trenches at night. Communication trenches very heavily shelled & very off to FRONT LINE - especially lower end of BOMB. BANK & STIRLING LANE near CANAL BANK - Working parties fail to report at FRONT LINE Enemy open a slight barrage on FRONT LINE about midnight. John Harvey wounded by shell fire.	Rwche

A5834 Wt. W4973/M687 750,000 8/16 D. D. & L. Ltd. Forms/C.2118/13.

WAR DIARY
or
INTELLIGENCE SUMMARY.
(Erase heading not required.)

Army Form C. 2118.

(115)

Place	Date	Hour	Summary of Events and Information	Remarks and references to Appendices
CHATEAU DE TROIS TOURS B29a.62. SHEET 28 BELGIUM. 1/40,000	15th July		Very little work done the previous night - (had) men (had) reserved fire & about 1 A.M. Sects VI & VII return from work and go straight to dinner. DE TROIS TOURS - Camp shelled all day, heavy shells - 7pm. are decide to look for a general place - when all ready ready regiment does sleep - have lunch at 8 p.m. I fill has moved near LAMBERTIN GHE CHATEAU about A3.a.01. - Very good night - now put to rest	RwMe
VLAMERTINGHE "E" do CHATEAU H.3.a.01. BELGIUM. 1/40,000	do		Arranged working party with 33rd Inf Brigade to work at sights also guy to be supplied by three platoons (1/1 EAST YORKS - capt Kingsmill) MAJOR FLEMING (6th EAST YORKS) found work in FRONT LINE between posts 11 & 11.A. Drilling party succeeded in all the advance com- artillery very quiet. Party of 100 from 33rd of brigade made tools at FRONT LINE at 10.30 P.M. 1 NO from EAST YORKS some between posts 11 & 11.A. starting at 10.30 P.M.	RwMe
do	16th	do	Very quiet progress made by both parties the heavier ones	RwMe

Army Form C. 2118.

WAR DIARY
or
INTELLIGENCE SUMMARY.
(Erase heading not required.)

Page 116

Place	Date	Hour	Summary of Events and Information	Remarks and references to Appendices
VLAMERTINGHE CHATEAU H.34.D.1. BELGIUM 1/40,000	17th July 1917		FRONT LINE between posts 11 & 11A now greatly enlarged. C.R.E. informs me we are to get parties from the 14th Yorks instead of from the East Yorks commencing on the 18th inclusive	Rw/Me
	18th	do	C/O night party received instructions from 33rd Infantry Bde. that East Yorks worked well	Rw/Me
	19th	do	Party of 30 men from 1/4 Gordons work in FRONT LINE in day 6/14 nights very much less. For the last few days two Corporals working with Regt. have assisted with 1/5/4 Gordons. 35 ranks LT BOYD at Post 11 & 35 ranks LT BENKEY. Capt. McKONE LT BENKEY, DOWNING & Maskell finished at A300 — Several NCO's from Coy. have now C.R.E. view that R.E. is being discharged at 1 A.M. the following morning it needed to stop all night working — not to be at 11.30 P.M.	Rw/Me
	20th	do	REME. & RENS. Fairly heavily shelled after gas raid — few dead hits on TRNCK 2. near VLAMERTINGHE CHATEAU — LT CLARKE to trenches at 7 A.M. working party of 30 men on FRONT LINE road LT CLARKE & not II	Rw/Me

WAR DIARY
or
INTELLIGENCE SUMMARY.
(Erase heading not required.)

Army Form C. 2118.

Place	Date 1917	Hour	Summary of Events and Information	Remarks and references to Appendices
VLAMERTI-NGHE CHATEAU H.30.D.1. BELGIUM 1/40000	21st July		Change in arrangements about working parties – Party A 55 men from 6 A.M. – 12 noon, Party B 25 men 1 P.M. – 7 P.M. – Party C 50 men from 10.30 P.M. to 2.30 A.M. the following morning. Day parties made considerable progress – Observation from enemy FRONT LINE not nearly so keen. Sect I relieved sect III at the CANAL BANK – ST DOMAIN taken over sect III from Lt BURKEY – Lt CONKEY took over sect III from Lt L Sect I in charge of right half sects II & III in charge of day parties. O.C. returned from leave to the O.K.	Pro /she
do	22nd	do	OC & CAPT MCCRONE to conference at CRE at 11 A.M. re sys of carry on fork on front line by day – Lt J wright Lt Horton goes FRONT LINE now twenty 5000 – Digging parties the hours arrangements made. little progress on account of ... Germans	Pro /she
do	23rd	do	FRONT O.B. to trenches at 9 A.M. – Inspection of work in FRONT LINE – Digging new trenches on enemy FRONT LINE at C19a across to R.N.O.C. Cashes. Tunnel at Bancroft farm for ... brass packs	Brushe

A5834 Wt.W4973/M687 750,000 8/16 D. D. & L. Ltd. Form/C.2118/13.

Army Form C. 2118.

WAR DIARY
or
INTELLIGENCE SUMMARY.
(Erase heading not required.)

Instructions regarding War Diaries and Intelligence Summaries are contained in F.S. Regs., Part II. and the Staff Manual respectively. Title pages will be prepared in manuscript.

(118)

Place	Date	Hour	Summary of Events and Information	Remarks and references to Appendices
VLAMERTINGHE CHATEAU. H.3.a.01. BELGIUM. 1/40,000	23rd July		Slow progress here, affairs too too slow - work just started - working parties for both sections II + III, commenced - heavy shrapnel + HE accounted for. Gas Shell bombardment on AMMI. Bank the previous night. O.C. returns to Horse Lines about 2 A.M.	Revd AC
	24th	do	O.C. moves to VLAMERTINGHE CHATEAU - Capt McCRONE returns to Horse Lines - Lt CLARKE sick after the previous day - Sect II gassed on the way to work at 5.30 A.M. near REIGERSBURG CHATEAU - 7"H.S.H. Raid enemy lines at 6 A.M. 5 prisoners taken - very little retaliation by the enemy - WILLOWS slightly shelled - Instructions received to take over Bn. H.Q. in right sector. 1 sect of 404th Field Coy attached - Shell falls in Horse Lines of R.A.M.C. about 50 yds from our wagon lines causing heavy casualties both in men + horses. 5 O.R. wounded 2 wrk 6NS 3 wrk shell fire.	Revd AC
	25th	do	To C.R.E. XEMR. H.Q. + 153 3rd Brigade - To trenches in afternoon - 1 Sect 404th Field Coy working from extreme right	Revd AC
	26th	do	Heavy rain - work greatly delayed	Revd AC
	27th	do	Work continued - interfered with at night by gas shells - attempt made	Revd AC

WAR DIARY or INTELLIGENCE SUMMARY

Army Form C. 2118.

(119)

Place	Date	Hour	Summary of Events and Information	Remarks and references to Appendices
VLAMERTINGHE CHATEAU. H.30.O.I. BELGIUM. 1/40,000	27th July 1917		to advance on our FRONT - Enemy found in force - Corpl Donald wounded CHINESE ATTACK - work continued - O.B. to trenches, to C.R.E. & REMR. H.Q.	P.S.O/Mc
	28th do.		Work as before - Sects II IV & I moved to CANAL BANK - Billeted with 401 F/Coy.	P.S.O/Mc
	29th do.		O.B. visited 152 & 153 Inf Brigades & talked over our position - putting finishing	P.S.O/Mc
	30. do.		touches to BOAR LANE BATTn H.Q. & FRONT LINE for accepth purposes	P.S.O/Mc
DUGOUTS AT C.29.a.9.7. BELGIUM 1/20,000	31st do.		XVIIIth CORPS attacked enemy positions at 3.50 A.M. - Good progress made 7 A.M. instructions received from 153 Inf Brigade to reconnoitre 23 METRE HILL for a STRONG POINT. O.B. Lt BLAKEY & small party proceeded to 153 Inf Brig at once - Instructions given to Lt CLARKE to proceed with Sect II & 2.5 supphrs into top of BOAR LANE where it joins our old FRONT LINE. Work to be carried on by the party. Reconnaissance made of ground between HINDENBURG FARM & 23 METRE HILL position for strong point finally sighted at C.8.d.84. - O.B. consulted with BLACKWATCH OFFICER digging in on BLUE LINE close behind - Sappers & work parties commenced work at 11 A.M. - Cruciform type of STRONG POINT constructed to hold one platoon - Work completed at 4 P.M. and handed over to O.B. troops on the spot - reported to Brigade	P.S.O/Mc

Army Form C. 2118.

WAR DIARY
or
INTELLIGENCE SUMMARY.
(Erase heading not required.)

(120)

Place	Date	Hour	Summary of Events and Information	Remarks and references to Appendices
DUG OUTS AT C.29.a.9.9. BELGIUM 1/20000	31st July	10am	regarding completion of work. – Small SPRING found while digging & will give enough water for garrison but apparently not capable of development. The STRONG POINT is on the REVERSE SLOPE of a hill & has a good FIELD OF FIRE.	Ph/MR
do	31st	do	Instructions received at 10.30 A.M. to construct STRONG POINT on CANE HY. O.C. 9 LT BLAKEY in conjunction with O.C. Troops on spot (5th Gordons) make reconnaissance facing ground with good FIELD OF FIRE in proximity to CANE AVENUE at C.9.a.60.75. Sect I & 25 Sappers & 10 men brought up. Work commenced at noon & completed at 4.30 P.M. Work handed over to O.C. 5th BORDONS in vicinity. – Completion reported to Brigadier 153 Inf Brigade. In both cases it was found possible to dig these STRONG POINTS to a depth of 4'6".	Ph/MR
do	31st	do	WATER POINT AT LANCASHIRE FM. – Work was commenced on this at daybreak – all ropes having been carried to the spot the previous night. – Heavy shelling in vicinity at first – 5 tanks punctured. Tanks placed on stands in two rows. – Water wheel had collected	Ph/MR

Army Form C. 2118.

WAR DIARY
or
INTELLIGENCE SUMMARY.
(Erase heading not required.)

Place	Date	Hour	Summary of Events and Information	Remarks and references to Appendices
DUG OUTS. AT C.29.a.97. BELGIUM 1/20,000	31st July 1917		Only sufficient materiel to fill three tanks — an attempt could be made to increase supply but this would mean stopping work supply for some days — Arrangements made to set up two tanks — Truck with tools laid & noted bonded to join with TRACK to VON BULOW F.M.-Point of junction of two tracks C.14.C.44. Work completed 5.30 P.M. & handed over to WATER POINT party & report made to Brigadier 153 Inf Brigade. Corpl Musgrove worn dead by shell fire.	Passive

RW McBrone
Capt. R.E.
for O.C. 400 th Highd Field Coy. R.E.

Vol 26

CONFIDENTIAL.

WAR DIARY.

OF

400th. (HIGHLAND) FIELD COMPANY, R.E.

FOR

AUGUST 1917.

Army Form C. 2118.

WAR DIARY
or
INTELLIGENCE SUMMARY.
(Erase heading not required.)

(122)

Instructions regarding War Diaries and Intelligence Summaries are contained in F.S. Regs., Part II. and the Staff Manual respectively. Title pages will be prepared in manuscript.

Place	Date	Hour	Summary of Events and Information	Remarks and references to Appendices
DUG OUTS at C.29.a.9.7. BELGIUM 1/20,000	1st Jany 1917		O.C. to Brigadier in morning – instructed to assist infantry at STRONG POINTS to clear water after heavy rains. – Sect I to STRONG POINT on CON E AVENUE clearing water, pumping and carrying out trench boards. Bn. H.Q. cleared of water & trench boards laid inside. Sect II doing similar work at 23 metre Hill – Sect IV continue work on WATER POINT at HAMPSHIRE FARM – Tunnel entrance closed & topboard. Well cleaned – storage tanks reduced to 5 as the supply is not sufficient to fill 10 tanks – meanwhile 9 tanks stored close by in case of emergency. Heavy rain all day made a trench in a fearful state.	AR
SHEET 28.N.W. do.	2nd do		Heavy rain continuous all day at 9 a.m. with S.W. wind – 68.7. 154 Bn. Inf. Brg. H.Q. instructions received to construct accommodation for 30 men new Brig. H.Q. – 3 sections & suffic. mates start work carrying of material accommodation for 15 men completion by night – work continues carried out on Brig. H.Q. – O.C. visited WATER POINT which had been cleaned & is now capable of giving a supply of 360 gallons	AR

Place	Date	Hour	Summary of Events and Information	Remarks and references to Appendices
DUG OUTS AT C.24.a.9.7. BELGIUM ZONE SHEET 28.N.W.	2nd Aug	12 hours	In 12 hours, there is sufficient to melt the elements mentioned. Instructions received from C.R.E. to reconnoitre the STEEN BEEK in left sub sector of 7 Div. LT. BLAXBY sent out to make the reconnaissance — he did same at night. The following are extracts from report by LT BLAXBY on river & bridges. STEEN BEEK. I looked owing to recent rains — width in some places as much as 20' — this is partially due to flooding & the banks being blown in by shell fire — average depth to the water level is about 3'6" — there is still about 1' of water & mud and 18'6" of top of banks — Current is very slight. Bed. This is soft especially at edges due to earth from road falling in & partly from in the centre. Banks. A fair number of shell holes, especially along the eastern bank - side of S. banks are not very steep - average height above water 4'6". Bridges. Two types of bridges — foot transport & the 10 canals in pile. Three heavy bridges & one light bridge. (6) They were about B28D.60-65 (PIUKEM 1/40000) in good condition — requires some minor repairs to roadway. (7) Military Road Bridge — was North about C4.B.55.95. requires repair in centre & has had a culvert put from a hill.	[illeg.]

Army Form C. 2118.

WAR DIARY
or
INTELLIGENCE SUMMARY.
(Erase heading not required.)

Instructions regarding War Diaries and Intelligence Summaries are contained in F. S. Regs., Part II. and the Staff Manual respectively. Title pages will be prepared in manuscript.

(124)

Place	Date	Hour	Summary of Events and Information	Remarks and references to Appendices
DUGOUTS AT C.29.a.97. BELGIUM.	2nd Aug.	10/17	Bridges (cont) — (c) Heavy bridge about C.5.a.15.19. about completely destroyed. Bridge light — There are designed to take infantry in files and constructed of trench boards or planks resting on small trestles — these organic refused. General. There is a wire fence extending along Divisional front on Eastern edge of what is about 15' thick — there are gaps in the opposite side of fence — heavy bridges 4 opposite two of the big trestles. The western bank has some trestles which would support a certain amount of foot-from view.	
25000 SHEET 28 N.W.				
do	3rd Aug.		G.S. visits 154 Inf Brigade — 10 mt uncensured or shelters — water except for OVERLAND TRACKS — WATER POINT patrolled — fairly heavy water during the day. HORSELINES in a terrible state — moved to another site.	
do	4th	do	O.C. + ST.BO.J.O. to FRANCOIS FM. — Search work could greatly be to a rate clearing CANE AVENUE TRACK to FRANCOIS FM. from again made over CANE AVENUE — Stables of truck — Weather still in favour.	
do	5th	do	Misty morning — 168.Divisional brigades shifting shifting — taken over recently back + bridges over the STEENBEEK — cont entrances to in custody of this	

A 5834 Wt. W4973/M687 750,000 8/16 D. D. & L. Ltd. Forms/C.2118/13.

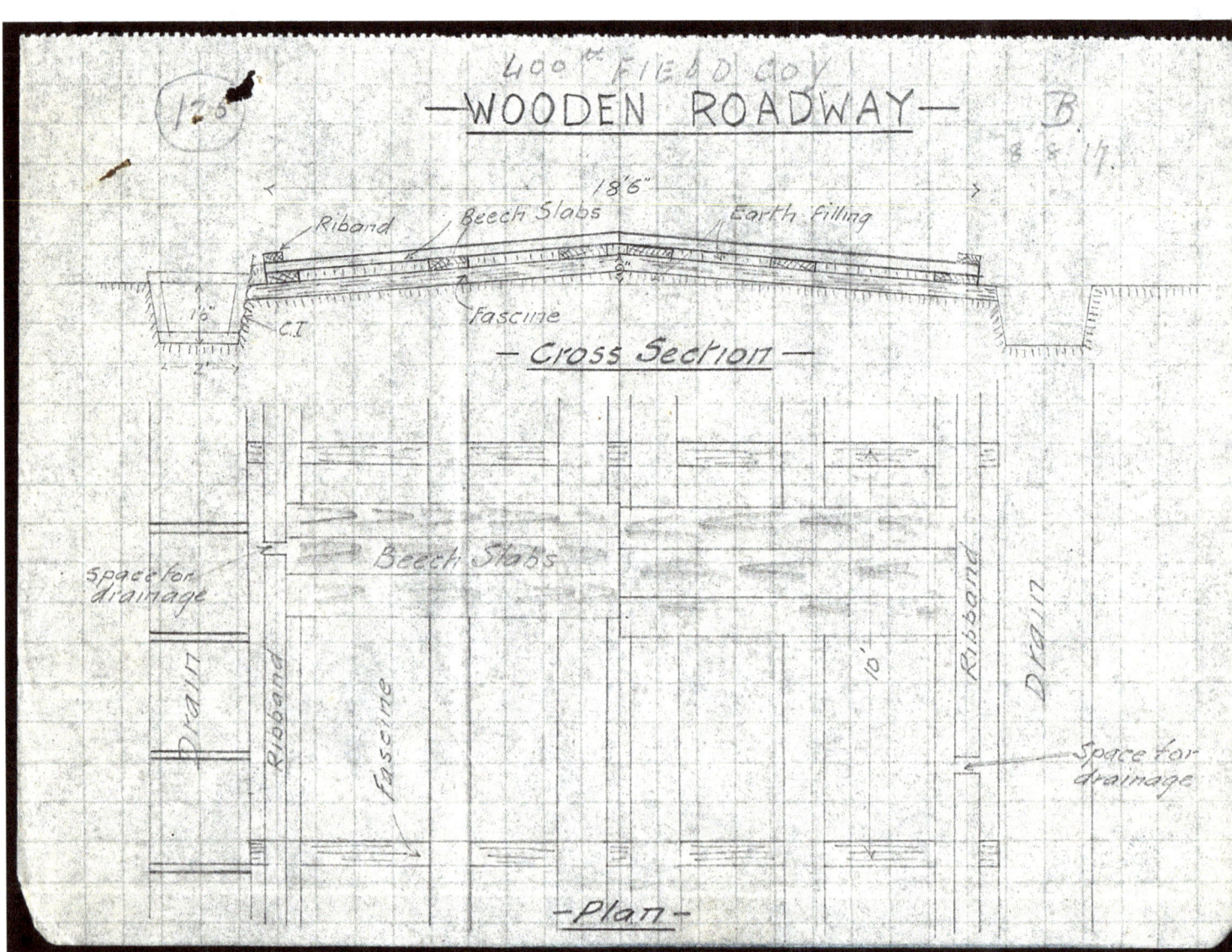

WAR DIARY
or
INTELLIGENCE SUMMARY.
(Erase heading not required.)

Army Form C. 2118.

Place	Date	Hour	Summary of Events and Information	Remarks and references to Appendices
DUG OUTS AT C.29.9.9.7.	5th Aug 1917		Work on CANAL AVENUE - Weather fine. O.C. to conference with CRE. of C.E.	
BELGIUM. 20000 SHEET 28.N.W.	6		Work in addition to CANAL AV + Traffic Bridges - Military Bridge has been hurried - laying or charges + numerous army bridges - Military Bridge is now unusable - No signs of any bridges or pontoons in neighbourhood - asked Adjutant CRE to ask for adoption of CRE's plan	
CAMP AT. B24d.25.70.	7th	do.	CAPT McCRONE took over work at advanced H.Q. - two miles further East working in the trenches - advanced H.Q. changed to a few hundred yards behind MARENGO DUMP about B.24.d.25.70. - A BLAKEY to REAR H.Q. to take over work at transport lines - work on roads handed over by O.B. 67 Field Coy at 6PM. - Very heavy artillery fire by our guns in answer to S.O.S. signal about 10 P.M.	
do	8th	do	Work started on PLANK ROAD running from C.20.c.6.65.45. to HAMMONDS CORNER at C.21.C.28.38. (Tracing of road attached). - about 80 yds of road taken up to start - drain dug and northern - roadway laid out, formed CE. + CRE. both inspected the work - Section work on this relief 5-12 + 12-6. Very heavy fall of rain about 7 P.M.	ATTACHED DRAWING MARKED B. 8.8.17

WAR DIARY
or
INTELLIGENCE SUMMARY.

(Erase heading not required.)

Army Form C. 2118.

(126)

Place	Date	Hour	Summary of Events and Information	Remarks and references to Appendices
CAMP AT B.24.d.25.70. BELGIUM 1/20,000 SHEET 28 N.W.	9th Aug.		Alterations in hours of work – Company all working on one shift from 8 A.M. – 2.30 P.M. – Road work continued throughout heavy & constant rain the previous night – C.E. Wagon completed the work. Vicinity of road heavily shelled about 2.30 P.M. 1 N.C.O. & 2 men & 5th horses. Weather better – good much firmer since morning	JH
do.	10th do		Work continued on road. Direct hits on road during the night – these had to be repaired & so delayed the part of present C.E. wagon completing the work. Weather – showers – strong N.W. wind dries the ground.	JH
do	11th do		Work continued on the road – Intermittent shelling all morning. 10 shrs a 22 men from 179 Tunnelling Company who took on road	JH
do	12th do		Work continued on road – good progress made. Lt. R.S. DOIG met Capt. STEVENSON from No 5 Survey Coy. at BRIDGE 4 at 9.30 A.M. – Position for O.P. reconnoitred and finally fixed at C.15.a central – Enemy aeroplane brought down about 600 yards from our camp at B.30.b.60.20. – Machine completely burned – airman killed. 9' single track being finished before 15' width commenced. 35 yds double width completed of 2 single of 15' 0"	JH

A5834 Wt. W4973/M687 750,000 8/16 D. D. & L. Ltd. Forms/C.2118/13.

Army Form C. 2118.

WAR DIARY
or
INTELLIGENCE SUMMARY.
(Erase heading not required.)

(127)

Instructions regarding War Diaries and Intelligence Summaries are contained in F. S. Regs., Part II. and the Staff Manual respectively. Title pages will be prepared in manuscript.

Place	Date	Hour	Summary of Events and Information	Remarks and references to Appendices
CAMP AT B.24.c.25.70. BELGIUM. SHEET.28.NW 1/20,000	13th July		Work continued on single track - progress about 40 yds per day. - C.E. & C.R.E. both inspect the work - C.E. wishes single track completed to HAMMONDS CORNER by the 16th - rather a big undertaking with men & transport available. LT DOIG and small party start work on O.P. - plenty material available for this work on site. - CAPT McCRONE to REAR H.Q. & inspect horses.	ff
do.	14th	do.	Work on road as usual - work stopped for a short time owing to shell fire - then again owing to heavy rain. - C.R.E. inspects the work - the framework for the O.P. completed. Heavy rain during afternoon.	ff
do.	15th	do.	Heavy rain over night - roads again very bad - Heavy shelling in vicinity of road work about 10 A.M. - men have to be withdrawn from the work for about 30 minutes - Officers from AT Coy are shown over the work with a view to taking over - Heavy showers all morning makes progress slow - C.E. inspects the work - C.E. wishes us to make a temporary track as far as HAMMONDS CORNER to let ambulance through. - CAPT McCRONE to conference at GHENT COTTAGES. B.28.b.70.95. - Coy to start work on road from KEMPTON PARK to HURST PARK on the 17th.	ff

Army Form C. 2118.

WAR DIARY
or
INTELLIGENCE SUMMARY.
(Erase heading not required.)

(128)

Place	Date	Hour	Summary of Events and Information	Remarks and references to Appendices
CAMP AT B.24.d.26.70. BELGIUM 1/20,000 SHEET 28 N.W.	16th Aug. 1917		Road connected through to HAMMOND'S CORNER by a temporary track. CAPT McCRONE & Lt BLAKEY reconnoitre new work, road between KEMPTON PARK & HURST PARK - small party start work. The following particulars of line taken to make a plank road maintainable for a 18' road with mineral sleepers were taken (sufficient for 2½ miles) (1) C.P.O. of men known for yard = 17. This includes all work on the spot, roof us handling of props in the returns to cross the trestles camel be retimered. (2) Labor was not necessary to rivet the sleepers. (3) If the weather had been very wet the time (?) of a stay had been made a good soil and rest on an old muddy road.	[signature]
do	17th do		Work started on new piece of road near HURST PARK and carried up to the place - all days spent on drainage - new piece between HURST PARK & BOCHCASTER marked out for 40 yds - work stopped for a time on account of shell fire. 18.401st Field Coy called at advanced H.Q. to make arrangements about relief of our Coy on the 18.19 by the 401st Coy. C.R.E. called about 2 P.M.	[signature]
do	18th do		Work on road as usual - O.B. 401st Field Coy takes over the work - C.E. & C.R.E. inspect the work. Coy relieved by 401st Field Coy & return to REAR BILLETS at 8.30 P.M.	[signature]

Army Form C. 2118.

WAR DIARY
or
INTELLIGENCE SUMMARY.
(Erase heading not required.)

(129)

Place	Date	Hour	Summary of Events and Information	Remarks and references to Appendices
REAR H.Q. A27b.2.3.	Aug 1917 19		CRO returned from leave - Maj Allan took over Coy at 9.30 p.m. Capt McEwan went	Appx
	20		Coy went on leave - Coy. Cleaning up & arranging camp in forenoon - no work afternoon. Lt Blakey looking after H.Q. - Lieut Clark to Sections & a Lieut Boyd to sections 3 + 4 - Inspection of kits - deficiencies noted - cleaning wagons - so men to baths + get clean clothes in afternoon.	Appx
	21		Section drill + Coy. organisation - cleaning wagons + inspecting camp in a.m + p.m. D.A.D.O.S. + I.O.M. - 100 men to baths & clean clothing in afternoon	Appx
	22		Section Drill + Coy. organisation - cleaning wagons + inspecting camp & Casuals to baths - horses sent to I.O.M.	Appx
	23		Section Drill + Coy. organisation - preparing for CRO inspection tomorrow.	Appx
	24		Coy. all ready for inspection & CRO at 10.30am. - Inspn came thro' CRO unable to be present. Carried out inspection of whole Coy.	Appx
	25		Coy Training continued - musketry - use of work parties + shoy mounts -	Appx
	26		Church parade - Gas helmet + Respirator inspection - Inspection of Camp - Lorries busy on work for Div H.Q	Appx

Army Form C. 2118.

WAR DIARY
or
INTELLIGENCE SUMMARY.
(Erase heading not required.)

(130)

Instructions regarding War Diaries and Intelligence Summaries are contained in F. S. Regs., Part II. and the Staff Manual respectively. Title pages will be prepared in manuscript.

Place	Date	Hour	Summary of Events and Information	Remarks and references to Appendices
REAR HQ A2/6.23	Aug: 1917 27		Instructed to move at 9 a.m. to line - preparing BORDER CAMP for Div HQ 2 Section with motor Transport taking down a Collecting hut. 3 Bessen huts at TROIS TOURS to MURAT FARM - Some huts got to Camp & 2 Sections commenced huts of erection - Issues of billets making tables, chairs, beds -	
	28		Continued work of collecting Bessen huts & erection - 2 completes - preparing to move Sappers to CANAL BANK.	
	29		Continued work on erecting huts - completed - tables, chairs, beds sent to BORDER CAMP for Div. H.Q. Sections 1, 2, 3, & H moved to billets in W. CANAL BANK near MARENGO HOUSE. 100 Sappers mates - 25 + 1 Officers from 6th Blackwatch) Reported at Horse lines & 25 + 1 " " 7 D°) marched with Sappers to 25 + 1 " " 5 Gordons) CANAL BANK - 25 + 1 " " 7 D° Black Watch billeted in W. CANAL BANK, S. Essex FM. Gordons in Bivouacs near MURAT FM.	

Army Form C. 2118.

WAR DIARY
or
INTELLIGENCE SUMMARY.
(Erase heading not required.)

(3)

Place	Date	Hour	Summary of Events and Information	Remarks and references to Appendices
CAMP BARK	Aug 30	1917	Sappers & mates divided into 4 Sections 6th B. No. 1 - 7th B. No. 2, 5th Jerdins No 3 & 7th Jerdins No 4 - attached to corresponding Sections. Sections 1 & 2 Sappers & mates continued fair weather track from GOURNIER to FM. S. past KIEST McDONALD WOODS to DEAD HORSE TPD. Sections 3 & 4 Sappers repairing & continuing duck track from E. end CANE AV to MILITARY BRIDGE. OC. visited Brigadier 152 for instructions.	fff fff fff
	31		Work arranged - Sections 1 & 2 - Repairing Duck walk track from CAFÉ = AV to MILITARY BRIG. - making track from GOURNIER FM to BRIG: H.Q. - Sappers & mates carrying up Trench Boards - Roads broken by shell fire & unfit for transport. (Sections 3 & 4 on night work.)	fff

J.H.Laue. Major R.E. ①

O.C. 490 (Highland) Field Co.

SECRET

CRE 61st Div'n

Herewith War Diary for
August 1917.

J.P. Arran
Major R.E.
OC 400(H) Field Co. R.E.

1/9/17

WAR DIARY

of
400ᵀᴴ (HIGHLAND) FIELD Cy. R.E.

For
SEPTEMBER 1917.

Army Form C. 2118.

WAR DIARY
or
INTELLIGENCE SUMMARY.
(Erase heading not required.)

(132)

Place	Date	Hour	Summary of Events and Information	Remarks and references to Appendices
YPRES CANAL BANK W.	Sept. 1917	1	Sects: 1 + 2 with 3 Sec: Sappers mates completing duckboard track from GOURNIER F"16 to BRIG H.Q. - Repairing tracks in left subsector - forming dump of duckboards at RUDOLPH FM. - O.C. spoke to BRIG 152 - Sec: 3 + 4 + Sec: Sappers moved taking duckboards to track forward of MILITARY BR. + keying - about 500 x laid forward. Horse lines shifted to A21b.9.3.	
do.		2	1 officer + 10 O.R. attached to Coy. at CANAL BANK. Two parties to reclaim dumps ont with CRE. at 6 am - inspected track to LANGEMARK RD - work proceeded as before.	
do.		3	With Lieut Bakey selecting positions for shelters in old BLACK LINE - 4 positions selected - (B) Track heavily shelled at MA Junction SHORT-LIU - much damage - Road in vicinity MORTELJE h. and shelled - mains unable to get up at night with French Loans. Duckboard single track completed to LANGEMARK RD.	
do.		4	Sects. on Batt. & Elephant Shelters - Sect 2 - wheel/tracks CAPE A" - Sects: 3 + 4 on Forward Track. MAJOR J.B. ALLAN goes on leave. CAPT E.M. MCCRONE to advanced H.Q. to take over work 47 PEBBLES taken on to work at the HORSE LINES. Lieut BOYD takes out jumping off point for Raid - see Appendix A.	Appendix A
do.		5	SECT I working on new shelters in CANE TRENCH SECT II on usll work on trench from 4 + B.H.Q. + refad of HD TRACK. SECT II on usll work on trench from RUDOLPHE FARM to the STEENBECK SECT II work along with sect III	

WAR DIARY or INTELLIGENCE SUMMARY

Army Form C. 2118.

(133)

Place	Date	Hour	Summary of Events and Information	Remarks and references to Appendices
YPRES CANAL BANK. N.	5th	1pt	Lt BOYD lays out tape for jumping off places for raid, like heap cut about 250 yds in front of PHEASANT TRENCH. (From great wounded) Shell fire engine taken up to Brig. H.Q.	
	6th	do.	Lt BLAKEY is in daylight. Sect I & duplex shelter move up to FRANCOIS FERME at 6 p.m.	
C14.c.25.20 ST JULIAN	7th	do.	Track running from SCHEMINS ESTAMINET to B.H.Q. handed over to 404th FIELD COY. R.E. Lt TELFER taken over the work by CAPT. McCRONE at 9.30 AM. Lt BLAKEY makes a further reconnaissance of forward shelter by night & reports Sect I start work on forward shelter.	
	8th	do.	C.R.E. inspects forward work lighting of Brig. H.Q. started. Good progress being made with shelter in CANE TRENCH. TWO BABY ELEPHANT shelter carried forward to shelters ND1&4 (A ready for erection) the near side.	
	9th	do.	Work now started on BABY ELEPHANT SHELTERS one about C.5.a.10.80 & the other about V.29.d.90.75. (POELCAPPELLE 1/10000) Work continued reclaiming shelter in LEFT BATT FRONT It.	
	10th	do.	Work continued on shelters in CANE TRENCH. TWO NEW SHELTERS started by Sect IV in forward area, these shelters are being built behind PILL BOXES so as to give them extra protection. Brigadier 154 Inf Brig. inspected trench	

WAR DIARY
or
INTELLIGENCE SUMMARY.

(Erase heading not required.)

(134)

Army Form C. 2118.

Place	Date 1917	Hour	Summary of Events and Information	Remarks and references to Appendices
YPRES CANAL BANK. N.	10th Sept		running from about V.29.C.80.40. to the LANGEMARCK RD about V.29.d.20.80. Same work as previous day - shelters in CANE TRENCH almost complete	AA
	11th	do	- shelters 24 in FORWARD AREA completed.	AA
C.19.C.25.20. ST JULIAN 1/10,000	12th	do.	Nos of shelters in Divisions are have to be altered to new numbers allotted by the Division. Work at CANE TRENCH had to be stopped on account of heavy shell fire. Instructions received from C.R.E. about screen required for artillery (59th Brigade) location of screen from point C.5.C.46.90. to C.5.a.80.15. & to 213069 supply PONCING. Wounded shelters	AA
	13th	do.	Capt Ohrtone to H.Q. 59th Brigade R.F.A. to make arrangements about screen. Major Davidson 59th Brigade goes over the work. Instructions received about clearing of STEENBECK RIVER. Work had to be done on shelters blown in the previous day at CANE TRENCH	AA
	14th	do	Material sent up for screen to MILITARY BRIDGE. Party of 70 men from 153 Brigade to stock forward dump. Major Allan arrived at ADVANCED H.Q. returning from leave.	AA

Army Form C. 2118.

WAR DIARY
or
INTELLIGENCE SUMMARY.
(Erase heading not required.)

(138)

Place	Date	Hour	Summary of Events and Information	Remarks and references to Appendices
YPRES CANAL BANK IV.	Sept 15 1917		Bn. continues laying tracks to LANGEMARCK Rd — Stocking forward Rd. Dump — Provision of Shelters —	
C.19.c.25.20	16		Work as before	
ST JULIEN 1/10,000	17			
	18		Bn. continues reconnaissance for operations in left Sub Sector Divisional Front. Much difficulty in getting stores through - began getting ditches - carrying parties busy direction. Stocking forward Dump in LANGEMARCK Rd completed.	
	19		Certain movements took place today. Casualties were disposed of as follows — Sections 2 + 3 Sub Sections at FRANCOIS FM — H.Q. + Sections 1 + 4 in Bivouacs — at C.14.c.37. — weather fine - preparing for operations tomorrow —	
C.14.c.37.	20		Some rain during night - troops in position — Zero hour 5.40 am — Attack began at 6.am on left - 1st Obj. 7.a.m - 2nd Eng. at about 10am observed (?) all batteries all ready known as follows — See Appendix B. — This also shows amount of hostile shell fire. Several counter attacks were led owing to sniping + shell fire. The conditions for work were bad owing to enemy observation + our men having to stand to relieve interfered with. Due visibility in afternoon.	Appendix B.

WAR DIARY
or
INTELLIGENCE SUMMARY.
(Erase heading not required.)

Army Form C. 2118.

Place	Date	Hour	Summary of Events and Information	Remarks and references to Appendices
C14.c.3.9.	Sept 21	1917	Work continued on declaved track to PHEASANT FM. Little could be done owing to heavy shelling. 150 Trench Boards got up to MILITARY BRIDGE. Attending to Batt. H.Q. maintenance of tracks. 50% of men resting.	App.
	22		300× Track laid towards PHEASANT FM. 150 duck boards taken up to MILITARY BRIDGE. Maintenance of track continued - average events made with the I/o Black watch to put in shelters near GOORIER FM. CAPE A. Heavily shelled. - Donald reconnoitred IEKKERBOTERBEK.	App.
	23		An Officer 68th Field Co. came to Birmans in connection with taking over. Lieut. Blakey took him over all works. Little work possible in daylight owing to heavy shelling + machine gun fire. # Shelters almost finished in CAPE T+R. Shifted down with H.Q. Sections 1+4 Sappers males to CANAL BANK at 3 pm. - Batteries near Birmans heavily shelled. Party sent up to be at 6:30 pm. at MILITARY BRIDGE in # notice boards + tapes for 152 Brigade.	App.
	24		Sections 3 + 2 Sappers males missed from FRANCOIS FM + H.Q. + Sections 1+4 + Sappers males shifted from CANAL BANK. The whole moved to Transport Lines - arriving at noon - at DROOMERDAK FM at A21.a.9.3. - Billets in CANAL handed over to 68th Field Co. - handed over 16 prs: Gum boots -	App.

Army Form C. 2118.

WAR DIARY
or
INTELLIGENCE SUMMARY.
(Erase heading not required.)

(137)

Place	Date	Hour	Summary of Events and Information	Remarks and references to Appendices
DROOGTEENTAP FM	Sept 1917		Plant (electric) removed from Brigade H.Q. CAMP POST - very hot weather - misty in morning. Lieut: CLARK returned from XIII Corps School.	ff.
A21 a.9.3	24			
	25		All men to baths + get clean clothing via POPERINGHE - wagons being cleaned + loaded up.	ff.
	26		Continuing work of preparation for move - section drill + Company organisation.	ff.
	27			
	28		Lieut: Doig & 3 men went forward as advance party. fine weather.	
	29		Marches to PROVEN + entrained with 3rd G. Div. Train - left at 7 p.m. 16. 40 mins late - fine weather - journey via HAZEBROUCK, BETHUNE, ST POL to BAPAUME.	ff.
	30		Arrived BAPAUME (WEST) 5:00 am Detained + marches to GOMIECOURT - Reported location to 153 Brig: (a) in bivouacs, tents + huts - Men in good condition - One horse sick.	ff.

J.J. Allen MAJOR, R.E.
O.C. 490 HIGHLAND FIELD CO, R.E.

400 Lt. Cay. R.E.

I beg to thank you
for the assistance given in
the preparations for the place of
[...]

Lieut Bere of your
unit laid a jumping off
tape expeditiously & well.

The troops advanced from
this tape and never once
lost direction.

J M Scott Lieut Col
1/5th Leas Rn.

O.C. 51st Divⁿ   (A)

For your information
+ return please.

J H Cman.
Major R.G.(?)
15.9.17
OC 400(H) Field Co.R.G.

War diary
JMC

OC 400 H Flight

[signature]

[signature] Capt
18/9/17   OC RAF S7(?)W

Orders by O.C. 400th (Highland) Field Co.

1. The Coy: will move as follows tomorrow 19th - all movements to be complete & reported before 7 p.m.

   Section 2. R/b + Sappers mates to FRANCOIS FM
   Sects 1 & 4 + Sappers mates to Birnais at C.14.c.30.70. near Old water point in front of LANCASHIRE FM.

   Sec: 3 + Sappers mates will remain as at present.

2. Work during operations is allocated as follows:-

   Sects 1 & 4 & Sappers mates
   (a) Continue Trench Board Track to PHEASANT FM & forward towards ROSE HOUSE -
   (b) Clear the ST JULIEN-POELCAPPELLE road from bridge at U.30.d.65.95. as far forward as possible
   (c) Repair bridge over LEKKERBOTERBEEK at U.30.c.55.55.
   (d) Maintenance of Tracks.

   Section 2 & Sappers mates { Reconnoitre & consolidate strong point at U.30.b.50.95

   Section 3 & Sappers mates { Reconnoitre & consolidate strong point at U.30.b.82.

18.9.17 — Copy to Capt: McCrae & Lieut: Doig

J.G. Cedar
Major R.E.
O.C. 400(H) Field Co R.E.

CONFIDENTIAL.

War Diary
of
400th (Highland) Field Coy. R.E.

from 1st October 1914 to 31st October 1914.

WAR DIARY or INTELLIGENCE SUMMARY

Army Form C. 2118.

420th (Highland) Field Coy. R.E.

Place	Date	Hour	Summary of Events and Information	Remarks and references to Appendices
GOMIECOURT	Oct. 1917			
REF. SHEET FRANCE. 51.B. 1/40,000		1	Coy. engaged overhauling wagons & making camp habitable. Five weather. Officers reconnoitring forward.	JJR
		2	O.C., Lieut. Boyd & 2.R.E.O.s went forward to take over work of billets N.7th Field Co - so the Dir. Coy. engaged in instructions & squad drill. Advance party proceeded as directed by C.R.E. to M.36.a.6.6. but found this a wrong location. Advance party then proceeded to N.2.b.d.b.8. (Where 7th Field Co. had been) billets. Inspected new camp at T.I.c.65.78. Horse Lines at T.7.a.75.15.	JJR
		3	Sent Lieut. Boyd back to GOMIECOURT with instructions as to movement of Coy. Coy. continuing section training. Sectns 3 & 4 moved forward to Mazen Huts at T.I.c.65.78. O.C. to trenches inspecting work in right sector of Div. front - inspected billets in HINDENBERG LINE & forward sections.	JJR
		4	Sections 3 & 4 moved forward to trenches - No 3 to dugouts at FOSTER CUCKOO DUMP 0.25.0.2.4. No 4 to HINDENBERG LINE at T5.b.4.6. Remainder of Coy. moved forward. Sects 1 & 2 & all Sappers makes to Mazen Huts at T.I.c.65.78. Transport to T.7a.75.15.	JJR

Army Form C. 2118.

WAR DIARY
or
INTELLIGENCE SUMMARY.
(Erase heading not required.)

400ᵗʰ (Highland) Field Coy. R.E.

(139)

Place	Date	Hour	Summary of Events and Information	Remarks and references to Appendices
N26.d.6.8 REF. SHEET 51 B. 	Oct 1917	5 6 7	Section 1, 2 & all Sappers makes moved forwards to N26.d.6.8. Took over billets from 17th Field Co. R.E. O.C. to trenches & took over all work with all section officers. also cushes at 153 Brig. H.Q. & arrays working parties. Took started as follows Sect. 4 with 75 men working by night clearing & with Lnr between Post 4 + 5 – Sappers & fay revetty between posts 2 - 3 & 4 25 men carrying by night. Sect. 3 with Sun Lnr took parties clearing & revetting Bn. Front Support. Sec. 1 Shelters at Right Brig. H.Q. & Cemetery & in COTEOT VALLEY Sec. 2 - Blanketing & numbering dugouts, also continuing work in horseshoe dump & at Nissen Huts – Sappers make Stations 3 & 4 Shelters to HINDENBERG LINE & billets beside Sect. 4. – Heavy rain. O.C. over trenches & night. – Heavy rain & wind – O.C. to Nissen Huts – Transport Lines & C.R.E. Work continued as before.	*[sig]* *[sig]* *[sig]*

Army Form C. 2118.

WAR DIARY
or
INTELLIGENCE SUMMARY.

(Erase heading not required.)

400th (Highland) Field Coy. R.E.

(140)

Place	Date	Hour	Summary of Events and Information	Remarks and references to Appendices
M26.d.6.8. Ref Sheet 51.	Oct. 8 1917		O.C. to meet C.R.E. at Prisor Huts - Received instructions to discontinue work on Horse standings at Camp. This to be continued later. C.R.E. visits billets at M26.d.6.8. Gave verbal instructions re work in Drmb. Park in Drum Line to be taken over by infantry - R.E. to work at Support Posts - trench boarding in between - Sect. 2 starts work on Duck board track for wet weather between Brig. H.Q. & entrance to AVENUE TRENCH. Very wet night.	Sgt.
	9		Work continued as before - O.C. round left Sub sector - this sub sector not so good as right - Over Trench's "subject to worse attention from the enemy. Batt'n Change over interferes with work. Went C.R.R. referring to new dead. Sect. 4 commences work on Suffolk Line - O.C. to Horse Lines - Brig H.Q.	Sgt.
	10		O.C. to trenches, visits Sec. 6th B.W. & 5th Gordons & made arrangements	Sgt.
	11		Be work at Support Posts - been round all Support Posts to work R.E. Officers concerned. Lieut. Hayward went on leave - Called at Brig: HQ C.R.E. went round Support Trenches with O.C. - Certain instructions & suggestions given to Section officers - work being concentrated on Support Posts in BROWN SUPPORT. Called at Brig: H.Q. & made necessary arrangements -	Sgt.
	12		O.C. Received instructions to proceed home & report to War Office -	Sgt.

Army Form C. 2118.

WAR DIARY
or
INTELLIGENCE SUMMARY.

(Erase heading not required.)

400th (Inglewood) Field Co NZE

(141)

Instructions regarding War Diaries and Intelligence Summaries are contained in F. S. Regs., Part II. and the Staff Manual respectively. Title pages will be prepared in manuscript.

Place	Date	Hour	Summary of Events and Information	Remarks and references to Appendices
Mob d.6.9 SHEET 51B.	Sep. 13	1917	Round Right Subsector Suffolk with Lieut. Boyd — looked up Lieut. Peebles & saw all other work — Lieut. BLAKEY went on leave — weather improving — highwind.	Sigg
	14		Weather fine — OC. received word to hand over temporarily to Capt. GLEGG — OC. went round 153 Brigade no 4 works with Captain Glegg — saw both sectors Officers in trenches — work as before.	Sigg
	15		Major Allan completed work of handing over to Captain Glegg. Work continued as before. Instrument returns for affiliated to two previous battalions to work in the line Nos 1+2 Sections returned Nos 3+4 Sections	IK
	16.		152 If. Pnr returned 153 If.Pnrs in the line Company billeted at NEUVILLE VITASSE.	W.
	17th 18th		Work on WRCN C.T., HINDENBURG LINE (New fronting entrance tunnel) + screens to destructions Trucks in COJEUL VALLEY.	W.
	19th		Forward Sections working am 12 pms only, Nos 12, 6, 7, 8, 12, 13, 14, 20, 21, 22, + "Model Post" SWIFT SUPPORT. Day 9 am — 3:30 p.m. Night 6 pm — 12 mn. Work consists of sloping sides of trench, cutting Cubby holes, Trimming & reverting mis-shape. Work on HINDENBURG LINE & COJEUL VALLEY continued. 9 O.R. Joined Co. from NZ. Base Depot to 19th 2 men detailed from Coy. A to work electric light plant in HINDENBURG TUNNEL	W.
	20th		Reconnaissance of dug-outs in Rue Ann commenced	W.

WAR DIARY
INTELLIGENCE SUMMARY

404th (Highland) Field Co. R.E.

Place	Date	Hour	Summary of Events and Information	Remarks and references to Appendices
N26d6.8.	21st		Work as on 20th. Major J.R. Riggall R.E. reported to take over command of company.	M.
Sheet "51.B"	22		Work as on 21st.	M.
	23		S.O.R. joined from Boulogne. Reinforcement of 1 O.R. from 102 F.d Co. R.E. Captain Glegg R.E. rejoined 401 Field Co. R.E.	M.
	24.		Work continues.	M.
	25.		"	M.
	26.		Lieut L.C. Blakey rejoined unit from leave to U.K.	M.
	28.		Pa/S 20, 21, 22 completed. Lieut Blakey accidentally injured – thrown off his horse whilst on duty & evacuated. Shwr Commission. Proceeds to Field Ambulance. Received orders to leave work after day shift on 28th. Preparations for relief by 209 Field Company 34th Div. G.II sections took over bathe at Neuville Vitasse. Work at Nissen Huts continued.	M.
	29		Sappers' Main reported unfit by 'bus. 209 Field Co. R.E. took over at Morchies to T.I.C.	M.
BEAULENCOURT	30th		209 F.d Co. took over from Horse Lines. Company paraded 7.15 am. & marched to Nissen Huts at Beaulencourt.	M.
Ref. Sheet LENS 1/100,000	31st		Company stayed at Beaulencourt. Refilling Point Bus (36th Div.) Advanced Pickett Party went on to YTRES.	M.

Major J.R. Riggall
O.C. 404th (H.d) Field Co. R.E.

Vol 29

CONFIDENTIAL
No 81 (A)
HIGHLAND
DIVISION.

Confidential

War Diary
of
400th (Highland) Field Coy. R.E.

for period

1st November 1914 to 30th November 1914.

400TH
(HIGHLAND)
FIELD COMPANY, R.E.
No.
Date. 1/12/17

Army Form C. 2118.

WAR DIARY
or
INTELLIGENCE SUMMARY.
(Erase heading not required.)

400th (H) Field Co. R.E.

143

Place	Date	Hour	Summary of Events and Information	Remarks and references to Appendices
BEAULENCOURT near BAPAUME	1 Nov 1917		Company moved by march route to LITTLE WOOD CAMP YTRES, billeting in NISSEN HUTS. O.C. attends conference prior to taking over HAVRINCOURT WOOD EAST. Repairs & erection of camp pump. Accommodation under LT PATERSON R.E.	
YTRES P.26.b.6.3. SHEET 57/C 1/40,000	2nd		1 Section of 404 Pats to R.E. & stores of HAVRINCOURT WOOD EAST. Lieuts BOYD & PATERSON & 2nd Lts PEEBLES & CLARK reinforced HAVRINCOURT WOOD EAST. Report reporting C.R.E. 6 p.m.	
	3rd		Work commenced in HAVRINCOURT WOOD by Sections 2,3,4 & Section 1 under C.S.M. Section 1 working in Camp fatigues et under C.S.M.	
do.	4th		Captain R.W. McCRONE rejoined company from Fifth Army. Section of 404 Pats to R.E. under Lt PATERSON R.E. billeted in Lechand at Q8d2.7 I.D.R. struck at the strength. billets at Q85.37.	Sheet 57/c 50.2 1/40,000
do.	5th		Section 3 under 2nd Lt PEEBLES R.E. billeted in Lechand at Q 14 c. 2.9.	
do.	6th		Section 4 under LT BOYD R.E. billets.	
			Lt Day R.E. relieves Lt PEEBLES & takes over command of section III. Lieut Pheteograph attack at full strength.	
do.	7th		Very wet morning – O.B. to inspect work in HAVRINCOURT WOOD at 5.30 p.m. D.m.e.s. Sat one of 36th Div Both House in YTRES. was reinforced with lints.	
do.	8th		Frost over night – clear stay morning – O.B. to work on road in HAVRINCOURT WOOD. – O.B. meets C.R.E. & E.S.O.I. & good round work with them.	

A5834 Wt.W4973/M687 750,000 8/16 D.D. & L. Ltd. Forms/C.2118/13.

WAR DIARY
INTELLIGENCE SUMMARY

Army Form C. 2118.

400th (Highland) Field Coy RE

(144)

Place	Date	Hour	Summary of Events and Information	Remarks and references to Appendices
YTRES. P.26.b.6.0.30	Nov 1917 9th		O.C. good round north at 8.30A.M. Section IV & section from 404th Field Coy R.E. to bath in YTRES - M. Dore & section III change their camp from PLACE MORTEMART to another hut of the wood alongside M. Boyol at Q.14.C.20.70. O.C. & CAPT McCRONE to H.Q. 147th I.T. Coy to get information about WATER SUPPLY from along the BANK of the CANAL DU NORD for a wholesale of 3000 gls towards our line. The water to pumped by 16 H.P. MERRYWEATHER engine with boiler and pump complete, the pump is designed to deliver 120 gallons per 1 minute against a head of 250 ft.	M
do	10th		M. DONALD CAMERON on will work on water supply - engine house footings excavation. The rest of the Coy still working on temporary the accommodation in HAVRINCOURT WOOD	M
do	11th		Instructions received from C.R.E. to reconnoitre the village of NEUVILLE (P.27.600) in view of increasing accommodation - Section I to reinforced on water supply by section of 404th Field Coy attached, this section starts work on part of pipe line running from the BRIDGE at J.35.B.3 forward. Work by sections II & IV in HAVRINCOURT WOOD is partially stopped as stores are not sent up by train. One other work struck off Company strength.	M

WAR DIARY or INTELLIGENCE SUMMARY

Army Form C. 2118.

400th (Highland) Field Coy. R.E.

Place	Date	Hour	Summary of Events and Information	Remarks and references to Appendices
YTRES. P.26.b.6030	Nov 1917 12th		O.B. reconnoitres NEUVILLE for accommodation. Section III moved & LT DOIG return to Coy H.Q. from forward billets in HAVRINCOURT WOOD — Stores for water supply drawn from 149th AT Coy R.E. Section I start connecting pipes for water supply. Sections II & IV still short of stores. LIEUT. L.C. BROWN struck off strength.	M
do.	13th		O.B. & CAPT MCCRONE inspect work on water supply — O.B. shows LT DOIG work in NEUVILLE. Section III take over work for the artillery from section I in the village of METZ (Q.19 & 20). Section II & IV supply men for work on OVERLAND TRACKS, in HAVRINCOURT WOOD for the artillery.	M
do.	14th		Section III start work on billets in NEUVILLE — Sapper Martin report in METZ — 100 are to work under our Coy. Section IV work LT BOYD return to Coy H.Q. from forward billets in HAVRINCOURT WOOD. Other sections work as usual. C.R.E. sends word at night that more shelters are to be made in HAVRINCOURT WOOD.	M
do.	15th		LT BOYD & section IV return to forward billets & start work again on shelters. LT DOIG & section III stop work in NEUVILLE VILLAGE & instructions from C.R.E. about forward shelters are as follows:— The camp at P.14.C.2.8. is to be increased to hold two Field Coys & 200 Sappers shelters & shelters have to be erected at B.W. 50 for 350 infantry. (Our later we were in No 401 FCRE)	M

Army Form C. 2118.

WAR DIARY
or
INTELLIGENCE SUMMARY.

(Erase heading not required.)

400 Field Coy R.E.

(46)

Place	Date	Hour	Summary of Events and Information	Remarks and references to Appendices
YPRES. P.2.b.6.0.30.	5/6/9/17	16th	O.C. working party reports for work on water supply – work badly delayed by receive instruction to move REAR H.Q. to NEUVILLE – orders finally received to the following day. O.C. to conference at C.R.E.'s in tree bow received for the coming operation as follows. N°s I & II sections have to work on road from Q.4.d.21. to K.29 central the sections have to come under the instructions of the 401st Field Coy. R.E. N°s III & IV sections have to assist the artillery in getting forward – N°s III are to be attached to the 255 & 256 Brigade & N°s IV to the 255 Brigade R.F.A.	M
HAVRINCOURT WOOD Q.11.c.4.8 Sheet 57C		17.	Accommodation in HAVRINCOURT WOOD interchanged of R.E. Camps, Limes sent to representative of Black Watch by O.C. NEUVILLE. Hope Lines and but 3 stoves at YPRES in LITTLE WOOD	M
		18.	Accommodation in HAVRINCOURT WOOD further hut complete Sections 2, 3 & 4 billeted in huts. O.C. lives at the hut. Lieutenant C.G.T. COSTER R.E.(T) joined Company for No. 401 & No. 404 to be in NEUVILLE also Hrinelin	M
		19.	Schme of 404 N°s report to companies. No work done H.Q. moves to NEUVILLE. P.O.R. reinforcement from R.E. Base Depot. C/o P.O.R. reinforcements Linmer Aller Sapper W/1153 M.S.	M
		20.	Dismal weather at 6.20 am took R.B.4 trench Remainder from Q.4.d.21 to arrive at K.35.c.2.6. Section foreman and truck in trenches broken had no men to cover & cut new in trenches undertaken trouble to in spent some making up the tunnel. Afternoon than request was training at am brought for some sanny the duty Section 3 at work on the Brigade bn fatigue from NEUVILLE following	M
				8 pm

WAR DIARY
or
INTELLIGENCE SUMMARY.
(Erase heading not required.)

Army Form C. 2118.

400th (S) Fd Co. R.E.

(47)

Place	Date	Hour	Summary of Events and Information	Remarks and references to Appendices
HAVRINCOURT WOOD Q.14.c.4.8 Sht 57c	21		Took over work from 401 FdCo. Same work as yesterday. O.C. reconnoitred FLETQUIERES and sent in report re C.R.E.'s Central Dump.	M
"	22		Section moved billets to HINDENBURG LINE about K.36.a. Cleaned out old German dugouts. Continued work on Ruth Section 374 yds. Working under R.A. Billets and returned into 356 Tun R.F.A.	M
HINDENBURG LINE K.36.a.	23		Hindenburg Line work to Camp Q.14.c.4.8 Fletquieres completed Company continued work from K.35.c.2.5 towards all trenches until about 300× and out proposed truck line 700× and taken infantry in file.	M
"	24		Orders received 12.30 am to go back to HAVRINCOURT road by 10 am + trenches at METZ at 6 p.m. lectures at START at 8 p.m. for FONSOMME Transport proceeded by march rout to BUSIGNICOURT at 1 p.m. Horses taken and Company marched and remb? picks, shovels etc. KIRSKI Road All 9 p.m. and men like this + mine was carried out they were known Moved into PLUNKET CAMP (R.26.S.85)	M
PLUNKET CAMP R.16 S.8.5	25		Orders received to take WL. General Damien ag Capt Guards Div. Crofts MacLong transport and men to DEMAIN CAMP KNOWLER CAMP bicycles) returned from DEMAIN CAMP forward to TRESCAULT hurry	1/10
	26		Stayed in PIONEER CAMP. horses recovered	

WAR DIARY or INTELLIGENCE SUMMARY

Army Form C. 2118.

Unit: 40th (H) Coy R.E.

Page 148

Place	Date	Hour	Summary of Events and Information	Remarks and references to Appendices
Havrincourt Wood	27.		O.C. sent O/S Guards Div. G. asking if Guards required us to maintain a camp near Trescault. Instructions recv'd - "Yes, 3 tractors & 15 tarpaulins to man. be sent to Coy. HQ. moved into billets at Q.14.a.6.4.	(1)
Q.14.a.6.4.			Night parties RE. hauling up timber to forward LT. DUG. + 50 horses brunt of North Hamburg at Ytres. Orders rec'd from C.R.E. Guards Div. to make an Overland Track from about Q.14.d.4.2 to about K.24.b.8.2. (Trescault to Flesquières). 2nd Lt. P.G. Clark R.E.(T) proceeded to England for duty with Tank Corps.	
	28.	10.0 a.m.	O.C. sent out 80 a.m. and started to reconnoitre track & recommended track K.h 3.30 p.m. Section 1+2 worked in camp.	(2)
	29.		Sections 1, 2, + 3 worked on track. Track was bridged at K.35c. to 15.45 and K.35.b 20.90. Lieut. Boyd R.E. proceeded on leave to the U.K. Leave granted 1.12.17 – 15.12.17. Lieut. D.B. Martin R.E.(T) joined Company from R.E. Base Depot. 1 O.R. reinforcement.	(3)
	30.		Sections 1, 2, +4 worked on track which was made passable to the road at K.24.d.35.75. E.W. trestles bridges were cut, & stores (metals) put out at 30 yd interval on hill B. Track (10" wide). Rear 800m. pervious (until then poorly in and bad pieces improved) & fencer bounded. Shell was still being fired in. Strength of Company 7 Officers 208 O.R.	(4)

Maxwell
Major R.E.
O.C. 40th (H) Coy R.E.

Confidential

War Diary

of

400th (Highland) Field Coy. R.E.

for period

1st December 1917 to 31st December 1917.

Army Form C. 2118.

WAR DIARY
or
INTELLIGENCE SUMMARY.
(Erase heading not required.)

400th (Highland) Field Coy. R.E.

Place	Date	Hour	Summary of Events and Information	Remarks and references to Appendices
HAVRINCOURT WOOD 57.c.b.64. Sheet 57.c. do.	Dec/9/17 1st		Orders from C.R.E. GUARDS DIV. that Coy is to stand by ready to move. Every other tent and billets in the wood. Verbal orders received that Coy will move the following day & take one from one of the field coys 56 or 58 Divs.	M
	2nd		Definite orders received to move. Major Heggelle & H.Q.R.E. to act as C.R.E. owing to absence of Lt Col Fleming. Capt Claiborne takes over the Coy. Coy moves to BERTINCOURT leaving HAVRINCOURT WOOD at 12.30 p.m. No definite orders what to do. BUCQUIERE to take over NFT billets of 513th field Coy R.E. O/C billets available for Coy in BERTINCOURT so Coy moves on to HEBUCQUIERE & finds billets there. Billets sufficient.	M
SHELTERS NEAR DOIGNIES J.16.b.70.50. do.	3rd		Coy also transport moves to forward billets at DOIGNIES by Govt service at HEBUCQUIERE in charge of transport. Lts Claiborne & McDonald & Coolful reconnoitre the line in front of GOUSIES & orders received from 154 Inf Brigade to start work on railway & communication for 150 men in trench running from Q.30.b.0.70. to E.19.c.40.20.	M
	4th		Sections III & IV leave billets at 8.20 p.m. made the Douite & Master shelters for shelter for 150 inf Brigade & and start work on shelters. Coy now to come under direct orders of C.R.E. Master.	

A5834 Wt. W4973/M687 750,000 8/16 D. D & L. Ltd. Forms/C.2118/13.

Army Form C. 2118.

WAR DIARY
or
INTELLIGENCE SUMMARY.
(Erase heading not required.)

H90 2 (Highland) Field Coy R.E.

(50)

Place	Date	Hour	Summary of Events and Information	Remarks and references to Appendices
SHELTERS NEAR DOIGNIES. T.6.b.7.80. Sheet 57C	Dec 4th	10.10	Moved to billets at 11.30pm as they are required for urgent work at night. Orders receive for the whole Coy to work at the village of BOURSIES. H durable apron fence to be put from T.6.6.50.0 to T.6a.25.50 a length about 850 yds. Wagons got heavily shelled at DOOVERVAL DUMP. Sgt. Brown & one driver wounded, four horses lost. 4 G.S. wagon built and one cart & two seconds at 11 P.M. What Coy is to move the following day transport gears move to FREMICOURT.	M
BEUGNY I.16.d.0.2. Sheet 57C	5th		Sections III & IV under Mr Gray & Martin are to to started to be ready by about Noon. No O.K. move to new billet at BEUGNY. Section I going by road to OP set to work if required at Martin & two field - rich.	M
Do.	6th		Section hutting continued in BEUGNY. Section I report to H.Q. in BEUGNY. N. Corpi takes charge of the horse lines have in FREMICOURT.	M
Do.	7th		Work on camp in BEUGNY continues - stables started. Section I under It Gowald start work on new support line under cover of noise made by R.E.	M
Do.	8th		Section I proceed to Lesbed return to cut old lout of BOISNES and some trench mortar of 401st (78th) Field Coy R.E.	M
	9th		CAPT McCRONE goes round work of various sections with the artillery	M

Section of Trench for Support Line.

Scale 1" = 6ft

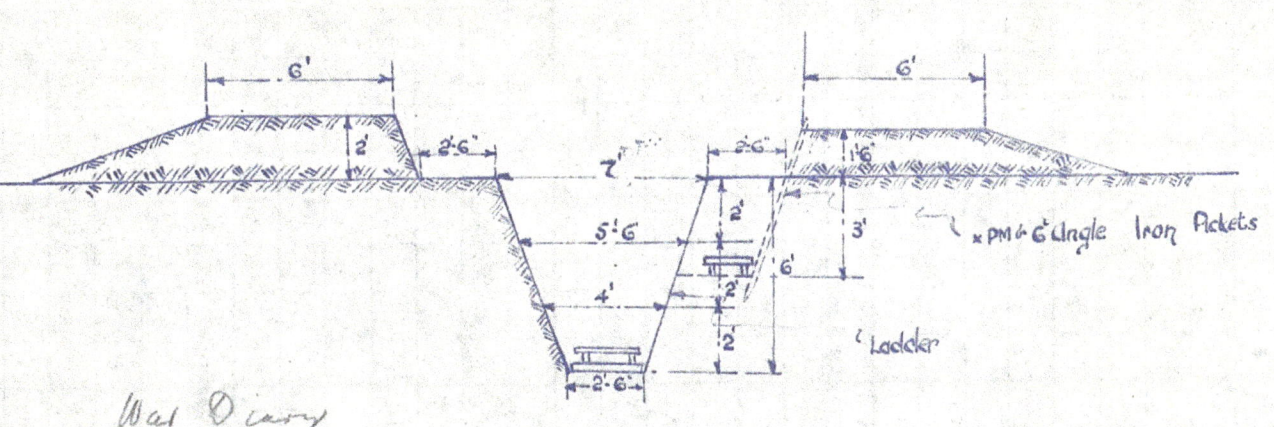

War Diary

400th High Field Coy. R.E.

Page 151   date 9.12.17.

Appendix E.

Instructions regarding War Diaries and Intelligence Summaries are contained in F. S. Regs., Part II. and the Staff Manual respectively. Title pages will be prepared in manuscript.

(151)

400ᵗʰ (Highland) Field Coy. R.E

Place	Date Dec 1917	Hour	Summary of Events and Information	Remarks and references to Appendices
BEUGNY I.16.d.0.2. Sheet 57ᶜ	9th		progress slow on account of small working parties. Section Ia II forming the support line to the necessary dimensions as shown on attached drawing.	Appendix E. M
Do.	10th		Section III start working by day on support line. Section III working on part of support line running from D.23.a.1.7. to D.23.a.6.6. section IV working on part of support line running from D.17.b.8.7. to D.23.a.1.7. Each section is to work on one post – each post to consist of four firebays & one deep shelter. great shortage of stone for work.	M
Do.	11th		Sections still on same work – 10 deep shelters being worked on for the artillery.	
Do.	12th		Sections as before. Box respirators of section III & IV & H.Q. examined by Sergt. from 5ᵗʰ Div. unserviceable ones condemned.	M
Do.	13th		Sections working as before. Section II get slightly shallow shelter work on new support line.	M
Do.	14th		Little progress is being made on shelters for artillery owing to no stone being available	M
Do.	15th		Some of our officers attend lecture by Div general commanding re. conference at C.R.E. He hopes to be allowed to work on new area	M

Army Form C. 2118.

WAR DIARY
or
INTELLIGENCE SUMMARY.
(Erase heading not required.)

400 (Highland) Field Coy. R.E.

(152)

Place	Date	Hour	Summary of Events and Information	Remarks and references to Appendices
BEUGNY I.16.d.0.2. Sheet 57c	Dec 15th		Work near the village of BEUGNY.	M
	16th		MAJOR KIBBELL returns to the Coy & takes over from CAPT MCCRONE & to OC 2/Lt as usual. I return to Coy H.Q. at BEUGNY. Section I & II taken over and being relieved by 404 M. Field Coy R.E.	M
do	17th		Moved to FREMICOURT to take over work and north of railway accommodation in the village. 8 Nissen huts to Mobile, waiting from of ? Prisrs. section II start work on the erection of Nissens on the BAPAUME-CAMBRAI road. O.B. marks out new NISSEN HUT Camp at MILL CROSS I.27.c.	M
do	18th		Small hutty camp on south Nissens — Work started on NISSEN HUTS at FREMICOURT. Work delayed owing to trainers not turning up to time. One hutr & the smith received from Mobile.	M
do	19th		Work on NISSEN HUTS near FREMICOURT as usual. Party working on Nissens withdrawn — Weather still very cold & frosty.	M
do	20th		Work on huts as usual — Work started on erecting a shed at the Batt. lines FREMICOURT. think no impt.	M
do	21st		LT BOYD returns from leave — 12 NISSEN huts near FREMICOURT now completed	
do	22nd		Work on NISSEN L.l. hutmt over to the Corps — Work to be started on the BEAUMETZ VAUX LINE — Stones for wearing not out to the mile about I.14.68.1.	M
do	23rd			M

WAR DIARY or INTELLIGENCE SUMMARY

Army Form C. 2118.

400 ᵗʰ (Highland) Field Coy RE

Place	Date	Hour	Summary of Events and Information	Remarks and references to Appendices
BEUGNY I.16.d.02 Sht 57ᵈ	Dec 23ʳᵈ 17		Enemy aeroplanes active - BEUGNY & FREMICOURT received air attack. Little done.	/h
do	24ᵗʰ		Work on recovery pumps St COOPER - 550 yds of double track above France put in - dummy started at I.14.b.0.3 a company on tramway. BAPAUME CAMBRAI road - Scrim from screens put up by Scots railway.	/h
	25ᵗʰ		Coy made party work on billets at DIV HQ. - the rest of the Coy Rose & Tidying. Div¹ Commander had whole Coy¹ party.	/h
No	26ᵗʰ		Work on hoving the BEAUMETZ VAULX MINE broad gauge. LT BOYD explosives LT DOE in own ds for the Rly [?] Reinstatement of the Cap¹ Karman by the R.E. at 3pm transferred him there with his Finnish R?. A_ pt in the ?pol?app ?	/h
No	27ᵗʰ		Screen on the BAPAUME CAMBRAI road. From now the Rly road "B" at DOUCHENS Finn ??? [?] Front R?L Road. 1000 yds of double upon put out dub by 26 troops + 10 Infantry We have to hire Jorm ??????	/h

Army Form C. 2118.

WAR DIARY
or
INTELLIGENCE SUMMARY.   466 (H) Field Co. R.E.
(Erase heading not required.)

Place	Date	Hour	Summary of Events and Information	Remarks and references to Appendices
BEUGNY I.16.d.0.2 Sheet 57c.	DEC 28.	1100	Working parties & men put out. Transport up into 108th Field Co. R.E. or Moncheit. Somewhat continued.	/11
"	29	500	Lorries put out. Strong wind. Out lorry unable to go as far as JIZa.1.6. returned to DONALD N.G. returned from Beaumez. 210' framework put up LAMBDA1 Room completed for 6 shelts camp instructional hutts. I.b-II Lain built	/11
"	30	1000	Spine put out. I6.b.6.7.- I7.b.25.85. IICPL ROUGH's pty completed lining opp. NISSEN HUTS with Althaia? marcenturia? it laken in about 1 piece of membranstin to 4m.s. & Tries Metzger withs ballasting it down to the purlins. C.E. IV Corps & GPO came to the camp I16.d.0.2. Two etc. about work	/11
"	31.		Os had remvt. the line from J.14.b.81. to about J.27.b. and thrown in siding & withdrawl have built C.S. IV Corps. 2a Cpl ANDERSON commenced to build food kitchen at BEAUMETZ, or foundations. 1000. Spine put out at BEAUMETZ line. Strength of Company. 4 officers 204. OR.	/11

Maggrell?
Major O.C. no
466 Field Co. R.E.

War Diary
of
400th (Highland) Field Coy. R.E.
for period
1st January 1918 to 31st January 1918

Army Form C. 2118.

WAR DIARY
or
INTELLIGENCE SUMMARY.
(Erase heading not required.)

Army_____ (Hqts) 1st Co. R.E.

 155

Place	Date 1918	Hour	Summary of Events and Information	Remarks and references to Appendices
BEUGNY T16d.0.2. Sheet 57c	JAN 1		No work. O.C. had meet the BEAUMETZ LINE, from the CAMBRAI ROAD to T28a. With B.G.G.S. IV Corps who wishes 4 sappers to carry round to put in pickets. The trench ..... to meeting ..... 450× on the top in afternoon. Mr Infantry & Sgt ..... digging near the Company had New Year Dinner at 1 Pm. Attached were Contained REGIMENT IPPMAC celebrated.	J.H.
	2		O.C. & 3 sappers ..... another 1800× of BEAUMETZ LINE with single tape. No Infantry parties available to bring up putting in 6 sappers put out 350× Then MG out and shirts knew has 6450× Cpl Roush puts continued work lining huts W. DJAKS Camp (LENDECQUARY) CAMPRAIT ROAD ..... to T13a.2.6.	
	3		OC. & 3 sappers marked out a further 1050× of BEAUMETZ LINE. 3 Battalion 2nd/1st Infantry in different clothes 1800× to line put out by Lt. LOFTUS & Park infantry ..... 500× KATCHLN BEAUMETZ ..... complete ..... way being waved	
	4		Major J. Hygell to h o/cpr during absence of Lt Col Fleming DSO Lieut G.E.T. Cooper Taken over company.	

(A7093) Wt. W12859/M1293. 75 5.0.0. 1/17. D.D.&L.Ltd. Forms/C.2118/24.

Army Form C.2118.

WAR DIARY
or
INTELLIGENCE SUMMARY.
(Erase heading not required.)

400ᵗʰ (Highland) Field Coy R.E.

(156)

Instructions regarding War Diaries and Intelligence Summaries are contained in F.S. Regs., Part II. and the Staff Manual respectively. Title pages will be prepared in manuscript.

Place	Date 1918	Hour	Summary of Events and Information	Remarks and references to Appendices
Bengying I16d.0.2 Sheet 57c	Jan 4ᵗʰ (cont)		Work done: 3 huts erected & 6 frames fitted at O'Shea Camp. 500 yds double apron fence hut out on corps line. 120ft screening erected on Cambrai Rd. Drainage of corps line work continued. Weather, cold, keen frost, snow at intervals.	
	5ᵗʰ		2nd Lt P. Donald met B.G.G.S. IV Corps at Beaumetz at 10am to go over corps line. Work done 2 huts erected at O'Shea Camp. 450ˣ wired on corps line. South Ritchen at Beaumetz completed. 60' screening on Cambrai Rd erected. Corps line:- 1600ˣ trench taped on left of Cambrai Rd - 300ˣ " " " right " " " Total taped out 5350ˣ Drainage in J.14 6 - 30% complete Weather Keen frost	
	6ᵗʰ		Work continued as on 5ᵗʰ Weather:- very cold in morning, keen frost during night 5/6ᵗʰ. rain came on at 8pm	
	7ᵗʰ		Work continued on O'Shea Camp, Wiring of corps line, Drainage of corps line & Screening of Cambrai Rd & Watson artillery small shelter. 4 O.R. & 5 1ˢᵗ Div Rest Camp - 40ˣ returned from 51ˢᵗ Div Rest Camp 1 OR. rejoined from IV Corps School of gas 1 OR reported from 51ˢᵗ Div School of gas soft ground in morning, ground softer after heavy rain Weather rain in morning	
	8ᵗʰ		Work continued until mid-day when parties were withdrawn owing to stormy weather. 2/st P Donald made reconnaissance for extension of light rly in Divn sector	
	9ᵗʰ		Reconnaissance for extension of light rly completed & plans forwarded to C.R.E. Work continued as on 8ᵗʰ Total Completed during week :- O'Shea Camp 52 windows barn huts 19 huts nearing completion	

Army Form C. 2118.

WAR DIARY
or
INTELLIGENCE SUMMARY.

(Erase heading not required.)

[157]

Army Form: 4th (Highland) Field Coy R.E.

Instructions regarding War Diaries and Intelligence Summaries are contained in F. S. Regs., Part II. and the Staff Manual respectively. Title pages will be prepared in manuscript.

Place	Date 1918	Hour	Summary of Events and Information	Remarks and references to Appendices
Beugny T16d02 Sheet 57c	Jan 9th (cont)		Section of Cambrai Road completed to T.13.a.7.8. Continued living 6 800 ft wire hut at Sidney wreck. Tracing & building of cabs tray completed. Drainage in J 9 & 6 completed. Section B.O.G continued work on dug-out for artillery.	
	10th		Work continued as on 9th. 1 GR wounded — at duty — shell fire. 2 GR returned with from R.E. Base Depot	
	11th		Work continued as above	
	12th		Work continued as before. Laying of huts on O'Shea camp at T.13.a 8.7 completed. Stacking of Cambrai Road completed. Shaw Instruction ordered at R.S.Day's ground from base Hq a. 2 Section half.	
	13th		Work continued on Stacking, laying of huts on 2 O'Shea camp — Instruction of IV Corps School at Guinon-le-Petit. B.O.R to train to Guinon-le-Petit. Orders received to move on 14th Day to Guinon-le-Petit.	HS
	14th		Work continued as on 13th. Party withdrawn from O'Shea camp. Lieut R. T. 3 L D humer. Walker Day- Threatening snow	HS
	15		3 L.D Enfield took entrance exam on 15th No 3rd Section retired third at 509 # F. L. Pl. called forming unit.	

WAR DIARY
INTELLIGENCE SUMMARY

Army Form C. 2118.

400th (HIGH) F.C. R.E.

Place	Date 1918	Hour	Summary of Events and Information	Remarks and references to Appendices
BEUGNY O.2 I.16.d Sheet 57C	Jany 16		Mr. 3rd 4th Section report Company from R.F.A. Returned parties from Search H.Q. H.P. arriving & are about normal R.F.A. unit. hope Repair return from C.R.E.'s. U.R. improvement from M.G. Area H.Q's Total work during week. Screening CAMBRAI RD. 600' erected since 9.1.18. Rail sum screening K.7/3.b.2.8 tonnage work not not during week 42,500'. DRAINAGE S.I.OF CAMBRAI RD completed except for 2 small pits. H.03.74 system carried out work for Artillery 100 tolow. – 12 dugouts – not complete. – 5 kilometres path of Splinter proof shelters completed at gun positions. Strong point Railway dram during 17th month.	R.G.R.
HOMET LE PETIT G.14.a.5.3 Sheet 57C	17th		Company moved to D.H.P. CERNAY ARHIET-LE-PETIT. OC. Part of 509 Fld. Co. to CATTENACH tempory attached and from them who attached 25th Dinst P. DUNLOP transferred 8 N.C.O's Argyll Treoung mentioned in herewith. Regt'l order by C.R.E. No. 409 159 4/Sergt. A. CHRISTIE mentioned in despatches in his Jan Honn prints. Commences work on Nothing Dry for in incomplete.	M
"	18th		S.D. 40.1 – 1 fiction new	M

WAR DIARY
or
INTELLIGENCE SUMMARY.
(Erase heading not required.)

(110th Foot ng)

(154)

Army Form C. 2118.

Place	Date 1/18	Hour	Summary of Events and Information	Remarks and references to Appendices
ACHIET-LE-PETIT	Jan 19		Carried on work in D.H.q. 2nd Lt T. WORKMAN (NZ E?) joined the Company. 3. O.R. joined from N.Z. Bno Depot. 1st Lt Atkins went on leave in England. Rde Pump Camps.	nil
G.14.a.53	20		mining against LEPETIT 1st Lt COPPER RE. S/L O.R.	nil
Sheet 57C			2nd Lt WATSON reported from Inf. Camp. Same work.	nil
"				
G.9.d.4.1.	21		1st Lt COPPER reported from CCS. Company moved to G.9.d.4.1. in BUCHANAN CAMP (152 Pde Group) work to begin operations of CHINESE Labour in BUCHANAN CAMP (G.15.a, 9.c?) Hutted CAMP (9.9.a.b, 9.3c). D.H.q. had entramp ministry Company. C.E. → DA HQ mg IV Corps Comm min Camp	nil nil
	22		Work as before. Cochairs 2nd CRE to willocal work	
	23.		1 Recce & Middle wk cafu BUCHANAN. Carry to Hq. Headman now with Camp Talks over work of BUCHANAN. 4 Sappers joined from N.Z. Bro. Depot. Pay'd Serjts (Priority)	
	24 25 26 27		Work continues. Army Hero Heard WLG put up daily Coke nutted in future from a menial Camp	nil
	28		1 O.R. reported from CCS 1 Lt reported from NZ Dino Dept (Leave & Meals rd Station Work continues. Competition Chinese + Chinese Nut Company ten 3 long h in complete hut with 8 min, warm turf than 55 minutes	nil

Army Form C. 2118.

WAR DIARY
or
INTELLIGENCE SUMMARY.
(Erase heading not required.)

(Aco FS ZNE)

(160)

Place	Date	Hour	Summary of Events and Information	Remarks and references to Appendices
GQ 41 Sh 57c	Jan 1918 29.		Sand ark. 10 linch TDM up	1/1 1/11 1/11
	30.		BUCHANAN CAMP Camp Left with Heaver hut with same help from Pioneers. Inspected in the Morning by Brig-Genl Gosset at 11 AM Billets 404 Billets 404 for Unit 3-0 PM	
	31.		No work.	
			COMPANY STRENGTH AT 31.12.17 = 7 Officers 204 O.R.	
			Decrease during month :—	
			1 Officer 6 O.R. – 1 Officer – 6 O.R.	
			Increase during month :—	
			1 Officer 13 O.R. + 1 Officer + 13 O.R.	
			Company Strength at 31/1/18 :— 7 Officers and 211 other ranks	

Confidential

War Diary

of

400th (Highland) Field Coy. R.E.

for period

1st February 1918 to 28th February 1918.

Army Form C. 2118.

WAR DIARY
or
INTELLIGENCE SUMMARY.
(Erase heading not required.)

(400 PSLNE)

(16A)

Place	Date 1918 Febry	Hour	Summary of Events and Information	Remarks and references to Appendices
G. 9.4. Bust 5/c.	1		Company training — Drill, Saluting, Trigger pressing, Aiming — Company fults and guards Junior NCO's. Communication drill under R.S.M. Swan. M.C., D.S.M., R.E. Weather — Cold and foggy.	Pistolle
-do-	2		Training continued. Section drill with and without arms; Instruction in care of arms. Loading drill. Firing position — Lying and standing. Sections I, II, and III firing on 30 yards range. Football — afternoon	Pistolle
-do-	3		Mounted Section, Sections I and II carried on with training. Sections 3 & 4 constructing Cook house in "BUCHANAN CAMP". 4 O.R. to 51st Divisional Rest Camp. 4 O.R. from " "	Pistolle
-do-	4		Sections 3 & 4 training; Sections I & II working on "BUCHANAN CAMP". Drums and hot Lotion firing on 30 yards range. Sgt. BUSHELL (MM) joined unit from R.E. Base Depot. 16 O.R. joined from R.E. Base. C.S.M. Clarke rejoined from 3rd Army Infantry School.	Pistolle
-do-	5		Company training continued. Kit inspection — afternoon. Capt. R.W. McCRONE rejoined from leave. Weather — very fine.	Pistolle
-do-	6		Company parade 9 am — ceremonial. Inspected by C.R.E. Training continued in afternoon. 152 2nd Patl Shots :- 3rd place :- Millinree Driver McFADDEN :- 3rd place — flat race for transport NCO's and men Driver CHAMBERS :-	Pistolle

Army Form C. 2118.

WAR DIARY
or
INTELLIGENCE SUMMARY.
(Erase heading not required.)

400² (Highland) Field Coy. R.E.

Instructions regarding War Diaries and Intelligence Summaries are contained in F. S. Regs., Part II. and the Staff Manual respectively. Title pages will be prepared in manuscript.

Place	Date 1918 February	Hour	Summary of Events and Information	Remarks and references to Appendices
G.9.d.4.1. Sheet 54S.	7		Ceremonial Parade in morning. Rigging hanging bits made into Special R.E features at Divisional Theatre. Commander-in-Chief visited Divisional Area. 1 OR joined from R.E Base Depot.	Note 1/2
-do-	8		No. 22,302 Bmr. Harry BROADBENT awarded the 325194 CROIX-DE-GUERRE for gallant conduct — PIONEERS. Rigging hanging bits — huts — forenoon. G.O.C. 51st (Highland) Division inspected Company at 3·15 p.m.	Bright
-do-	9		Orders received to move on 11th to BEUGNY. Weather fine — men at intervals working on bomb slits — huts. Divisional R.E shooting competition on 30× range at G.14.d.n.n. Score :— 400² Field Coy RE — 278 points 404² " — 259 " 401" " — 201 "	Bright
-do-	10		Football with 401² Coy — afternoon — at home put 8 area — tied. Company paid at 5 p.m. 1 OR evacuated to BEUGNY to go on one OC, 2nd Lieut WORTMAN, and 5 NCOs went forward to BEUGNY to go our works of 12H. Field Coy, RE — 6th Division and prepared to move to BEUGNY. Company finished bomb slits — huts, afternoon — away —. Football with 401² Field Coy — afternoon — away —. 404,71 HCPL B.J. HALE to ENGLAND for RE Commission. 1 OR evacuated out of Divl. Area — sick.	Note

(A7092.) Wt W12539/M1293. 75.10.0. 1/17. D. D. & L. Ltd. Forms/C.2118/14.

Army Form C. 2118.

WAR DIARY
or
INTELLIGENCE SUMMARY.
(Erase heading not required.)

400 H/(Highland) Field Coy R.E

(163)

Instructions regarding War Diaries and Intelligence Summaries are contained in F. S. Regs., Part II. and the Staff Manual respectively. Title pages will be prepared in manuscript.

Place	Date 1918 February	Hour	Summary of Events and Information	Remarks and references to Appendices
BEUGNY T.15.d.9.0 Sheet 57 C.	11		Company moved off, from BUCHANAN CAMP, at 9 am, arrived BEUGNY 12-15 pm. Sections I, II & III moved to forward billets – SUNKEN ROAD north of BEUGNY (T.5.c) at 4-30 p.m. Work, and billets of 124th Field Coy, (G.S.D.) taken over. Disposition of Coy:– HQ., Transport, and No IV Section at BEUGNY, Nos I, II & III Sections in SUNKEN ROAD at (T.5.c.) Weather:– very fine.	Ruoth
Do.	12th		O.C. goes round the line – a small party from Section II work at night on INTERMEDIATE MINE near POST 26, cutting out trench to connect trenches & relaying duckboards.	Ruoth
Do.	13th		Section II carry on work started the previous day – Section III start work in relief of ROOK TRENCH	Ruoth
Do.	14th		O.C. & CAPT McCRONE go round the work. Section I start work in relief of continuation of shells of intermediate coy HQ – & this section working in 2 previous day. 2.S.R. evacuated out of Bird Lane - P.o.C.	Ruoth
Do.	15th		Sections work on before Section II had a party on SUPPORT SIDE or general things.	Ruoth
Do.	16th		Work as usual. Considerable gas shelling round forward billets (& Sunken Road at T.4d and T.5c)	Ruoth

Army Form C. 2118.

WAR DIARY
or
INTELLIGENCE SUMMARY.
(Erase heading not required.)

450th (Highland) Field Co. R.E.

Place	Date February 1918	Hour	Summary of Events and Information	Remarks and references to Appendices
BEUGNY I.15.d.9.0. Med 57c.	17th		N.G. Tyree on leave to U.K. Capt R.H. McCrone taken over. 2 O.R. to Hospital suffering from pneumonia. 1 O.R. in infirmary. Section IV in the forward hills - Pelz-Fiction IV relieved Section III in the forward hills - Bright Lake one from 1st Divn. Small party of sappers assist Coy in return of tools.	R.W.W.R. Pte W.R.
	15th		SUPPORT LINE - Wire sections work on ROOK AVENUE SUPPORT LINE in front of victim. IV would mining trench on shelters in ROOK AVENUE - SECT III assist on shelters in SUPPORT LINE 1 O.R. & Hospital suffering from flu, foraging hard front delays work on the trenches. The RESERVE LINE running from "ROOK AVENUE" D.78.a.50.00. To "RABBIT AVENUE" D.28.c.50.30	R.W.W.R.
do.	19th			R.W.W.R.
do.	20th		LT BOYD & SECT IV with a party of 150 infantry dug 2000' of revving from D.28.a.38. To D.22.c.12. A length of 320 yds - infantry parts work exceptionally well. CAPT McCRONE goes round line with Brigadier 150 Inf Brig & 2.OC. 51st Div. 1 OR to Hospital suffering from flu poisoning.	R.W.W.R.
do.	21st		Lt WORKMAN & section II finish off new C.T. dug the previous night held in ROOK AVENUE completed and handed over to the Brig. 1st task of 350 yds in RESERVE LINE dug. 1 OR evacuated but pneumonia.	R.W.W.R.
do.	22nd		Men skilled for M.G.s marched out while HERRING SUPPORT crossed PICCADILLY. 2nd task of bunch stores up the previous night finished. 10. O.R. to Hospital suffering from flu.	R.W.W.R.
do.	23rd		Work on new shelters for M.G. in HERRING completed. Section II working chiefly on relays of different line shelters in ROBIN support in HERRING.	

WAR DIARY or INTELLIGENCE SUMMARY

Army Form C. 2118.

400th (Highland) Field Coy. R.E.

Place	Date	Hour	Summary of Events and Information	Remarks and references to Appendices
BEUGNY	23rd Feb		Progress. 1&2 L.GR. Hospital suffering from Gas Poisoning.	
T.15.d.9.0. Ypres Sec.	24th	do.	CAPT MCCRONE goes round wiring with R.S.O. 153 Inf Bry. Party of 50 non work from 4pm to 6pm. cutting new RESERVE LINE to protect new party of 500 non from front to back.	Bank
do.	25th	do.	18.3.0. Inf to Dt. RESERVE LINE in hilltops. 8.SR Inf to Dt. wiring to Inf & finishing cat the trenches down from Battery dug outs work started on excavation of Posts in RESERVE LINE - Dug out parties Being made on M.G. Dug out T.29.C.50.50. IT COOPER returns LT WORKMAN on the forward shelter - Section to take over from sector T. 3 men go to Infield Coy. from job.	Bank
do.	26th	do.	Work continued. In account of shortage of Inter Parties digging slackens up to RESERVE LINE & system S.F. carry parties of Mining Platoon 1 R OK that R.E. dump sketch for Batt. HQ at T.3.C.90.50. Water in R O & M support complete except for treads. 18 men to Installed Battery on OGR.	Bank
do.	27th	do.	Conference at C.R.E. where the recommendation of the Div. was Front 153 Brig taking in more line on the right of 16R.	Bank
do. SHAMROCK AVENUE			5.G.R. Highland Inf carrying from Ypres Poison	

Army Form C. 2118.

WAR DIARY
or
INTELLIGENCE SUMMARY.
(Erase heading not required.)

420th (Highland) Field Coy R.E.

(166)

Place	Date	Hour	Summary of Events and Information	Remarks and references to Appendices
BEOGNY. I.15.d.9.0. Maps 57c.	28th Feb.		LT WORKMAN & 20 ORs taken over from 2nd Lt McKAY to continue work of wiring North of MOEUVRES BRIDGE. 2nd Lt MINERS & 7 ORs to continue work of wiring South Mound from MOEUVRES. 2nd Lt WATSON & 8 ORs .... 2 Coy HQ & BEOGNY. Parking party of OR's sent back by train at late hour and bringing total.	
			Company Strength at 31.1.18: 4 / 211	
			Decrease during Month:—	
			Wounded – {Gas poisoning – shell (early)} 1 Officer 49 ORs ---------- -1 / -49	
			Evacuated out of Div. Area – Sick ---------- 7 OR -7	
			To England for Commission ---------- 1 OR -1	
			Increase during Month:—	
			40 OR joined from R.E. Base Depot ---------- +4	
			Company Strength at 28.2.18 6 / 158	
do.	28th Feb.		Report on GAS BOMBARDMENT on the 16th & it effective & situation	Application to attached

400TH (HIGHLAND) FIELD COY. R.E.

APPENDIX TO WAR DIARY DATED FEBRUARY 1918. F.

Report on Gas shell bombardment of area in which Company forward billets are situated (in SUNKEN ROAD near BOURSIES at J.4.d. and J.5.c.) on the 16th February 1918.

There was some gas shelling between 4-15 p.m. and 5-15 p.m. about 200 or 300 yards in rear of Sappers billets, a strong breeze was blowing the gas in opposite direction. No action was taken during this period.

Shelling near billets started about 6-30 p.m., Officer i/c Detachment (Lieut. R.S. DOIG) issued orders for all men to get into Dug-out, drop gas-blankets, and to wear Box Respirators. The Corporal of the Guard was sent round to see that these orders had been complied with.

The dug-outs had not been quite completed with gas blankets.

Shelling continued heavily until 6-45 p.m. At 8-30 p.m. it was thought safe to remove Respirators, and orders were issued to that effect. The gas, however, must have been lying in the SUNKEN ROAD, and possibly in the dug-outs. On the 17th two Sappers reported sick, they were diagnosed as suffering from "Gas poisoning - Shell. (Lethal)"

The gas took effect on the men at different dates, numbers admitted to Hospital, suffering from Gas poisoning, subsequent to the shelling, are shown in the War Diary, and total 1 officer and 49 other ranks to date.

28/2/18.

Rw McBrone Capt. R.E.
for O.C. 400th High Field Coy

51st Divisional Engineers

WAR DIARY

400th FIELD COMPANY R. E.

MARCH 1918

Confidential

War Diary

of

400TH (HIGHLAND) FIELD COY., R.E.

for period

1st March 1918 to 31st March 1918.

WAR DIARY
or
INTELLIGENCE SUMMARY

Army Form C. 2118.

(Erase heading not required.)

400th (Hyland Field) Co. RE

Place	Date	Hour	Summary of Events and Information	Remarks and references to Appendices
BEUGNY I.15.d.9.0. SHEET.57C	1st March	8	Section IV working on repair of ROOK AVENUE — shortage of duckboards. The work for the III working on roads in RESERVE LINE. Section I in CRESCENT TRENCH. Not so much to do as last. Shelling until CAPT MCCABE — only 3 ripples available for the work of Section	Puckle
do.	2nd	do	The night parties to the magazine very dangerous of [illegible] of the Sections. Work carried on despite intense [illegible] in RESERVE LINE 2. Received the orders to return to the 238th at 6.45 PM. It was so dark at night it took the party (parties etc) arts and our replacement at D.78.d.63. A total of the replacement Men men so & handled affecting the 2nd Tanks went out to 16th.	Puckle / Appointed to establish
do.	3rd	do	Working party photos made to the events of the smoke shot fallen fell at CAMERA hut attended 2 when LT. R. S. DOIG R.E. learns the log in the 232 W x 13 R. Morning when then to hospital suffering from SEA	Puckle
do.	4th	do	Was the usual company duty & to ambulance to CRESCENT RESERVE Line. Matriage [illegible] trenches now held up again many ARTY 42.	Puckle

WAR DIARY
or
INTELLIGENCE SUMMARY.
(Erase heading not required.)

Army Form C. 2118.

(168)

400th (H) Field. Co RE

Instructions regarding War Diaries and Intelligence Summaries are contained in F. S. Regs., Part II. and the Staff Manual respectively. Title pages will be prepared in manuscript.

Place	Date	Hour	Summary of Events and Information	Remarks and references to Appendices
BEUGNY I.15.d.9.0. SHEET 57 C. do.	5th March		After the clean up top the work above ground by day. First entrance to dugout in NEW HERRING completed. Major Kibbell rejoins the coy from leave	Rw.dle
	6th	do	MAJOR KIBBELL taken round the work by CAPT McCRONE ... with RSE women not removing the ... from shaft dugout in NEW HERRING No 400,291 2Corpl ED PAXTON B ENGLAND for officer cadet unit ... LIEUT SE MOSS rejoins the coy from the ... coy RE.	Rw.dle
do	7th	do	OC & CAPT McCRONE go round the fine work ... on ... of SUPPORT LINE by AT ... TE 153 Inf Bdg ... night working parties on SUPPORT LINE as the men are required for wiring. 4 OR return from 51st Div but with I&D not to mobile.	Rw.dle
do.	8th	do	OC goes round the line in the morning. 4t SERRY report from 232nd AT Coy RE to replace LT RE DOIG 51st Div ... new drawing of how they with fine ... constructed. 1 O.R. wounded by shell fire.	Rw.dle

Lt Moss relieves Lt BOYD in the trenches

(A7092). Wt. W12839/M1293. 75 ,0.0. 1/17. D. D. & L., Ltd. Forms/C.2118/14.

Army Form C. 2118.

WAR DIARY
or
INTELLIGENCE SUMMARY.

(Erase heading not required.)

408th Field Co. RE

Place	Date 1918	Hour	Summary of Events and Information	Remarks and references to Appendices
BEUGNY T.15.d.9.0. Rear Sec	March 9	9.15	1 OR. wounded (shell fire)	
		10.15	Lt GERRY return to WATSON on another tank. Sinuka Road at [illegible] having met Mr GERRY to complete Feb 2 + Mar 3. Infantry have compressed casualties - no Offr. with him	
		11.15	Lt ASHTON returns to Company in the trenches.	
		13.15	Section found small F.O.W.'s at corner of all roads in BEUGNY & S.W. cor. of enemy attack.	/M
		14	Draft of 51 OR join Co. from R.E. base depot. Work on elements hindered by Bright putting in men to line before complete	
		15.15	Sect III (up the line) reinforced by men of Hrs. Draft	
		16.F	2nd Lt. J.B. LONGMUIR joined Company from P.S. Base Depôt. This has been strength almost Slated - am in RAVEN, to one near ISTRAND for M.9. Sect. Anticipation except the new instructor out.	
		17.F	CRE. & G.O.C. 51 Div to round up put in this undertaking the mark ammunition hereabouts excepted.	
		18.F	2nd Lt LONGMUIR takes over cart of Sect 3 from Lt MOSS. Sect 4 under Lt BORD stays work at AGIAN HUT for the week near MILL COTTS	
		19.15	Sect 4 commence repair of screens in CAMBRAI RD	
		20.15	Major Kiggell arranges to take over present works from Lt NAPIER to sect of all remaining batten - but is asked KG Ru Div to take over new area bne	

Army Form C. 2118.

WAR DIARY
or
INTELLIGENCE SUMMARY.
(Erase heading not required.)

400 1/5 (Highland) Field Co R.E.

Instructions regarding War Diaries and Intelligence Summaries are contained in F. S. Regs., Part II. and the Staff Manual respectively. Title pages will be prepared in manuscript.

(70)

Place	Date 1918	Hour March	Summary of Events and Information	Remarks and references to Appendices
BEUGNY T.15.a.9.0 Sheet 57 C.	21st		Enemy attacked on a 60 mile front. Bombardment had continued barrage, BEUGNY standing shelled principally with shrapnel at 5.0 a.m. Enemy tanks commenced fire (1 & 3) under Lt WATSON & 2/Lt LONGMUIR stood to in the chapel in an important post set out into the wood over the barrage. At about 10.0 a.m. an Infantry Officer called down the dugout that the enemy were advancing at WATTEN & 2/Lt LONGMUIR led the way out & the trench just in front of the wood into the line. The enemy from Corporal RAVEN TRENCH began to come down the road from BOURSIES towards LOUVERVAL HOOD R.E. & MILLS in the trench returned the our horses trying up to spoken in Lorraine in front LOUVERVAL at LATEAN has been moving up the trench to the Southwards; enemy were in this trench & was moving to the stuff severely ranged in the shoulder at the top of the trench and to LONGMUIR into stuff severely ranged in back a message by N° 400059 Spr. Musson Holden killed. Lt BATTEN sent back a message by N° 400059 Spr. Musson & N° 402319 Spr BARCLAY C. " Enemy is advancing. Am holding Thompson F.Y. & Sgt. CHRICHTIE are forward bombing & is moving trench. Any R.E. men got away held up just to the LOUVERVAL road mentioned down to the BERTINCTZ - MARCOING LINE N° 250272 2/Lt FUGGLE A. was returned to the & men get in, having no ammunition returned and 3 drums into the stores with them the fire was blown up in the LOUVERVAL line. Lieutenant was taking the gun & men in those forward locations (& all ranks) 1/4 reported 28th and 6 privates all were wounded. Major RUSSELL returned to the Co. S in BEUGNY, fell in all available dismounts from & riding men went the transport back to I21 a 5.5 just N. of FREMICOURT reported Coy. for further orders at 5.30 P.M. Transport (under Lt COOPER) in ammunition for support. #34C 15o at LE PERONNE full of BARAUME. This morning was in position by 2.30 P.M. 3 Casualties to Drivers in BEUGNY 1 died & 2 wounded, Also 2 horses killed & 3 wounded.

Army Form C. 2118.

WAR DIARY
or
INTELLIGENCE SUMMARY.
(Erase heading not required.)

405 th Field Co. R.E.

Place	Date March 1918	Hour	Summary of Events and Information	Remarks and references to Appendices
BEUGNY I.15.d.9.a.	21 (contd)		At 12 noon Capt R.W. McCRONIE M.C. took command of 405 Field Co R.E. vice Major WATTERSON (wounded). Major KIGGELL assumed Temporary Command of Section at BEUGNY under Major KIGGELL. Section Commander Sect 2 under Lt BOYD at I.16.d.2.2. Commenced GERMAN Road Sect 4 under Lt BOYD at I.16.d.20.75 to cover VAUX Road with MORCHIES Valley. GERMAN under A.W. MOTT holding Strong Point I.15.d.8.2 covering MORCHIES. Remainder under A.W. MOTT holding position & valley this morning. After dark From men withdrew leaving position & steps in old built.	
	22nd		Stood to at 4.30 am. No increased enemy pressure fire on Cois. to have been taken at ... S.P.S about MILL at I.15.d.35.90. Cut into trench W/F of R.W.F. (19th Div) where was supporting BEUGNY with battalion. He was digging in on line I.15.d.27. – I.16.c.20 – 5.0. and I.16.c.2.7.5 to I.16.d.00.65 – 40.20. Owing to Enemy men to centre not yet further mv Aerodrome I reconnoitred the mound near I.15.d.85.90. but not very happy. Posn into improving the Trip-pit Run. In the evening retired to R.E. Ditch I.15.b.47 (this posn has not linked) as soon as reported to have vacated. They made a ... VAUX route it about I.15.d.4.7 (this post was not linked) with from I.16.c.5.2 to I.16.48. to R.E. ulk 2 sects at Truncation on the head from I.16.d.5.2 to I.16.48 about 300 * Co NE under Lt in height to a huge ... This entanglement from St was in the ... mentioned. Ours my carried be Let at Lt procured in BEUGNY Dump the enemy now mentioned. No. 405.496 M.G. post from enemy infantry. employees & Rifle per This body taken Spr McKenzie to bring Batal R. Lts. A.D.S. at BEUGNY	

WAR DIARY
INTELLIGENCE SUMMARY
(Erase heading not required.)

Army Form C. 2118.

Unit: 400th Field Co. NE

Place	Date	Hour	Summary of Events and Information	Remarks and references to Appendices
I15d 9.0 B205 H30 Sheet 57c	22nd (contd)		Transport shelled & 1 horse wounded. 11 pm Transport went to Bertincourt GRÉVILLERS & RUES have evacuated. 2 am 23rd. On information 41st 153rd Bde & from Div Reserve Coy put under orders of 74th Inf. Bde. at about 8 pm. Major Haigh received a message that the enemy had broken through near CAMBRAI Road and from MURCHIE's to sustained new to come CRITICAL Road. M.G. fire distant there was many men coming that to after a numerous shower there was no movement, damage they were rifled to have smaller trench & steep, from a T.M.B. bullets cracks deeply in Every PREVSNY 20 stray shells hurtling	/A
	23rd		Starts to at 6.10 am Sec 4 to tour out British trench T.K.2 British troops line TRMF at I.16 @ 17 & I.15d B0.75. Sr Ms still in Reserve Dep at I.15d.02.2 Sit was in the morning that enemy was breaking roads south of the villages. from LEBUCQUIERE Infantry (Rifles) hidden went I.22a70 - I.22.d04. Infant retiring on their men NE to move all NE except Lt Ross to improve & hold trench men with party working at I.21.d 4.6 where Faulkner Boxall was with stood empty. Most British trench from I.22 a 6.0 this 4 into saw Bayville in was warmed 28 that they floored fall back as up to between Sow Cont Infantry retiring in I.22.d stopped & continued Infantry line, very important to hold PREVSNY for a time to Save our men in I.16d. Enemy within 30 & 4 lumps in I.22.d heard several rounds of Mont, All was quiet until Newt R.E. brought his men across to South Bengay being [?] heard shells & Stokes into 5.9" Support trench I.16 & 17 4th F 4.2 + 77 cm	/A

WAR DIARY or INTELLIGENCE SUMMARY

408th Field Coy R.E.

Place	Date	Hour	Summary of Events and Information	Remarks and references to Appendices
BEUGNY	March 1918 23 (cont)	about 6 p.m.	Received orders from Lt Col KING (R.W.F.) that we has orders to evacuate BEUGNY + draw to start taking up new posns in the ARMY LINE behind BEUGNY at once. Descending's reserve the Infantry on front, halted there along railway southward T.21.c.2.1. There were several OR, talked with Lt PRESSICOURT to see if he could get into touch with Division. PRESSICOURT back. brought about an hrs communications cut. No 400.869 Spr THOMPSON F.N. + another Sapper sent back with a note to CRE at GREVILLERS, explaining position. – The only men of 51 Div + other Div Infantry in the trench. on landward (WEST) side his patrols have found out for him to go back but has never reached Bn Hqrs. Horbman N.E. arrived at about 2.0 am. whereas to make back to	
GREVILLERS	24 R	CH 11.30 am	GREVILLERS begun transport. HALL (401 Fd. Coy RE) First SPRAY (400 Sd) went out into 10 OR. + party under 2/Lt men in BEUGNY front formed under Lt 400 Ord 4 b/Cpl McDonald. J. in front of BANCOURT. At 12.30 pm returns of	
			Major Hopper arrived at 9.2 D 8.1 about 4.0 am. Things written in for him. Major Hopper came back to GREVILLERS + stayed any with CRE 2/Cp M:Donald J arrived back about 1.0 am. His turn he learn't 3 of BADAVKIE failed find Sappers so has changes return if M have even a 3 man even picked up. Orders received at 4.30 p.m. to move to MIRAUMONT & mod. 9 OR. start 10.0 + East of J. in MIRAUMONT (Rail LENS 14)	M M

Army Form C. 2118.

WAR DIARY
or
INTELLIGENCE SUMMARY.
(Erase heading not required.)

406th Field Co. R.E.

Instructions regarding War Diaries and Intelligence Summaries are contained in F. S. Regs., Part II. and the Staff Manual respectively. Title pages will be prepared in manuscript.

Place	Date March 1918	Hour	Summary of Events and Information	Remarks and references to Appendices
FORCEVILLE	25		Orders received to move back FORCEVILLE at once. Marched off 1.30 am arrived FORCEVILLE 6.0 am. 252 Tunnelling Co. R.E. attached to Field Co's all under command of Major Riggall. Major Riggall put billets for all ranks in FORCEVILLE. Orders received 7.10 p.m. to move to FONG VIS VILLERS. Moved off 9.30 p.m. Traffic control very bad. Early arrival at 5 am 26th Tunnelling Co. R.E. left behind took under Capt. ——— Transport less and full between FONQUEVILLERS + SOUASTRE between BOUTTILLE – HENU.	/M
PAS	26	9.0 am.	Under Capt. NIVEN 9/40 R.E. N.C.O. to behove BOUTTILLE – HENU.	
		At 1 pm.	A fresh was carried by transport that arrived early. Small branch Transport moved off at 2 p.m. to BAVINCOURT Bois DE BOUILLERS. Suspend been to L'ARTILLERIE DE LA MAIS hear FONQUIS WILLERS at 5.0 am at	
		7.30 am	orders received to concentrate for South of SOUASTRE + marched to SAILLY AU BOIS + were Brigade about any supper it being they might have left nature until ——— from G.S.O.	
		At about 10.30 am	Hants + Cardiffs through Man Lardry opened the ridge to the SAILLY over a mile away. All troops under direct 51st Div. Staff at once extended ——— to villages or stored 11.15 R.E. + 16 Royal Scots from kitchen most the back of thr village tick up position cover STAMFORDS	
		At about 3.30 pm	and moved from the ——— SOUASTRE.	

WAR DIARY
or
INTELLIGENCE SUMMARY.
(Erase heading not required.)

Army Form C. 2118.

4th Fusiliers

(173)

Place	Date	Hour	Summary of Events and Information	Remarks and references to Appendices
PAS	26th March 1918 (cont)		Demand for ponies but R.E. moved to PAS. 2nd Battalion all ranks.	I/I
BARLY	27th		Orders received about 1.0 am to move down 154 Bde to NEUVILLETTE area starting 7.15 am. 154 Bde arrived at 7.15 pm. that in several trf. lorries from PERNINISTER and 1.15 pm. Lt COOPER went a two do billeting and all the men who could march marched off there. Remainder got a lorry into first difficulty at 1.0 pm came on to NEUVILLETTE. Billets at BARLY. Supplies mounted a lorry sent back to help HQE POLANE. Transport arrived 5.30 pm. No billets for Drums. Billeted and R.M. call 10.30 am.	I/II
			Casualties from 21st to following O.R. Officers 3 — Killed 1 11 Wounded 1 2 Wounded remain 1 34 Missing — 50 Total 2	III
BARLY	28th		Orders received 11.30 pm. to move to 5 Corps area on 29th. Ist German Ret. attack FORMS 2/XA MGS 5/709 FORMS. Army F. Ambulance Hoffrees	I/IV

WAR DIARY or INTELLIGENCE SUMMARY

Army Form C. 2118.

(Erase heading not required.)

405 F Field Amb

Place	Date March 1918	Hour	Summary of Events and Information	Remarks and references to Appendices
BARLY	29		Transport moved off 8.30 am under 153rd Bde via FREVENT – ST POL – KTARRAS to harass on via HUCLIER + CONTEVILLE. Transport parked in field ½ mile South of E. in GUERNONVAL. 1 Driver billeted in CONTEVILLE. A very bad march – no chance of watering the horses & too long an interval between halts – once 2½ hours. Dismounted marched to FREVENT, arrived 6 pm to entrain at 7.15. Finish entrained complete including officers horses carts + men's big rail via ST POL to LAPUGNOY arriving just after dawn.	/M
LAPUGNOY Slag Heap Barrack Sq.	30		Good billets in LAPUGNOY. In all ranks. Transport moved off 10.20 am marched via VAUTHUN – CALONNE RICOUART to LAPUGNOY. Halts more frequent. C.I. HQ order No. 107 a heavier – Some rain & dull.	/M
"	31		Drill during morning & cleaning up & prepare to hospital. Sick on Strength. Events up & permanent hospital x full reversal.	/M

Company Strength on 28.2.18 — 6 158

Decrease During Month
- Killed —
- Wounded — 3 or
- Missing —
- Wounded + Missing — 1 off. 02 2 or, 2 off 2 or
- Evacuated – sick — 70 r
- Transfers — 10 offrs. 3 or

Total decrease 3 offrs 65 or -3 -65

Increase During Month
- Reinforcements 3 offrs 55 or +3 +55

Company Strength 31.3.18 6 148

(A7092) Wt W12839/M1093/75. 10.0. 1/17. D.D. & L.td. Forms/C.1118/14.

INTELLIGENCE SUMMARY

(Erase heading not required.)

405(b) (Highland) Field Co RE

Place	Date	Hour	Summary of Events and Information	Remarks and references to Appendices
LAPUGNOY	31st March	1918	Notes on part taken by 405 Field Co RE in the battle commencing March 20th. The Company was put under orders of 153 Inf. Bde when Pans Ridge was withdrawn to give Div Reserve on 22nd. The Co'y was put under 74 Bde, 25 Div with orders — confirmed by 74 Bde — to continue disposal of BEUGNY, being held by a battalion of RWF, 19th Div. The meeting the p.m. was that the Co'y was employed solely on Infantry defence were unable to do any work except rig up emergency defences from that moment. Orders hom [?] received from Bde, and no there[?] were but in accordance with the scheme drawn up then of disposal of BEUGNY by Battalion Cmdr of RWF. They were not asked upon most satisfactorily to take over with the battalion arrangements as the situation was not [illegible] suddenly. On return of a small party of sappers to bring up [?] protein [?] they were found small officers there were manipulated in [illegible] found Company cmdrs designs thus somewhat unwilling to use except in emergency trapped in emergencies. From my own personal knowledge I saw at the battle, it appears that the Field Company Commanders had been at Bde H.Q. with his company about Bde HQ with transport en to two [illegible]	

INTELLIGENCE SUMMARY. 405th Field Coy RE

(Erase heading not required.)

No 8

Place	Date	Hour	Summary of Events and Information	Remarks and references to Appendices
LAPUGNOY	March 1918 31		It would seem that we have been an fact into the situation & have been able to employ his section to mining ground, whilst the majority of MIRAUMONT & MIRAUMONT IRLES & MIRAUMONT have been employed pm IRLES & MIRAUMONT on destruction of bridges & dumps & holding of the enemy's advance with D.Coys moon effect there coincide with acting as Infantry. My own feelings in the line were that the infantry could have done very well without us some moreover there rather worried them at times.	

31.3.18

Magnell Major (Hopkins) Freeman RE
OC 405 Field Coy RE

APPENDIX G.

400th West Riding Coy R.E.

2·3·18

Anti-Tank Gun Emplacement

Direction of Gun-fire
Angle of Fire 30° each side of C

51st Divisional Engineers

WAR DIARY

400th (Highland) FIELD COMPANY R. E.

APRIL 1918

CONFIDENTIAL.

WAR DIARY.

OF

400TH (HIGHLAND) FIELD Co. R.E.

FOR APRIL 1918.

Army Form C. 2118.

WAR DIARY
or
INTELLIGENCE SUMMARY.
(Erase heading not required.)

400th (Highland) Field Coy R.E.

Place	Date	Hour	Summary of Events and Information	Remarks and references to Appendices
LAPUGNOY	1st April		Drill for dismounted in the morning. Cleaning & overhauling wagons in the afternoon. Orders to be ready to move at one hours notice.	
HAZEBROUCK 5.A.	2nd do		Box reinforcements in the tea by Divisional Bus Officers at 2.30 P.M. Orders to be ready to move at one hours notice recalled from the Coy.	
	3rd do			
CAMBLAIN-CHATELAIN	4th do		Coy. moved to CAMBLAIN-CHATELAIN leaving LAPUGNOY at 12.40 P.M. arriving at 2 P.M. Orders received at 1 P.M. to move to BURBURE & wagon stores by motor at	
CHATELAIN HAZEBROUCK 5.A.	5th do	2.40 P.M.	arrived BURBURE 5 P.M. Coy 9.30 18 & this billets LT GAUD & LT VICKERS	
BURBURE	6th do		Mounted engaged in cleaning up from losses. Dismounted then engaged loans to Rlb. Draft of one officer report LT BLANCK	
HAZEBROUCK 5.A.	7th		Coy. wagons. As part of portable bridge in this area sent to Comdr. orders received for the Coy to move to ROBECQ by motor bus. First 500 yds from BURBURE on VICKERS Rd. at 10 A.M. Lt. GAUD in G. 2nd Lt. VICKERS Bde. Engr. LT GAUD dismounted & to North field by RE. Stores at 10 A.M.	
	8th		Coy. move off from BURBURE at 9.30 A.M. march via VICKERS, BURNES, to near ROBECQ at 12.30 P.M. Drags of S.O.R. report	
ROBECQ SHEET 36 A 1/40000	9th		Heavy bombardment... attack by the PORTUGUESE. From the little information available as all communication had been cut off 10.30 A.M. other... Bombardment continued all day...	

Army Form C. 2118.

WAR DIARY
or
INTELLIGENCE SUMMARY.
(Erase heading not required.)

Place	Date	Hour	Summary of Events and Information	Remarks and references to Appendices
ROBECQ SHEET 36A 1/40000	9th April		O.C. written down at right Infantry Bde H.Q. on the line held by LTS LAURIE & MOSS neither of whom he had been able to find. He was told by B.G.C. 153 Inf Bde to get in touch with the 10th R.W.F. LTS LAURIE & MOSS went to 153 & 151 Inf Bdes H.Q. & the 552 A.T.Coy.R.E. at 3 P.M. LT MOSS went to bridges at R.21.b.36. & R.21.b.37. & got in touch there with CAPT HARPER 552 A.T.Coy.RE. CAPT HARPER informed LT MOSS that bridges already mentioned should have been prepared for demolition by ⟨crossed out⟩ by the PORTUGESE but were not. LT MOSS was instructed by Col. 1/C KING EDWARDS HORSE to prepare these two bridges, preparations were completed by 10 A.M. on the 10th. The bridges immediately north of the two already mentioned had been prepared by CAPT HARPER & two sappers were at each bridge with instructions to blow as soon as the infantry had crossed. LT LAURIE reported to O.C. 552 A.T.Coy.RE. at RUE DELANNOY R.15.C.1.2. at 5 P.M. O.C. 552.A.T.COY.RE. had instructions to blow bridge in 153 Bny sector on receiving orders from 151 Inf Bng or at his own discretion LT LAURIE proceeded to 153 Inf Bng at Q.23.C.8.6. & reported position to them. B ny had orders LT LAURIE to get in touch with CAPT HARPER & report. LT LAURIE got in touch with CAPT HARPER	M

WAR DIARY
or
INTELLIGENCE SUMMARY.

(Erase heading not required.)

Place	Date	Hour	Summary of Events and Information	Remarks and references to Appendices
ROBECQ SHEET 36A	9th April 1918		at bridge at R.15.d.24. & two other bridges by them. The other bridges in the 153 Inf Bde Sector were not hostile. R.8.b.6.8. - R.9.d.19. - R.9.b.85. - R.15.d.24. all these bridges were closed down for which the full demolition charges retained & ready for firing the night. Draft of 4 O.R. joined the Company	
D.O.		13:00	LTS. GERRY & WILKIN move off from billets at 153 H.Q. with orders to maintain bridges at W.4.C.38 - W.11.a.60. W.11.c.25.15 & assist as report in possible crossings at W.10.B. - W.9.B. - W.9.B.21 - W.9.D.21 all bridges to be demolished. No crossing to be made at W.10.B.8.6. CBE. G.O. to keep in touch with 4th GERRY, the Cr Inf Bde from off touch by the R.E. Officer and pushed forwards to LILUE Sector return to the CO.R.E. line out of 8.15 P.M. O.P.T. HARPER 5.32 AT C.O.R.E. His to tr return to 153 Inf Bde HQ. in the morning & report on 15.3 Inf Bde HQ. The reads the proton & the 1.53 Inf. Bdy	W

Army Form C. 2118.

WAR DIARY
or
INTELLIGENCE SUMMARY.
(Erase heading not required.)

(182)

Place	Date	Hour	Summary of Events and Information	Remarks and references to Appendices
TROBEC.Q. SHEET 36A 1/40000	10th April	9/8	LT LAURIE to inform the C.R.E. & to ask for men to complete the work. LT BOYD & retn to Bn. LT BOYD proceeded on his return journey to endeavour to develop in daylight by reference at R.9.a.18. to get in touch with LT MOSS & give him any assistance. LT BOYD reported to O.C. 1/15th B.W. (Lt. CAMPBELL) he sent him to the company commander & to find LT BOYD forward, the infantry holding the road running through R.9.a.d. & a LEWIS GUN was in action. He finally located LT BOYD & carried on daylight work at the bridge. LT BOYD was never located by O.C. 1/15th to the bridge at R.7.d.535. When the former Lt MOSS & others were sent for & were at LT. MOSS, but before they arrived it became found necessary to blow the bridge. The final instructed LT BOYD there were there to blow the R.P.C.I.R.1. & when asked was hereby not lightly asked some one to come up & see that Lt. LT BOYD cleared. LT BOYD & some 20 yds away, the Cpl. commander reported himself unable to report the Lt. LT BOYD cleared with him to await in the defence of the Batt HQ. in the command at 11/9 MB.H., LT BOYD & written force returned & relieved & retiremen on the fields.	

WAR DIARY or INTELLIGENCE SUMMARY

Army Form C. 2118.

Place	Date	Hour	Summary of Events and Information	Remarks and references to Appendices
ROBECQ SHEET 36A 1/40000	10th April	9/12 a.m.	Section reached billets in ROBECQ about 3 P.M. 11.4.18. Lt BLACK was sent out at 4 P.M. to reconnoitre & report by 8 P.M. on possible crossings between ROBECQ & BAQUEROLLES FM. across the two CLARENCE. He reported good crossings at B.19.d.5.2 & B.14.c.5.8. The former being a wooden cart bridge the latter a footbridge. Both crossings were reported up to carry full guns & infantry in forces.	
Q.D.	11th April		Section standing ready to move all morning, no orders looking. B.B. goes up the line in the morning to see 153 Inf. Brig. at Q.27.a.4.7. Orders sent back at 12 noon by B.G. – two officers & 24 men. I met him at B.21.b.52 with explosive stores & made 2 N.C.O.S. BLACK & WILKEN to — B.G detailed to following work: Lt. BLACK with 8 sappers to prepare for demolition small bridge at Q.4.c. Central. Lt. WILKEN to prepare for demolition road junction on QUENTIN at Q.22.b.32 & small bridge near LE CORNET MALO (Q.28.) at Q.28.a.4. Lt GERRY & Section worked out at 5.30 pm & prepare for demolition two bridges at BAQUEROLLES FM. Q.14.c.72 & two bridge at Q.14.c.65. All our work being of all bridges with mine or...	

WAR DIARY
or
INTELLIGENCE SUMMARY

Army Form C. 2118.

(184)

Place	Date	Hour	Summary of Events and Information	Remarks and references to Appendices
ROBECQ Sheet 36.A. 1/40,000	11th April 1918		As the situation deteriorated Lt. Headquarters transported 1M/S Officers Men & Kit left ROBECQ at 11.15 A.M. & moved to L.E. CORNET BRASSARD under Lt COOPER, arrived 2.30 P.M. CAPT MCCRONE gave round the work under LTS BLACK & WILKEN arranging men to made to prepare the bridge of CALONNE to demolition (Q.38.4.3.) This work however was taken over from us by the S.D.O. in. Cl. Petrol wagon was detained near bridge at Q.28.c.11, the sapper in charge of bridge was instructed to destroy the at some time as the bridge. CAPT MCCRONE called at 153 Inf. Bgde HQ. & got orders to send two sections Nos 4. 5 of MERVILLE at K.35.a.2b. & K.35.b.38. LT MOSS and two subalterns at once to report to S/LT HQ. at Q.11.b.28. LT MOSS to make arrangements for the sections to meet him. No further orders the been received from LT.MOSS re the two subalterns. 10.30 P.M. Large Shell fell outside of M.O.II. section Billet wounding one O.R. & destroying the villa. 9.30 P.M. Orders were received that convey at L.E. CORNET BRASSARD was to come under orders of 153 Inf. Brig. Traveller the following message received from C.R.E. at 9.30 P.M. "St. Q. is to made responsible for defence as to the mines to be employed by the 51st Div. 153 Inf. Brig. will be responsible for defence of NIEPPE ROBECQ & Canal	⋁

Army Form C. 2118.

WAR DIARY
or
INTELLIGENCE SUMMARY.

(Erase heading not required.)

(185)

Place	Date	Hour	Summary of Events and Information	Remarks and references to Appendices
ROBECQ SHEET 36A 1/40000	11th April 1918		Bank. at K.36.a.4.6. Wkr Brig's are in position 61st Div will relieve 51st Division troops east of them N. of an E. & W. line through L'EPINETTE. On account of this order bridge at CALONNE at Q.30.d.3. was handed over to the 61st Div.	M

WAR DIARY or INTELLIGENCE SUMMARY

Army Form C. 2118.

407th Field Co. R.E.

Place	Date	Hour	Summary of Events and Information	Remarks and references to Appendices
ROBECQ	12 April	7:30 a.m.	C.R.E. told O.C. that enemy was just entering village but some stragglers & after him. 404 Field Co. R.E. under Lt. PATTERSON to defend ROBECQ. Also had 4 Lewis guns of K.O.Y.L.I. Dispatches sent a runner to Shrapnel & 2 Lewis guns in Reserve. It took extra few Si Dn men on the left. Found the left flank to put 2 officers & 30 stragglers on left of M.G. at P14.c.0.6. Found 1 section of 407 Pts. Co. R.E. under Major PATTINSON with some M.G.'s defending bridge at P36.a.87. Sent by this time enemy reaching from head to section I who went to put out posts in ROBECQ. A certain amount M.G. m.g. fire.	Markers H
nr P36 a 5.5		10:30 a.m.	About 10:30 a.m. 1/4 R. Berks. R. (61 Div) took over defence from CAPTAIN to P14.d.8.2. Saw them O.C. & got him keeping this line he had 154 Berks. about P36.a.87. The N.E. were their collected. From a Lt. head to succeeded in road P14.d.8.2. Berks. arrived from 153 Berks that they would bridge as crossed O.C. saw representative of one 61 Div who prepared for demolition to prepare bridges P31.a.8.1. & P14.c.6.2. 404 Field Co. R.E. & to bridge at LT. PATTERSON to put heavy cover southwards. bridge on P36.a.86. Told Lt. PATTERSON a Company bridge to prepare it for demolition (by Capt. DUKE R.E.) that at P36.a.0.8. to make a Company bridge from C.R.E. (by Capt. DUKE R.E.) that In the afternoon received word from C.R.E. 3 Field Capt. R.E. who were also to assist heavy guns our count over to him prepared for demolition - both to be circled up between the 3 Field Capt. R.E. in their efforts.	

WAR DIARY or INTELLIGENCE SUMMARY

Army Form C. 2118.

(1st Field Coy N.Z.E.)

Place: ROBECQ
Date: April 12
Hour: p.m.

4 O.R. Tks bridge Q31 a 8.2 & P36 a 8.6 — 404 Pl.w. tk P36 a 0.8 &
In tk P4 c 8.1 & P27 b 3.5
Company disposed as follows:- Hq. 404 & 2/604 Pl.ws P35 a 60.85.
1 Section four N. of majic head consists in defence on N.E. spur stream bank
last in area of recently tpm. Llument for demolition. 1 Section on
atttached of the main in P35 a in finding Coy Hq. to assist Lt
NW flank. 1 Section - prepare bridge for demolition in Ruenne P35 a 1.2.
1 Section under Lt BOYD N.T.S. of bridge P17 b 3.5.
O.C. first began to make a reconnaissance of interior of 404 Platoon of
defences of the CLARENCE R. from P35 b 3.9 towards GONNEHEM
in case the canal was broken further East & N means necessary to
oppose a flank. We took two heavy report 6 pr. to hand over all
demolitions to Hq Field Coy NZ withdrew the 1st BYNES.
He arranged this with O.C. 407 Pl.w. at Q31 a P.2. Enemy sniping
this point from NLR 30 VINAYES.
Company withdrawn at nightfall (billets) in BYNES. HQ P26 c 2.2.

1 O.R. Wounded
Lieuts MOSS and WILKEN rock #12215 2/3rd arrived and 50 2.389 Leyton Garce
reported missing

Army Form C. 2118.

WAR DIARY
or
INTELLIGENCE SUMMARY.
(Erase heading not required.)

Instructions regarding War Diaries and Intelligence Summaries are contained in F. S. Regs., Part II. and the Staff Manual respectively. Title pages will be prepared in manuscript.

(188)

Place	Date	Hour	Summary of Events and Information	Remarks and references to Appendices
BUSNES. P.26.C.34. SHEET 36A 1/40,000	13th April 1918		Coy rests at BUSNES. Section which reports from those sents? & recon and the advanced H.Q.	
	14th	do.	Orders received about midday to wire the front line in front of ROBECQ from P.24.C.18. to P.24.C.82. B.E. & LT BOYD go forward in the morning to reconnoitre the work. Three motor wagons report with wire at 4.30 P.M. & are with recon picket at 10 P.M. These wagons are taken forward to ROBECQ. 4 G.S. limbers from 51st M.G. Batt. take the store from within wagons to the wet long screw pickets are very scarce. Sections II III & IV put out the wiring picket return to billets at 4 A.M.	
ST HILAIRE T.6.C.21. SHEET 36A 1/40,000	15th	do.	Capt. McCRONE & two O.R. leave BUSNES at 7 A.M. by motor lorry & arrive at ST.HILAIRE at 10.30 A.M. CAPT NILSON. 183 Inf Bry meets the party and allots to Coy billets. Coy arrives 12.30 P.M. Billets fairly good.	
	16th	do.	Orders received at 12.30 P.M. to send 50 men and one officer at T.35.d.33 to work on bridge across the river LYS. Coy parades 2 P.M. for one hour drill two returns until M. HAIRIE. bar by Rail way at 1 P.M. for work on bridge. Message received at 3.30 P.M. cease work and rendezvous for one officer & 50 O.R. party withdrawn ready to M. and a rendezvous a bridge at T.28.d.41. for Cambo.	

Army Form C. 2118.

WAR DIARY
or
INTELLIGENCE SUMMARY.
(Erase heading not required.)

(189)

Place	Date	Hour	Summary of Events and Information	Remarks and references to Appendices
ST HILAIRE T.6.C.2.1. SHEET 36A 1/40000	17th April		The range at T.9.A.8.2. is allotted to the Coy from 4 P.M. till 7 P.M. All available men sent. 3 rounds grouping at 100 yds & 5 rounds application at 200 yds.	
	18th do		Fictions held in the mornings. Section officers was lecture subject on the use of explosives. From 14.00 to a demolition scheme in the Field.	
	19th do		Drill in the morning for all sections, instructions in demolitions. Firing the afternoon on the range wrote Lt Coombs at 4 P.M. Draft of 1 OR joined the Company. No 414329 2/Corpl Broomes J. transferred to H.Q. 3rd Boy R.E. Lt Bridgs Lts Mansfield + Buxton are now resuming instruction.	
	20th do		Company completion of 3 P.M.	
	21st do		Drill & LG instruction	
LABIETTE FARM P29.b.80	22nd do		Coy. Les H.Q. transfer from to billets at P.29.b.80 in a convoy under the orders of the C.R.E. 3rd Div. H.Q. remains at + O.R. remains at FORTES. O. des officers Lieut Behind in Billets Lieutenants CAPTAIN M^cCRANE, LT LAURIE + LT NAPIER remain behind.	
	23		OC went with work party parties to jobs on the Railhead. Took over A guard + demolition of bridges from 3.55 – P.26.c.05.20 – P.27.b.4.5. Arrangement changed immediately Leave today - recall up to C sections but now cut of Leave 1 each phase No. 1 to 3 post. Sgt 2 Bar 1/2 hours P.24.c.57 & 1/2 hour P.19.a.3.3 Posts 1+4 Post 1/5 double upon turn up from P.24.c.47 – P.24.c.13 P.30	

(A7092). Wt. W12359/M1393. 750,000. 1/17. D. D. & L., Ltd. Forms/C.2118/14.

WAR DIARY
INTELLIGENCE SUMMARY

ADS 2 (Rd Claus) Field Co 165

Place	Date APRIL	Hour	Summary of Events and Information	Remarks and references to Appendices
LAQUETTE FM P27 d 80 Sheet 36A 1/40,000	24		Sect 2 flattened known burnt sanctuary & (Studs) cellar near CP HQ. P24 d 85. Improved shelter & made rodent protector for men using buildings. HQ5c P27c 7.17 - P24 d 5.13. Thinned wired Sect 3 trenches in Midgis town near tactics - Wiring charges various kinds. Stores up P27 d 48 for electric fuses. Sect 3 i/r4 removed wire to 3 belts from P30c 3.5 - P24c 51. 1 p+ and Sandbag apron from P24 d 9.5 - 4.3 (320') O.C. returned to the CRE 61 Dw in St Venant.	/A
	25		400,183 Sergt. R. Brown transferred to 184th Tunnelling Coy R.E. for examination. 404 Field Co relieved 406 Field Co on out post to head line with Sect 2 + 4 under CRE 61 Div for work. Under instruction of CRE 61 Div on 400 sq grs. site a trench line N of RUISSEQ from HAZEBROUCQ + ARMENTIERS line on the canal or 400 decauville that work will be divided from 400 to link up improvements of trenches by the ROMFARECQ 404 to take on new Sects. All motor van lorries commenced trips from P24 c Cnts + RUINES recommitting by LTS 3000 cy TRAPPER, Import and 5 CRE 61 Div. per DUNNING came by Ads 2 + 3. up from two lines.	/A
	26		Rent ward of 2 Ports of thiern Stephens F.L. Coughill. 1 Pol (4 bays) in thieren by LT Meera line P29 d 3.7 cleared out ruts' by matty by No2 bolt sector in DUNNING Lr Boyd had done to rescuing castin in billets for sheep fire 7.30 pm. No 400,031 Sapper CAMPBELL killed 4 or wounded (402,896 Sapper Jack D. Stroll if wounded at A.D.S. (Can in de four)	/A

APPENDIX I.

400 #High Field Coy. R.E.
Maj Denny
27.4.18.

SKETCH B. TYPE OF BREASTWORK. ROBECQ. APRIL 1918.

Army Form C. 2118.

WAR DIARY
or
INTELLIGENCE SUMMARY.

(Erase heading not required.)

Instructions regarding War Diaries and Intelligence Summaries are contained in F. S. Regs., Part II. and the Staff Manual respectively. Title pages will be prepared in manuscript.

400 W(A.y(Low)) Field Co RE

(191)

Place	Date	Hour	Summary of Events and Information	Remarks and references to Appendices
P276 80 Sheet 36a 1/40000	26 APRIL	(cont'd)	CRE 61 Div came round, proposed MOBICap site bet: DC 400 7454~ approved by SRE. 480H commenced work that afternoon. Eng.(61) 48rcs	W
			RATACp expr. W-DC 400 & opening up proposed track	
	27		Insp obtained from 2/Lt. Gittelson (61 Div) 180 men & 400 P.Co. N.G. 40 gun. A.ead of duty 29.3 upon a laying of 50 ft³ - very sticky clay. Men worked @ Pits 1.2.3.7.8 in Reserve System T.L. completed (Main line 3 pr.ls taken for wire-cast). Planned line (No. 1841 - attempt Attempted Tramway out not between pip Proposed cut to b/h extended to Lysette camp up from horse lines G.L. had mud made bypasses from made a tracked.	W Appendix India I
	28		Same work continued. Planking of all S. pits in Reserve System T.L. completed. Revetment of Cap N°.1 in Reserve line completed. Late continued.	W
	29		Same work. Drainage for pits completed. Beer heavy rains during morning.	
	30		Infantry direct hit Casualties 3 OR. wounded. Roller going on in 2 huts at P.32c7.8, HQ. 12 buts & horse-lines P.3a.5.5. N° 400.17 a/4r.	
			INNES killed by shell fire in horse-lines upper line	

W.R.M (signature) P.L.C.

400th The5 Field Coy R.E.
War Diary
30.4.18.

Company Strength at 31.3.18

	Officers	Other Ranks
	6	148
Reinforcements from R.E.B.D.	+ 6	+ 68
Killed		– 2
Wounded	– 1	– 9
Missing { 2 Officers	– 2	– 2
{ 2 Other Ranks		
To Hospital 7 Other Ranks		– 7
Transferred { 2 Officers	– 2	– 3
{ 3 Other Ranks		
Company Strength at 30.4.18	8	193

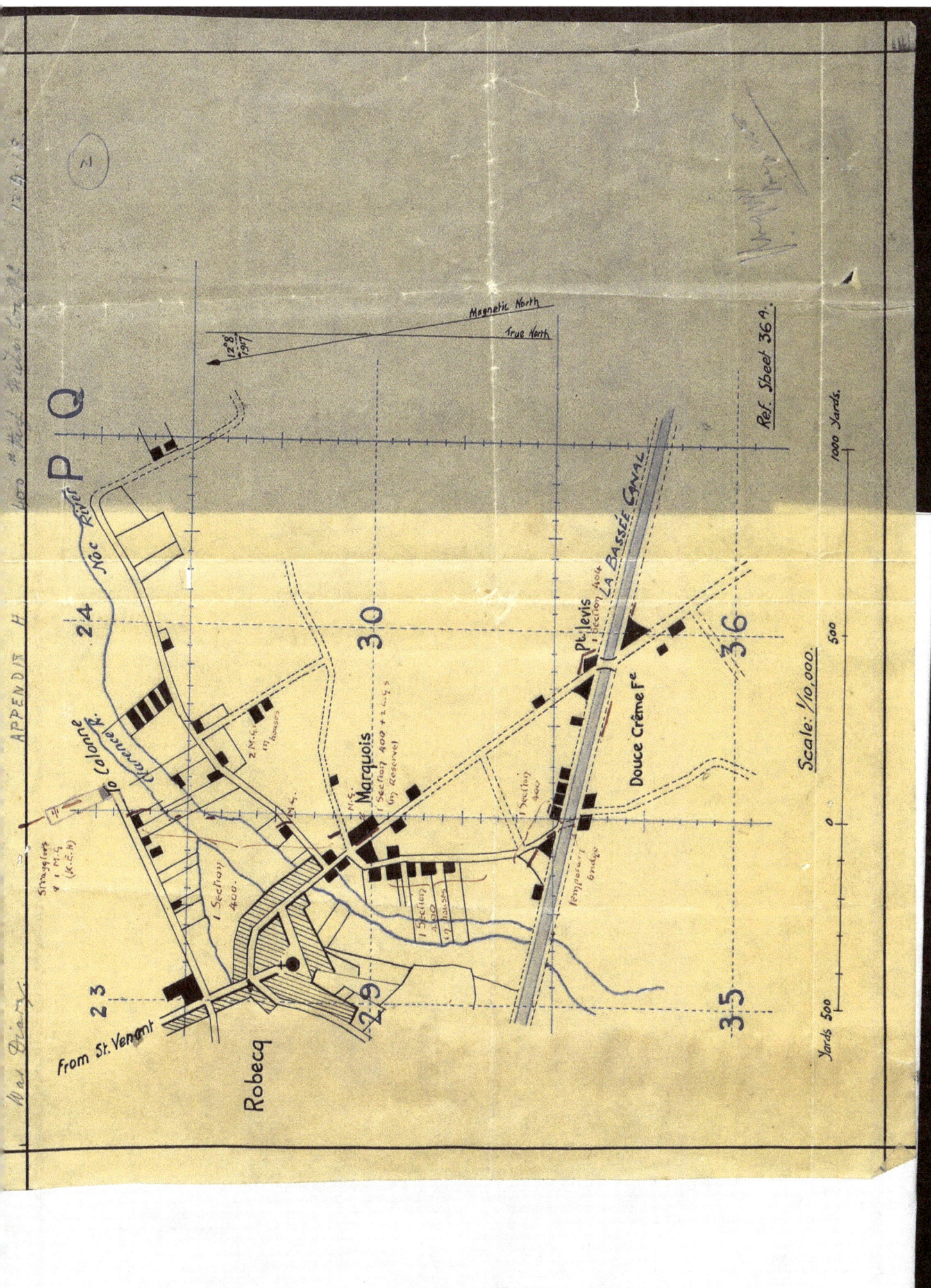

CONFIDENTIAL.

WAR DIARY for MAY, 1918.

of the

400th (HIGHLAND) FIELD COMPANY, R.E.

CONFIDENTIAL.

Army Form C. 2118.

WAR DIARY
or
INTELLIGENCE SUMMARY.
(Erase heading not required.)

400th (Highland) Field Coy R.E.

(192)

Place	Date 1918	Hour	Summary of Events and Information	Remarks and references to Appendices
LA PIERRE. P.19.a.S.S.	1st May.		Sect IV under LT DUNSIRE start work on trestle bridge across the CANAL at P.27.5.9.1. Very few men available for the work. Site of bridge heavily shelled all day.	JB
Do.	2nd May.		Lt BOYD takes over Sect IV, & the foot bridge nearly completed. LT GERRY wounded by shell fire while working in front of ROBECQ. 5.30 P.M. orders received to stop work and hand over to Field Coy from 61st Div. LT BOYD and a party guarding the bridge remain behind, the rest of the Coy move to BOURECQ leaving at 8.30 P.M. LT BOYD first sent to FONTES and forms the dismounted at BOURECQ (HQH+H(HQ1) Field Coy RE. Lieut Gerry wounded by shell fire received from 153 Inf Bgde received first to move	JB
BOURECQ. U.I.C. sheet 36 B. 1/40000	3rd	do	Transport moved off at 2.30 P.M. and joined 153 Inf Bgde column at 2.55 P.M. at V.I.C.2.7. Orders for sappers to move received at 12.45 P.M. Transport arrived at DIVION at H24b7 7 P.M. I.O.R reinforcement from R.E. Base Depot, joined Coy.	JB
Do.	4th	do	Transport moved off from DIVION at 9.55 A.M. and arrive ECOIVRES at 5.20 P.M. Damaged en bream at HIRE at 7.8 P.M. O.O. & LT LAURIE go on in the morning by bus in an advanced parties. HOO.103 Capt Bellew returned on damaged billets and continued M.S. Oct of 1916.	JB
ECOIVRES. F13.C.5.5. sheet 51e 1/40000	5th	do	Damaged bed continue 1 A.M. LT LAURIE made Coy at station and guide them to billets. Orders received to find forward two sections under LT'S BOYD & BLACK to take over work from the 11th Field Coy. (Canadian) Forward billets are at A.P.O.A.9.5. Sappers take over trenches at Croys roads	JB

Army Form C. 2118.

WAR DIARY
or
INTELLIGENCE SUMMARY.
(Erase heading not required.)

(193)

400th (Highland) Field Coy R.E.

Place	Date	Hour	Summary of Events and Information	Remarks and references to Appendices
ECOIVRES. F.13 central. SHEET 1/20,000 MAROEUIL.	5th Aug 1918		at A.8.c.6.9. and A.11.a.9.9. and Electric Light Plant at 153rd Bg. H.Q. at A.6.c.9.2.	JB
Do.	6th	do	Mr BOYD shown over the trenches by Officer of 11th Field Coy R.E. IT BLACK & Section IV work on "AIRPLANE TRENCH" at night.	JB
Do.	7th	do	Section IV take over work on dugout at TIVED POST. Party from No. 1 IV clearing water out of BEEHIVE TRENCH & laying duckboards & BLACK working on dugouts and laying duckboards on AIR PLANE TRENCH.	JB
Do.	8th	do	Sects III & IV warned to parade fully equipped at 5.30 A.M. & proceed to ARGYLLE CAMP at A.29.b.90. to take down 5 NISSEN huts & erect same at C.R.E. Fd H.Q. at F.18.a.9.2. All arrangements cancelled & No.1 FIELD COY CAMP at A.27.a.81. allotted to the Coy. Party would LT. LAURIE working on NISSEN huts move into the camp & the work not 8 P.M.	JB

Army Form C. 2118.

WAR DIARY
or
INTELLIGENCE SUMMARY.
(Erase heading not required.)

400th (Highland) Field Coy RE

Place	Date	Hour	Summary of Events and Information	Remarks and references to Appendices
ECURIE. SHEET MAROEUIL 1/20000 Do.	8th May 1918		Section I & transport move from Camp at ECOIVRES to new real H.Q. at M.27.d.8.2. and arrive at 11.45 P.M. Sections III & IV hand over work & billets to Sections of 52nd Div and no no billets are available in 153 Inf Bgde billets these sections return to Rear H.Q. at ECURIE	Photo
Do.	9th do.		Sections III & IV move up to forward billets and take over work & billets from 404 Field Coy RE. Section III work by day in OUSE trench and reliefs demolition parties at Gloriclane road mine (G.6.c.2.9.10.) Bridges at BULLIO (H.1.a.3.5.70.) and Bridge at B.26.b.90.40. Section IV work on AIRPLANE trench where it joins the front line. Section II make LT J.NDRIE Erect W.55EM Hot Camp for 153 Inf Bgde H.Q. at M.22.d.9.0. I.O.R. transferred to 209th Field Coy RE.	Photo
Do.	10th do		Work as for 9th advance party from 401st field coy RE school at real H.Q. at 9.30 AM to take over work & billets	Photo
Do.	11th do		Sect II under Lt DUNSIRE take down huts at Corp's camp and then to 51st Div. H.Q. at MAROEUIL, Lt DUNSIRE with return S/O. proceed to MAROEUIL at 2:30 P.M. & take over work & billets of 401st Field Coy. RE. Section III working in OUSE ALLEY Section IV working on AIRPLANE tunnel, POST LINE & Leach DUGOUT at B.9.C.3.2. Two sections from Rear Field Coy. RE. take over forward billets & work. Lts BLACK & BOYD return to Rear H.Q. in the evening.	Photo

Army Form C. 2118.

WAR DIARY
or
INTELLIGENCE SUMMARY.
(Erase heading not required.)

400th (Highland) Field Coy R.E.

Place	Date	Hour	Summary of Events and Information	Remarks and references to Appendices
ECURIE. SHEET 51 20,000	12th May		Coy moves to MAROEUIL to take over work & billets from 401st Field Coy R.E. Two sections working on road for 51st Div. H.Q. at MAROEUIL.	People
MAROEUIL	13th	Do.	Lt LAURIE & Sect III leave at 9 a.m. & proceed ECURIE to finish work on Div Hutts. It Corpl will section II & II work on 51st Div dump, and a Cpl. held up for want of stores.	People
MAROEUIL F.27.c.6.6.	14th	Do.	Work as usual. Hutts completed. 10.R. transferred to 20120 Field Coy R.E.	People
	15th	Do.	Sect I work in tunnel on Div dump. Section II, III & IV "Coy from H.Q. R.E. 51st Div." manage in the morning from tow equipment recovered from railway this is to replace equipment lost on the SOMME on 21st March.	People
Do.	16th	Do.	Sect II & Lt LAURIE to ROCLINCOURT DUMP to take machinery. Lt BLACK & sect III on 51st Dis/Camp. Lt COOPER machine SODA WATER FACTORY at DUISANS. Lt DUNSIRE meets the D.A.D. Q.M.G. to make arrangements about carrying out work. L.C.S.H.F. came out 2.00 P.M.	People
Do.	17th	Do.	Officer from 404th Coy R.E. reports at Coy. H.Q. to take over work. Lt Corpl. leaves at 9.30 A.M. to take over forward billets of 409 Raleigh Parish. 1st parties & sections I & II leave MAROEUIL at 1.20 P.M. & proceed to 404th Coy R.E. forward Billets in the Railway cutting at A.28.b.5.3. J.Q.R. sends bombcombs from R.E. Park Dept. leave MAROEUIL at 7.30 P.M. & sent forward to take one march from 404th Coy R.E. & to recommide the returns transport & colum III & IV leave Park MAROEUIL at 10 P.M. & arrive new Park H.Q. (A.27.C.6.6.) at 12 Midnt.	People

(A7092). Wt. W12839/M1993. 750,000. 1/17. D. D. & L., Ltd. Forms/C.2118/14.

Army Form C. 2118.

WAR DIARY
or
INTELLIGENCE SUMMARY.
(Erase heading not required.)

400ᵗʰ (Highland) Field Coy RE

Place	Date	Hour	Summary of Events and Information	Remarks and references to Appendices
MAROEUIL	18ᵗʰ May	1918	New C.T. dug from F.L. at B28 d.9.6. to trench T200 yds & task completed.	people
M27.6.6.6. M7 ROBOIR SHEET I 25000	19ᵗʰ May		New F.L. north of THAMES 150 yds. 1ˢᵗ task completed 4 OR from cleaned in the POST LINE. 1.O.R. (H.L.I.) attached company reports the unit. Preliminary orders about new extension of the R.E. works on new F.L. & new C.T. N.P. of 450 from BRS in R line 400 from BRS to reach for POST LINE FRONT 4 in 2 days by 152 1ˢᵗ Bge too narrow & too L to be widened, wheel, escalators difficult. 2 & OSM CUBRICK wounded by shell fire on the railway embankment. 2nd Corpl Mills killed. Sh.L Lce 229A after Kent pulled Ret fire.	post R post R
Do	20ᵗʰ do		Forming up line came up & only 3b at N.C.S. Left Lt Harris & required to take as far the 19ᵗʰ Platoon Bge III down to reach HQ at ECOURIG. Whilst postling work over by 404 Field Coy. 1ᵗʰ & 11ᵗʰ Field met, last part of our Company billets 398.424 H22.535	people
Do	21ˢᵗ do		Time work. Quotations of wiring TONS & T.N.T.A.N.B.S.	post R
Do	22ⁿᵈ do		Work on new CT new F.L. THAMES & TONS continued. N.P. now only 300 from O.B. Entire cut of 145 yds of new F.L. & N.E. W.C.T. Jones old F.L. near BAKKENH TRENCH	people

Instructions regarding War Diaries and Intelligence Summaries are contained in F. S. Regs., Part II. and the Staff Manual respectively. Title pages will be prepared in manuscript.

197

Place	Date 1918	Hour	Summary of Events and Information	Remarks and references to Appendices
H 27 c 6 6. MARŒUIL SHEET 1 20,000.	22nd May.		Orders received from C.R.E. to start work on cold string bath at H.1.a.6.1. Forward work continues. W.P. now only 300 owing to Bde. being disposed in a Battalion front. OC taped out 175 y of new Front Line & new CT joining old F.L. 25 x south of BAILLEUL Trench. 400.010 Sergt. Webster W. appointed Acting C.S.M.	/M
	23rd		1 O.R. joins Coy from R.E. Base Depot. H1H 378 Corpl. Cunningham G Day parties now 4 Platoons cleaning duckboarding new F.L. new C.T. THIMES + TOW. 2 O.R. transferred from 1179th Field Coy R.E. join Company.	/M
	24th		Ditto	/M
	25th		400.127 Farr Sergt. McNeil C. appointed Farr Staff Sergeant. Enemy more active. Considerable shelling of all areas F.L. shelled with gas. Infantry commands moving new F.L. from the night (TOW) under their own arrangements. N.C.O. + 2 O.R. commenced extending dugout for B.E. H.Q. near front of TOW + BROWN LINE 3. O.R. join Company from R.E. Base Depot	/M
	26th		1 O.R. slightly gassed in the line. This man had his gas respirator at the time no one else was affected. Region of CUTTING (forward billets) shelled nearly all night. Some gas detected. Wires from parados to parados with canvas threaded on to pull out as required.	/M
	27th		2 O.R. join Company from R.E. Base Depot. Capt. McCRONE M.C. relieves OC. Enemy attacked between RHEIMS + SOISSONS Work on new F.L. continues, extending northwards + widening	/M

WAR DIARY or INTELLIGENCE SUMMARY

Army Form C. 2118.

400th (Highland) Field Coy. R.E.

Place	Date	Hour	Summary of Events and Information	Remarks and references to Appendices
PT466 MAROEUIL SHEET 1/20,000	May 1918 28th		Sect 4 laying duckboards in New F.L. by day & clearing Sect 3 Supervising digging of New F.L. at Hotton Pond from heavy trench mortar fire. Parapet of platform at 10.30 pm — mostly struck 20' ↕ over the RFT. Any one Casualties (6 Wounded)	1/A
	29th		Work started on 6 culvert holes in New F.L. & ME & 12 Infantry to each in 2 m.p.h. 154 Bn. relieved 153 Bn HQ M.P. at Capt W. in LW BLACK come down to Men billets — sick permit P.U.O. in LW DUNSIRE head up to take Ptr 3. Same work continues. Capt.	1/A
	30th		McKown recommatics drill in BAILLEUL repairs to cable lines posting for cable lines in New F.L.	1/A
	31st		Work as per last Enter home (Cont'd) Ono workers 12 in all.	1/A

Company strength at 30th April 1918.   OFF.   O.R.
                                                      8   193
Increase 30 O.Rs joined Coy on transfer   + 3
          190 O.R. reinforcement from
               R.E. Base Depot   + 19
          2 O.R reinforcement from Hospital   + 2
                                                   8   217
Decrease 1 Officer wounded   — 1
          2 O.Rs killed   — 2
          1 O.R. wounded   — 1
          11 O.Rs evacuated sick   — 11
          2 O.Rs transferred   — 2
                                          7   201

Company strength at 31st May 1918

400TH (HIGHLAND) FIELD COY R.E.

WAR DIARY

JUNE 1918

Army Form C. 2118.

WAR DIARY
or
INTELLIGENCE SUMMARY.
(Erase heading not required.)

403rd (Welsh) Fld. Co. R.E.

Instructions regarding War Diaries and Intelligence Summaries are contained in F. S. Regs., Part II. and the Staff Manual respectively. Title pages will be prepared in manuscript.

Place	Date 1918	Hour	Summary of Events and Information	Remarks and references to Appendices
A.27.a.6.6. MAROEUIL SHEET 1/10,000	1st June		Capt. Watson M.C. takes over 200ᵡ N.F.L. from B.29.a.1.13. SECT 3 under 2/Lt Bowers improving deep dug outs B.29.b.9.4.32 & B.N.F.L. at Northern end, New C.T. connecting old Front Line to New Front Line. Company dugouts Sect 4 under 2/Lt Bryant improving dugouts enabling N.F.L. S.3. & Thames, Lancast D.O. & Cubby Holes. En Cooper forward on Line.	JB
	2nd	do	Work as usual. Sapper Keir No 3 Sect. wounded by shrapnel	JB
	3rd	do	Railway Cutting shelved with H.E. for gun places. Sect 3rd working on New F.L. & New C.T. in Dugout. Widening & deepening N.F.L. S.3. Thames, dovetailing & Cubby Holes. Working party strength about 310.	JB
	4th	do	O.C. takes over Forward report for Capt. Watson. Lt. Boyd & Dawson arrived 3rd after 2 work on night 4/5th return to Rear Hqs. Echuie. Lieut Cope McCrohl unable to take rest – sent forward. Sect 1 reg under 2nd Lt. Laurie and 2nd Lt. forward bridge. Sect 2 remain at forward pass 3rd.	JB
	5th	do	Rly Cutting near forward bridge shelled all morning of 4/12.30 am (B.26.a.7.2.) Work on N.F.L. continued southerly southwards. Forward bridge moved to H.1.c.4.5. in the afternoon.	JB
	6th	do	Capt Watson goes to Rayfine (P.U.O.) Work as reported. Sect 1. deepening & widening & deepening N.F.L. & new ground being continued of 1. Sect 2 on dugouts, duckboarding, Cubby Holes & repairing well at BAILLEUL	JB
	7th	do	Same work continued. 3 new cavalry horses arrived. Horses arrived very great. Reinforcement of S.O.R. arrives from R.E. Base Depot.	JB

WAR DIARY or INTELLIGENCE SUMMARY.

Army Form C. 2118.

700 = (1892) Field Co. R.E.

Place	Date	Hour	Summary of Events and Information	Remarks and references to Appendices
A 27. c. 6.6. MARŒUIL SHEET 1/20,000	JUNE 1918 8th		LT. BOYD takes over forward work from O.C. – SECT.1 – Burying + reinforcing N.F.L. by rapped wooden knife rests + deepening by day – SECT 2. Working on dugout, Bgde HQ. GLENCREIG + LAUNCESTON – BAILLEUL WELL reported to Sample of water taken; also working on cable poles.	JB
	9th	do	O.C. Lieut BECK (Pub) at EOURIE. Sans work continues near LAURIE – CANTEEN in Ry CUTTING (B.27 a.4.6.) – 2 New (6839 INNES) commenced – New B.T. (BAILLEUL EXTENSION) trench boards complete. Gas beam freq reported from BAILLEUL vicinity. No night parties.	JB
	10th	do	Forward work continues – CANTEEN at B.27 a.4.6. commenced – Good progress on Dugouts Bde HQ'rs + GLENCREIG – 152 3rd Suff Bn. relieved 154 3rd Suff Bn – Night party of 50 men of	JB
	11th	do	LT. BOYD types 300+ N.F.L. from B.29 a. 15.40. astride NATHAUSER + NORWICH R. Lines staged B.25. – 130 Infantry dig 15 Task on Enemy side of ground. 130 Infantry Labouring N.F.L. – Ammunition dump work N.F.L. + carrying Trench Boards. Enemy frequent – Cable Noise.	JB
	12th	do	LT LAURIE with Sect. 1 + 2 after usual on surface of N.F.L. returns to EOURIE + are relieved by Sect 3 + under N.B. BLACK who now night Labouring + work reversed	JB
	13th	do	Sect 3. Strenuous digging, burying + deadening N.F.L. – also GLENCREIG Dugout. SECT.2. Work on CANTEEN Hut S. Bde HQ + LAUNCESTON Dugouts. N.C.O. materials reinz Bottn during = 2 New Cable huts commenced – Road on left by 6th Blackwater intrepid mist representations – Sgt M Scott attention from Niel tat.	JB

(A 3099). Wt. W12839/M1193. 75,000. 1/17. D. D. & L., Ltd. Forms/C.2118/4.

WAR DIARY
or
INTELLIGENCE SUMMARY

Army Form C. 2118.

Place	Date	Hour	Summary of Events and Information	Remarks and references to Appendices
A.27.c.6.6. MARUEUIL SHEET 1/20,000	14th June 1918		2nd Lieut. Dennis count forward & taken over No 1 Section. Night-party consisted on way to road by 15th Division to next night. - N.F.L. complete & thickened & lowered. Section 3 commenced widening & deepening BAILLEUL C.T. starting at B.26.B.1.7. & working forward. MAJOR KIGGELL leaves the Coy. & take over the duties of DC RE SUSSEX Coy.	JB
	15th	do	CAPT McCRONE takes over work from 17Boys & when lent by Hoy. as No. 1. Sec. 2nd Lt M.G.B. 3 O.R. join deal unit from R.E. Base Depot	JB
	16th	do	Work on CANTEEN in the valley complete and 4' duckboard to D.C. and to myself D.D. of entrance of TOMS MECHANIC HOLES by N.F.L. Sect II & 40 x BOOT TRENCH 16.10 BAILLEUL C.T. & BOIS CANTEEN 10 DUGOUTS & cutting working parties of 200 at work on N.F.L. 200 on N.F.L. & 50 on BAILLEUL C.T.	
	17th	do	40 OR on improv. Blue & BLACK finds charge of night parties on N.F.L. & BAILLEUL C.T. Lieut. Cooper returned from leave	
	18th	do	New work started on C.T. from BROWN LINE to FIRST TRENCH. to be tp 200 long. 20 x wide x 2' deep w. 1' top. Rest 135 on BAILLEUL C.T. 3 40 x 2' deep & 1' top & cut of BOOT HOLES incurred the N.F.L. Shelts Sect 3 improv. deepening and widening BAILLEUL C.T.	
	19th		CAPT gone around the work & with Capt McCRONE nearly all the jobs reviewed. Have about 30 OR, B.877 H.Q. mountain well of hilly at A.26.9.5.5 1 O.R. join from R.E. Base Depot.	

Army Form C. 2118.

WAR DIARY
or
INTELLIGENCE SUMMARY.

(Erase heading not required.)

202.

Place	Date	Hour	Summary of Events and Information	Remarks and references to Appendices
H.Q.75. BAILLEUL	20th [illegible]		[illegible handwritten entries]	
Do.	21st [illegible]			
Do.	22nd do.			
Do.	23rd do.			
Do.	24th do.			

Army Form C. 2118.

WAR DIARY
or
INTELLIGENCE SUMMARY.

(Erase heading not required.)

Instructions regarding War Diaries and Intelligence Summaries are contained in F. S. Regs., Part II. and the Staff Manual respectively. Title pages will be prepared in manuscript.

Place	Date	Hour	Summary of Events and Information	Remarks and references to Appendices
H.10.95.	24th June		[not readable]	
B.A.12.46.0.b. 1/75,000	25th June		Work started on new R.O. for M.G. Batty at H.3.D.3.3. and that this D.O. to be named "HAMPSTEAD HAMPLEGAUNTS." Trench about 70 yds. in length, D.O. to be roofed & floored with 1ft. of earth covering or [?] The trench is to be 7 ft. wide & 7 ft. high. Two [?] entrances [?] to be put at each end of trench. G.O.C. Division called up [?] it is hoped to [?]	
Do.	26th June		C.R.E. gave round the work with Capt. McBane. Slight alterations made in the making of GULLY LOCALITY. 6.E. 51st M.G. BATT calls at advanced H.Q. were about trimming of old spur dug D.O. at H.3.C.3.3. The D.O. has two shafts + about 15' of harness, all the timber has been removed. CAPT McBANE reports on the D.O. to the C.R.E.	
Do.	27th do.		LT COOPER starts work on further in FIRE BAYS + preparing trenches at B.22.C.5.1. + B.22.C.90.00. Tunnels for defense of FIRE BAYS marked	

Army Form C. 2118.

WAR DIARY
or
INTELLIGENCE SUMMARY.
(Erase heading not required.)

Instructions regarding War Diaries and Intelligence Summaries are contained in F. S. Regs., Part II. and the Staff Manual respectively. Title pages will be prepared in manuscript.

Place	Date	Hour	Summary of Events and Information	Remarks and references to Appendices
H.Q. 7.5.	29th June		Out at B.29.d.6.6.8. Getting Lewisth and Lagging T.B. to GULLY LOOP N.	No. 46
BAILLEUL			All working parties now busy on JECT II pulling out of the front lines at H.Q.75. of DUNSIRE Relief by D. & Y. on the McEwen trench.	
H.Q. 7.5.			2 R.E. maps on modern Reims we do not want. No. 7 to stand side R.Q. at H.30.33. Changing the whole width of 7.6. No. 69	
Do.	29th	Do.	Do. on the 29th.	
Do.			Work as usual. Capt. McCrone arriving bring & make them work on another portion. N.O. more wanted. Parties now working on BAILLEUL CT. through Infy to NEW C.T. must amount to fairly often, have not counted. This night before a new party arrives, too much.	No. 46
Do.	29th	90	Work on "CHU" D.O. (H30370) commenced. The night on the parties at BULY LOOP N11 cancelled on account of much to infantry along TYNE ALLEY, and up a parties, and so many were demand.	Rough
Do.	30th	90	Lack of Duds in front of GULLY ALLEY N11 was kept until return parties with H.Q. near 3. Nearly sudden all day. D.R. more of them than H.O. since	

(A5092) Wt. W12539/M1293. 750,000. 1/17. D. D. & L., Ltd. Forms/C.2118/24.

Army Form C. 2118.

WAR DIARY
or
INTELLIGENCE SUMMARY.
(Erase heading not required.)

Instructions regarding War Diaries and Intelligence Summaries are contained in F.S. Regs., Part II. and the Staff Manual respectively. Title pages will be prepared in manuscript.

Place	Date	Hour	Summary of Events and Information	Remarks and references to Appendices
M.C.T.S. BAILLEUL 10/300	30th June		(05) JB numbers kept up to 200 OR & 6 UGs (locality to form a ?) El 7th went to the rifle range. No OR wounded or killed during the last 3 weeks officially, but some twenty have been slightly wounded 300 yds. Officers completely rested & trained.	Purple
			COMPANY STRENGTH JUNE 1918	
				Officers	Other Ranks
			Company Strength at 31st May	7	201
			INCREASE		
			Reinforcements from Base		+15
			Hospital		+6
			Joined on transfer fr Corp		+2
				7	224
			DECREASE		
			Wounded		-1
			To hospital and evacuated		-15
			By transfer to other units		-3
			Officers transferred on A.G.'s authority to Cadet School in England	-1	-1
			Company Strength at 30th June	6	204
				Rifle Range Capt X.	
				Jn 25, 400 m field range M.E.	

Divisional Engineers

51st (Highland) Division

400th FIELD CO., R.E.

JULY, 1918.

CONFIDENTIAL

WR 37

400th (Highland) Field Coy. R.E.

WAR DIARY

July 1918

Army Form C. 2118.

WAR DIARY
or
INTELLIGENCE SUMMARY.

(Erase heading not required.)   400TH (HIGHLAND) FIELD Co. R.E (T).

Instructions regarding War Diaries and Intelligence Summaries are contained in F. S. Regs., Part II. and the Staff Manual respectively. Title pages will be prepared in manuscript.

(206)

Place	Date 1918	Hour	Summary of Events and Information	Remarks and references to Appendices
H.I.C. 45 BAILLEUL 1/10,000	1st JULY		Capt. McCRONE visits work on GLENCRAIG DUGOUT. The line of shafts had not been properly manned up.	Ruothe
	2ND		LIEUT. COOPER out with night party on POST SUPPORT. Good progress being made with wiring. Orders from C.R.E. to start work on Dugout in POST SUPPORT at 10 P.M. on the 4th. Working party arranged. LIEUT. LAURIE taking out a track from about B.29.a.3. to POST SUPPORT about B.28.a.35.15. Gully of dugout out all night filling shell holes & erecting bridges. This will save a carrying party of 20 from Brigade.	Ruothe
Do	3RD		All spoiling parties out down. LIEUT. DUNSIRE takes night party. Quite a good night's work done. LIEUT. COOPER out with day party on GULLY LOCALITY. LIEUTS COOPER & DUNSIRE feeling their touch of P.U.O. CAPT. McCRONE takes out night working parties. 154TH INF. BRIGADE relieves 153rd in GAVRELLE SECTOR.	Ruothe
Do	4TH		C.R.E. calls about increase in working parties. The Brigade being relieved has to send 1 Battn. as working parties before leaving the line. This makes night party over 400 strong. 150 of party work on NEW C.T. running SOUTH from RAILWAY. C.T. nearly 300 yds. opened up (1st task). Some of the work had to stop owing to men going to Hospital. No night wiring party.	Ruothe
Do	5TH		New Dugout "CHIN" in GULLY LOCALITY started. The men are being worked on shifts of 8 hours. Capt. McCRONE visits Brigade about working parties.	Ruothe
Do	6TH		Work as usual on GULLY LOCALITY. Night working party places out junior track.	Ruothe
Do	7TH		Work as usual.	Ruothe
Do	8TH		Work on GULLY LOCALITY as usual, nightly working party very poor. Warning orders about relief by CANADIANS received about 10 P.M.	Ruothe
Do	9TH		Officer from 4TH CANADIAN BATTN reports at forward Billets about 2.20 P.M. CAPT McCRONE takes him round the work; all jobs examined & all details about work handed over. LIEUT. LAURIE takes night party on BILLY C.T. Slightly better night's work done.	Ruothe

(A7092). Wt. W12839/M1293. 750,000. 1/17. D. D. & L., Ltd. Forms/C.2118/14.

WAR DIARY or INTELLIGENCE SUMMARY

Army Form C. 2118.

(Erase heading not required.)

207

Place	Date 1918	Hour	Summary of Events and Information	Remarks and references to Appendices
H.1.c.y.3 BAILLEUL 1/10,000	10TH JULY		CANADIANS take over working party work taken over by midnight. Orders received from C.R.E. about 10.30 P.M. about move to BEUGIN. Dismounted to move by Light Railway, entraining at ECURIE at 5.45 A.M. Travelled to move by Road starting point road junction 1 Kilo N.W. of MONT ST ELOI at 9.12 A.M. Lieut BOYD proceeds on leave.	Route
BEUGIN LENS 11.	11TH "		Company moves as ordered. LIEUT. COOPER takes charge of the Transport. Other officers all by train. Dismounted arrive at BEUGIN about 1 P.M. Mounted about 2 P.M. Billets are poor. The 401st & 404th Coys + C.R.E. Also billeted in BEUGIN.	Route
	12TH "		Company rest at BEUGIN. Parade 9-30 A.M. Inspection of Kits & making out deficiency lists for Lorocart. Conference at C.R.E. at 6 P.M. to discuss schemes for training.	Route
	13TH "		Company drill and knotting & lashing. Training scheme about move of the Division. received 8 P.M.	Route
	14TH "		Company drill in morning. Details of entraining received 7.30 a.m. to entrain at TINQUES at 10 a.m. 15th Company BLACK proceeds to reconnoitre TINQUES RAILWAY STATION & facilities for entraining. Lieut LAURIE & one man for action go ahead in advance party leaving TINQUES at 1 p.m. At 10 a.m. move received from Brigade altering time of train to 9.38 a.m. Entraining Station unknown O.C. 401 & 404 Coys so made Officers Commanding No 18 train.	Route
do TINQUES	15TH "		Transport leaves BEUGIN at 4.45 a.m. Rail units leave 5.45 a.m. & march to TINQUES STATION. All arrangements about entraining are very good & train leaves to time. No 3 Coy A.L.C. & one Coy 1/1 TH GORDON HIGHLANDERS travel by same train. Horses & men are served with train & tea on route to the night of the 17th. Transport at NOVELLE for 3/4 hour to water the horses & feed the men.	Route
CHAT	16TH "		Train stops at CHAT at about 2 A.M. Horses watered & men served with tea. About 2.15 p.m. CAPT. CHAPMAN from DIVISION boards train & warns others detraining station is NOGENT. Officers have to move by Bus from NOGENT to an area ATHIS-TOURS-SUR-MARNE MAREUIL about 50 miles N N E of NOGENT. Transport to move by road under LIEUT COOPER. Transport leaves NOGENT about 6 p.m.	Route
NOGENT	" "		The Buses are hung round by the FRENCH to Buses arrive on 16th & happen spend the night	Route

WAR DIARY or INTELLIGENCE SUMMARY

Army Form C. 2118.

Place	Date Hour	Summary of Events and Information	Remarks and references to Appendices
NOGENT	16th July 1918	In a field near NOGENT STATION	Route
"	17th	Transport arrived at BARBONNE about 2 A.M. French Officer reports to CAPT. McCRONE that Busses are available & wishes men to move at once. O.C. arranges with the French that men can wait till 4.30 am as Americans are about to start before we leave by Busses at 4.30 am. Route NOGENT-VILLENAUXE-SEZANNE-FERE CHAMPENOISE-BERGERES-VERTUS. Busses left 3 kilometres of GRAUVES. It part from 153 INF. BRIGADE informs O.C. that Company is to be located at PIERRY. Reported arrival the Coy. 10 kilos to PIERRY. LIEUT LAURIE has guides out searching for Coy. Billets. Billets are very bad. The men are very exhausted due to the journey & shortage of rations. Transport leaves BARBONNE and arrives at VERTUS. Corp. ROBERTSON sent forward to reconnoitre & bring up a lorry containing C.R.E. annexe on Johnson to be billeted at MOUSSY.	Route
PIERRY	"	Inspection of the Coy at 9 a.m. No rations. 118th Coy received "Iron Rations" & Transport arrives at PIERRY at 4 p.m. Rations for 18th received about 2 p.m. O.C. visits C.R.E. arriving in orders yet received.	Route
do	18th		Route
do	19th	Orders received at 5 a.m. for the Company to move off at 7.45 a.m. Coy to move to CUMIERES route EPERNAY-DIZY-MAGENTA-CUMIERES. Coy arriving about 1 p.m. & encamps in field in S.E. corner of village. C.R.E. calls about 7.15 p.m. bearing orders to move to BELLEVUE received the 51st DIV. M. & N. an attack from the BOIS DE COURTON & the Coy is in readiness to do any work required. Final orders received at 9.30 p.m. Coy moves off at one ton & one mile N.E. of BELLEVUE. Coy arrives about 1 a.m. Coy preparing to transport up rifle orders for work on 20th received with movement order at 9.30 p.m. The Coy to be prepared for the construction & keep of a route from 500 metres No 7 first O on CORMOYEAU through the BOIS DE COURTON to a point near HUNTHOUSE - thence N.W. of JOINES rondo, thence N.E. to OM COURTON - thence H.W. to LANEUVILLE-CHAUMUZY Road.	Route
CUMIERES REF "CHALONS SUR REIMS" 1/50,000			
"	20th	Coy with section leaders move off at 5.45 a.m. C.R.E. calls at 6.15 am. O.C. leaves at 6.30 am & goes ahead to reconnoitre the route. No work & requires a road until H. COURTON & learning route to be made there both H.OO & Johnson & Shepard.	Route
N.E. OF BELLEVUE			

WAR DIARY or INTELLIGENCE SUMMARY

Army Form C. 2118.

Place	Date 1918	Hour	Summary of Events and Information	Remarks and references to Appendices
N.E. OF BELLEVUE	20TH JULY		O.P. reports to C.R.E. Orders sent for the Coy to withdraw to the transport lines, as they are bound back on line. 2/Lts gave orders every two hours, having been previously sent to sit on top of parapets, the attack at the 153RD BRIGADE were not very successful as they had only gained their first objective. CORPL ROBERTSON J. wounded	Further.
WOODS WEST OF MAN(Z)EUIL "REIMS"	21ST	"	Orders received at 9.30 a.m. for Coy to move at 10 a.m. to rendezvous W. of MANZEUIL. Coy arrived at rendezvous at 2.30 p.m. & left at 4 p.m., marched on into Bank. Reconnaissance made. Camp hastily pitched from 2.30 p.m. to 4 p.m.	Further.
CHÂLONS	22ND	"	Heavy bombardment about 3.30 a.m. Orders received at 7 p.m. from C.R.E. to reconnoitre & report for water supply for points at Cm = CORMOYEUX at corner of wood S.E. _____ of M. COURTON.	Further.
60,000 R.F.	23RD	"	Enemy bombarded about 6 am. The Germans again make an attack but without much success. Section IV start work on water points near Cm CORMOYEUX. There is a plentiful supply of water about 20 to 30 gals. per minute. Section III relieve Section IV on the work at 3 p.m. The following facilities for watering were made: 1 tap for filling water bottles & dixies. 2 pipe filling water cans. Section II work, cut matroval on work point at Cm = MOTCOURTON. The scheme is damaged at 4.40 g.c. & a tank is used, each tank being fitted with a tap for filling water bottles & dixies.	Further.
do	24TH	"	Enemy aeroplane flies over camp killing one, after alighting wounding a driver. Enemy at heavy bombardment of billets about 10.30 p.m. Ambulances hit about 3 am. The following morning all transport moves to ST. IMOGES in the evening. Enemy shelves about ST. IMOGES killing a about 30% of men & horses.	Further.
B/W BOIS de QUENTIN	25TH	"	Coy change from 153 INF. BRIGADE to 152ND BRIGADE. CAPT. McCRONE goes to the end in the morning with 2/Lt. Geen from the 152ND BRIGADE and arranges to work on improvement of the Coy H.Qrs. in the front line to the left of the BOIS DE L'AULNAY. LIEUT BLACK takes up Section I at 12.50 p.m. & starts work on repairing holes. Coy move to billets 2 & 3 in BOIS DE QUENTIN. MAJOR ARGENT reports to take over command of the Coy from Capt. McCRONE	Further.
do	26TH	"	O.C. CAPT. McCRONE & LIEUT. BLACK leave H.Q. at 6 am. to reconnoitre the W. side of the BOIS DE L'AULNAY. Shell pits to have to be made on the edge of the wood to give men cover during the attack. Arrange for the 2/Lts Section IV & III to arrive about 9.30 a.m. & carry out the work. LIEUT BLACK. Orderly from C.R.E. about mid-day to start work, splinter proof cover for an O.P. in the wood due E. of MARFAUX. 1.N.C. 084 Sappers do this job, finishing after midnight.	Further.

WAR DIARY or INTELLIGENCE SUMMARY

Army Form C. 2118.

Place	Date 1918	Hour	Summary of Events and Information	Remarks and references to Appendices
BOIS DE QUENTIN	27th JULY		The Division attack in the morning. Meet with very little opposition. ESPILLY & NAPPES captured in the morning. At 1pm patrols pushed forward & captured CHAUMUZY without opposition. Orders from C.R.E. in the morning to reconnoitre & report on opening near BULLIN FARM, not having made a recce. point. C.R.E. called at 3.30 p.m. at Coy H.Q. & Coy to prepare for dry weather track on S. side of RIVER ARDRE joining NAHTEUIL & CHAUMUZY. Recce. parties out & men redid out at night. Work completed as far as the corner of the BOIS DE L'AULNAY.	Rouille
REIMS & CHALONS 50,000 1	28th "		Orders received from C.R.E. Coy to concentrate in their billets. Went to 10 A.M. orders received from C.R.E. to move forward to CHAUMUZY. O.C. 4 LIEUT DUNSIRE O.C. 4 went to reconnoitre positions for Coy. Took up a position on CHAUMUZY-NEUVILLE ROAD ½ Kilo WEST of the former transport moved from ST. IMOGES to the BOIS DE L'AULNAY arriving at 8pm. During Coy. to take advantage of horses & vehicles belonging to No.3 Section are left at NAHTEUIL. Orders from C.R.E. that the Coy. is to be responsible for the repair of the CHAUMUZY-NEUVILLE ROAD from CHAUMUZY to a track ¾ of Kilometer S.W. of CHAUMUZY.	Rouille
CHAUMUZY.	29th "		Coy. working in afternoon the road ordered this work & also to see that no one camped on the bringing up horses in the morning village of CHAUMUZY.	Rouille
do.	30th "		Coy. working on improvement of the road worked on the previous day. Orders from C.R.E. to concentrate at old pd. horse lines & then move to ST. IMOGES. Transport arrived at ST. IMOGES about 6.30 p.m. Sappers about 8.30 p.m. Camp at E. in ST. IMOGES.	Rouille
ST IMOGES.	31st "		Sappers cleaning wagons & equipment preparatory to the inspection of the Divn. on the 1st Augt. by the G.O.C. VIIth FRENCH ARMY.	Rouille

RW Metcalfe Capt. R.E.

for Lt. Col. 400 W Hyl. Field Coy. R.E.

WAR DIARY
or
INTELLIGENCE SUMMARY.

Army Form C. 2118.

Place	Date	Hour	Summary of Events and Information	Remarks and references to Appendices
211			**COMPANY STRENGTH JULY 1918.**	
			OFFICERS. OTHER RANKS.	
			COY STRENGTH AT 30TH JUNE 1918. 6 204	
			INCREASE. REINFORCEMENT FROM BASE 1 5	
			" HOSPITAL 11	
			TRANSFER TO COMPANY 7 220	
			DECREASE KILLED 1	
			WOUNDED 17	
			HOSPITAL 54	
			TRANSFERS FROM COY 1	
			CADET SCHOOL 1	
			SUBSTITUTION 1	
			"MISSING" 3 58	
			COY STRENGTH 31ST JULY '18. 4 162.	

CONFIDENTIAL

WAR DIARY

— OF —

400TH (HIGHLAND) FIELD COMPANY. R.E.

FROM 1ST to 31ST AUGUST 1918.

Army Form C. 2118.

WAR DIARY
or
INTELLIGENCE SUMMARY.
(Erase heading not required.)

400ᵗʰ (HIGHLAND) FIELD COY R.E.

Place	Date	Hour	Summary of Events and Information	Remarks and references to Appendices
ST IMOGES. (Marne)	1/8/18		Marched to PIERRY - Monsieur Prof. Gen. BERTHOLT. G.O.C 4ᵗʰ FRENCH ARMY set work at DIZZY MAGENTA.	/h
PIERRY.	2/8/18		Ponteens & peoples received from 404 Field Co R.E. Lt BOYD - 5 O.R. proceeded to advance billeting party with 153 Brigade for VERTUS to BOUVIGNY. 2/Lt LANOIS billeted as Liaison officer at OIRY STATION. Transfered with Capt McCRONE marched to OIRY at 7.10 p.m. via EPERNAY	/h
PIERRY	3/8/18		Remainder met with O.C marched at 1.30 a.m at OIRY - Coy retained at left 2.15 [?] as rear	/h
CHILDNNE- EROUNAY June 2	4/8/18		Coy released at 4 p.m. & marched to BOUVIGNY - BOYERUEIS during midnight. Temperary Hd-qrs put in order -	/h
BOUVIGNY.	5/8/18		Coy Recce at 11 a.m. & began making cleaning of equipment. Wash & Bath. Cooks at - Cpl MATHESON & others evicted of Insubordination at Cham. de la HAYE.	/h
"	6/8/18		The following ree promoted to Sergt. SPR. 476/12 ROMPLING. W.1794236 KOYTE. T. - 576190. JONES. A.J. - 428313 TURTON. J - 213561 SHACKLETON A. WRIGHT G. Dr 400140 WRIGHT G. Reinforcement from WOOLWICH Dr 400140 WRIGHT G. Cpl MATHESON at CHAN de la HAYE. 2 hrs Extra Parade & section Drill -	/h
"	7/8/18		Coy Parade - Section Drill - Football included feature No 1 Th & No 3 Th selection 400461 & CARSON T refused a employment. C.S.M. BYRNE G. Area Sup. Corps left for Hd-Qrs - Arrived in outskirts of CHAN de la HAYE.	/h
"	8/8/18		Coy Parades - 2 Lecture Pte T Bayonet various under CSM BYRNE. 2 hrs. extra drill. Football Selection match to flames.	/h

Army Form C. 2118.

WAR DIARY
or
INTELLIGENCE SUMMARY.

(Erase heading not required.)

400TH (HIGHLAND) FIELD COY. R.E.

Place	Date	Hour	Summary of Events and Information	Remarks and references to Appendices
BOURIGNY	9/5/18	-	Training continued - reinforcements from base - 9487 spr FEVER W. - 160431 spr GRIFFITHS G. - 491734 spr SMITH L. - 231120 spr JACKSON G. - 446901 spr SAVAGE F. - 45040 spr KENNEDY D.J. - 402215 st TPSGN Q.P. 420051 S/spr COOPER J. - 388294 D. MERCHANT A.	J.L.
"	10/5/18		Training continued - 9 L.D. recruits marched	J.L.
"	11/5/18		NCOs personal P.T. OS Training under C.S.M. BYRNE of A.G.S. CHURCH PARADES - FOOTBALL	J.L.
"	12/5/18		Parade in morning - 600 Company to MARQUEFFLES RIFLE RANGE Shoot. 100 "group" 200" Afficial & S.R. Rifle. 300" Official & S.R. Rifle.	J.L.
"	13/5/18		Training continued - Lecture by C.R.E. to R.E. Mess & Cooperation of R.E. & Infantry.	J.L.
"	14/5/18		Training as usual - FOOTBALL & by Various Theatres at CHATEAU de la HAYE.	J.L.
"	15/5/18		" " Lecture by O.C. on French Systems.	J.L.
"	16/5/18		" " P.M. DUMMIE PARTIES went to ST MICHAELS Field or Army Athletic meeting.	J.L.
"	17/5/18		O.C. & Lt BOYD & 2 sergeants instructors to ST MICHAELS Field or 1st Army Athletic meeting. SOS Date to R.E. - Company Batten at BOURIGNY. An Pay Parade. - 210A94 S/Sgt SIGNS COLL McCRONE & Sgt LONEZ	J.L.
"	18/5/18		Transport Instruction to 505 Duke & Billet of ROZEN wk. Call McCRONE & Sgt LONEZ. Company of Town under 2Lt. LAURIE - MCLELLAN O.C. 6,16 & 77. Wed ST. B. N4. 2L COOPER reported to Not section & Dreuch Billet at AIC.60 35. VA. ST. B. N4. CRE to date - No 2 section hosts to B. Awl Alarie Anjues Lavey as Operator in ropey of 19th (at look ft of overhear - trip has lost brick.	J.L.

Army Form C. 2118.

WAR DIARY
or
INTELLIGENCE SUMMARY.

(Erase heading not required.)

400TH (HIGHLAND) FIELD Cy R.E.

Place	Date	Hour	Summary of Events and Information	Remarks and references to Appendices
G16f.77 (ST MICHAELS)	18/9/18		The following issues killed to Home Establishment:— 187238. PEARCE.A. - 153901 WILCOCK.J. - 557167 MYERS.G. - 422616 BRUNSHURST.W. 470507 HUTCHINSON.G. - 420287 McQUEEN.T.	A
"	19/9/18		No 1 Section issued to R.A.P. EFFIE TRENCH & MG's at M2d.4.87 also S.A. ammunition dump for R.M. for AMBULANCE RD & RY BRIDGE at M1d.4.0. also making forward rd. " No 4 Section took over B Gerd demolitions & CHARLES TUTOR dump. No 2 & 3 issued a travelling CHANTECLER SWITCH The following Repairs for R.O.C.A. reinforcements :— 14966 6727 COLLYER.A. (P.T. & S. militants) - 457 690 GREEN.J.K. - subspar 134618 MARCH - H. 245064 ALLARD.R. — 241319. BURFORD.S - 183 940 WILLIAMS.S.L. - 50025 BREWSIDE.G. 69 695. BOOLS.J. - 148722. MARTIN.C.H. - 496390 BARTLEY.N. - 434 531 HEWITT.T. - 434 491. WILLIAMS.T. - 495109. OLD.W. - 414 524 CULLEN.M. - 504 524 MASLEN.C.W. 457141 HARDING.T.F. - 572499 PASCOE.W.H. - 557077 SIMONS.A. - 145 437 ROEBUCK.H 154 336 WYATT.A. - 474 409 STAINFORTH.G.A. - 400126 COOPER.F. - 494443 MIDDLE.A. 412 724 PEACOCK.D - 426 550 PEPLOE.H. - 145 605 PACEY.W. - Pioneer. 550 660 OLIVER.R. 69545 BENTLEY.P.P. DRIVERS 412362 CRAIG.S. - 412599 FULTON.J. 412604 BAXTER.A. No 1 & 2 Sections in store - No 2 & 3 Travelling CHANTECLER SWITCH. III Issue of curb cells for CRP - Gas helmet inspection to be first 7.30 am 21/9/18	A
"	20/9/18			A

WAR DIARY
or
INTELLIGENCE SUMMARY.

Army Form C. 2118.

400TH (HIGHLAND) FIELD COY. R.E.

Place	Date	Hour	Summary of Events and Information	Remarks and references to Appendices
2/9/67.7.	21/8/18		Sector. Owing to a storm — F/LT LAIRIE & 2.NCOs taken out to replace of our own & enemy trench around THE SNOUT (in front of our Operation here) at the 7th R.H. Cmd.— Sector 2 Lent. gun guard posts to H.Q. for instructions— Rest completed — 2 L.O. NCOs wounded & POSHA VET. sector. — Rest completed. —	A/
"	22/8/18		F/LT LAIRIE & 12 O.R. prisoners in front operation with 7th R.H. Also 3 sections & tapes. No 1 commenced trucking a new trench to take another sector at forward line. Morale always good of operation — 2/Lt. EWEN McGREGOR FIELD FERGUSON replies as reinforced for home. The following hampered Spurs identified. 400274 Pte. BELL, J. — 160257 Pte. EWING, J. 250272 L/cple FURSLE, J.— took 2 other men who NO 4 sector continued work. 253 Bgde R.F.A. M.G.E. worked a 22/8/18	A/
"	23/9/18		M.G.E. Conference — 253 Bgde H.Q. Conference — No 2 worked in Horky trench a 2nd line Broughty Squad. No 1 preparing charges. Places & CHANTECLER sector Brophty trench. —	A/
"	24/8/18		Pte. GLASGOW S. & 3 sappers sent out with mobile charge of destroying enemy dug out — an operation of 7th R.H. in morning of 25th — As last reported — received orders from CRE to place a section at disposal of 256 Bgde R.F.A. for lifting trenches, to a end of move forward — (No 1 section). Also another at disposal of 153 Bg. Bypass in search for Booby Traps etc. (No 2 sections & mines & forward billets. Carried on in CHANTECLER sector.	A/

Army Form C. 2118.

WAR DIARY
or
INTELLIGENCE SUMMARY.
(Erase heading not required.)

400? (HIGHLAND) FIELD CO. R.E.

Instructions regarding War Diaries and Intelligence Summaries are contained in F. S. Regs., Part II. and the Staff Manual respectively. Title pages will be prepared in manuscript.

Place	Date	Hour	Summary of Events and Information	Remarks and references to Appendices
2nd Fd A G.16.E.77	25/9/18		The following OR Joined & Home Establishment. 82922 Spr LEWIS. E. — 134225 Spr KEYTE.T. 422535 Spr HERD. D. No 2 section constructed French Obs. TOMY TRENCH Sheet 51 Corps GAVRELLE R2. Other section work by fn. roles.	/3
"	26/9/18		Coy moved forward to forward section H.Q. H.1.C. 60.35. Section 1. made crossings of trenches in CAM VALLEY for 283 Bde RFA. " 4 reconnoitred work Valley 3/R forward of BETTIS Trench to GERMAN LINE (GREEN LINE) to ensure passage for transport. " 2 + 3 held in reserve for C.R.E. work.	/3
" H.1.C.65.35	27/9/18		Section 3 put works in water supplies for 2 Hrs. " 2 Cleared NORTHUMBERLAND LANE + FRED LINE FAMPOUX + FAMPOUX to ARRAS ROAD for fn. mph. Foot much traffic - heavy motor traffic. The following are recommended for late Mr. M. 218497 HASTINGS T. Section 1. Works for fn. roles for 286 R.F.A. Brigade. 216910 PALMER JR. 420263 WALKER D. 230789 HEGELTING.T. 241262 CAHILL M. 480721 HURST.C.W. SPENCE JERRY W.	/3
"	28/9/18		Section 4 + 3 Works in Water Supplies. " 2 Cleared NORTHUMBERLAND LANE. Section 2 works by fn. roles for 256 Bde RFA in H.I.R. A. Section 2 Works by fn. roles for 256 Bde RFA. 1 motor tank + heavy.	/3
"	29/9/18		Section 2 - 3 + 4 Works in Water Supplies. Other advance tank force in NORTHUMBERLAND LANE. N. enabled to put on Pluage period & Delice Salt. Section 1 Water Supplies for H10 E 65" + Wells for 237 Bde RFA for Horsey Fork. Major Curry to Hosptl Change to JR ALLARD. R. 7050 to Hospital - Shock of Trench.	/3

No. 285 O P4. (A7092). Wt. W12899/M1293. 75,000. 1/17. D. D. & L., Ltd. Forms/C.2118/14.

Army Form C. 2118.

WAR DIARY
or
INTELLIGENCE SUMMARY.

(Erase heading not required.)

400th (HIGHLAND) FIELD COY R.E.

Instructions regarding War Diaries and Intelligence Summaries are contained in F. S. Regs., Part II. and the Staff Manual respectively. Title pages will be prepared in manuscript.

Place	Date	Hour	Summary of Events and Information	Remarks and references to Appendices
#1.C 60 35	30/8/18		2 O.R. Section on half shifts.	ft
			3 Officers.iew Closing Road in FAMPOUX.	
			1 artillery Track.	
			217 261 Spr PARNELL G. L'Hopital Etablished	
			40076 2/Cpl ROBERTSON. W.R. proceeded to 2/Course.	
			400110 Spr GLASGOW S. " " 2/2/Cse.	
			400035 Spr FISHER A.C. " " 2/2/Cse.	
			400 113 Spr DUNCAN A.G. " " 2/2/Cse.	
			TRANSPORT LINES moved from L28 S2 5 - G 16 ? 77. Sheet 57 B. N.W.	
"	31/8/18		No 2 OR Section clearing road in FAMPOUX.	ft
			No 4 " " in water supply.	
			No 1 " " Sully H.Q.F. X2 Bridge L.P.A.	

COMPANY STRENGTH AUGUST 1918

	OFF	O.R.
STRENGTH AT 31st JULY	7	163
INCREASE		
Reinforcements from Base	+1	+50
	8	213
DECREASE		
Wounded (Gas shell)	—	-1
Evacuated Sick	-1	-6
STRENGTH AT 31st August	7	206

WD 39

CONFIDENTIAL

War Diary

of

400" (Highland) Field Coy R.E.

From 1st September to 30th September 1918

Army Form C. 2118.

WAR DIARY
or
INTELLIGENCE SUMMARY.
(Erase heading not required.)

400TH (HIGHLAND) FIELD COY. R.E.

Instructions regarding War Diaries and Intelligence Summaries are contained in F. S. Regs., Part II. and the Staff Manual respectively. Title pages will be prepared in manuscript.

Place	Date	Hour	Summary of Events and Information	Remarks and references to Appendices
41 c 60 35	1/9/18		Bt. Commenced f. BATH HOUSE to PAMPOUX. Sections 2 & 3 commenced Byre H.Q. in CAM VALLEY. Section 4 worked on watertable. Section 1 Railway H.Q. f. 256 Bgde R.F.A. Capt. McCRONE R.E. proceeded to England on one month leave — 420574 Sjt HENDERSON A. Gratuity to UFTON Reformatory.	A/2
	2/9/18		Sections over watertable where & CORPS were Engineers. Sections 1, 2 & 3 as above — section 4 worked in MQ Billet O.C. walked over proposed line of light railway forward from PAMPOUX with 3rd CANADIAN RAILWAY BATT. Co.	A/2
	3/9/18		Section 2 as above — section 3 on channels clearing light Railway feed from PAMPOUX working with 3rd CANADIAN RY. BATT. Section 1 attached to Inf. H.Q. from 256 B.U. R.F.A. 400174 Cpl LAMB N.— 487909 Spr JONES.E. Notes 5 hrs Rickelund	A/2
	4/9/18		Section 1 & 3 worked on light Railway — 2/H in Byre H.R. in CAM VALLEY. Lt BOYD — 400576 Cpl. McCRACKEN. J. — 400100 & Cpl GLASGOW to Rest Army Self Camp	A/2
	5/9/18		Section 2 Yesterday —	A/2

Army Form C. 2118.

WAR DIARY
or
INTELLIGENCE SUMMARY.
(Erase heading not required.)

400TH (HIGHLAND) FIELD COY. R.E.

Place	Date	Hour	Summary of Events and Information	Remarks and references to Appendices
H.C 65.x5	6/9/18		Work as before –	
			The following O.R. returned from base. Septhers – 442854 INMAN F. 426390 WEST A.	1/5
			108129 LEWIS A. 496657 CARTER G.A. 448710 FOYSTER F.	1/5
	7/9/18		Work as above – company Bathed before return –	A
	8/9/18		do	A
	9/9/18		do	A
	10/9/18		do	A
	11/9/18		Sections 1 & 3 worked on Railway as usual	A
			" 2 on Rd. No1	
	12/9/18		Section 2 & 4 worked on Railway. O.C. 57 Field Coy R.E. & 2 Officers came &	A
			3 " on Repair of Plank Road were round work in hand –	
			1 worked & took lime covered portions begun x	
	13/9/18		Coy relieved by 57 Field Co CE & marched to DOUGLAS CAMP VILLERS AU BOIS	A
			No 519991 Spr TAYLOR J broke to use Picturshard –	
			400135 C/Sgt GILLESPIE W. & 450080 Spr KENNEDY D.J. struck off coy strength	
VILLERS AU BOIS X 19 Sheet 44B.	14/9/18		Coy Paraded labor report – &c	A

Army Form C. 2118.

WAR DIARY
or
INTELLIGENCE SUMMARY.

(Erase heading not required.)

400th (HIGHLAND) FIELD COY. R.E.

Instructions regarding War Diaries and Intelligence Summaries are contained in F. S. Regs., Part II. and the Staff Manual respectively. Title pages will be prepared in manuscript.

Place	Date	Hour	Summary of Events and Information	Remarks and references to Appendices
VILLERS AU BOIS	15/9/18	9.30 am	Coy Parade 9.30 am. Balance of day spent testing equipment & stores	ff
"	16/9/18	10.50?	The WESTON S. Retd to duties with detachment.	ff
			Training commenced - Staff Sgt. BURTON + G.S. attached to 2 Coy for instruction. A Bryce NCO attached took a Reveille class of 2 hrs for instn. No 3 Sectn. attended a tent. Sub Class for instruction. Balance of Coy on sector company fates.	ff
"	17/9/18		Training carried on. Officers + NCO's prepared demolition scheme for Roque. in ECOIVRES.	ff
"	18/9/18		Musketry shoot. S.R. Smk. - 100 - S.R. Applica 100 + S.R. Rapid 100 S.R. Sgt 2 + 300 at CAMBLAIN L'ABBE Range. Football + training. No 474409 the STAINFORTH G.A. transferred to 529 Field Co R.E.	ff
"	19/9/18		Training continued - 496657 Sgt CARTER G.A. Struck off strength - Wiring nets received from ORE that Sec had relieve 499 Co. in Line.	ff
"	20/9/18		Training continued - 21 Bryce + 2 Ors. from ??? Heavy R.E. Coast.	ff
"	21/9/18		O.C. + Lt FERGUSON + 4 O.R. to PONT de JOUR ? blow in? ? and ? from 458 Field Co. R.E. Training continued - Football in afternoon.	ff
"	22/9/18		Abracourt ? Lieut 5 + 3 O.R. (field S7 B) transferred and to ECOIVRES (+27 F. field 57 B) + Lieut via to L2 PENDU Station to entrain - all other Cancelled + all returned to VILLIERS AU BOIS. 91st DIVISL RE schedule from MARKY INFANTRY SCHOOL	ff

Army Form C. 2118.

WAR DIARY
or
INTELLIGENCE SUMMARY.
(Erase heading not required.)

400TH (HIGHLAND) FIELD COY. R.E.

Place	Date	Hour	Summary of Events and Information	Remarks and references to Appendices
VILLERS AU BOIS	23/9/18		Company Clearing Repair to all Roads in Brigade Yesterday.	/r
			O.C. + 2 Lt. FERGUSON to Div. H.Q. in connection with proposed Pipeline.	
			2 Lt. LAIRD to base L.U.K.	
	24/9/18		Coy hired a/follows:- Tunnel HQ & No 1 & 2 Sections & 6 carpenters work on pipeline Site 6 (incl. 2 coopers)	/r
			ECURIE Balance of 3rd section to PONT DU JOUR #3 C 57 (57 B)	
			12 carpenters worked at JEN MULE. Scottish Coy. plated in Cruciales into Pipeline.	
			400 014 Spr McDONALD J. - 167970 Spr OAKLEY C.R. 498109 Spr OLD W. 184003 Spr CORNELL E. 341 SPT. 61 VICKERS N. wound of shrapnel.	
			241 9441 Spr DAVIDEY A.G. injured useful & dangerous to the chest box expert.	
ECURIE	25/9/18		Section 1 & 2 & Carpenters spent morning filling in old J.O. of CHINESE FIGURES in 22 of 7 and a Outfield with Coal & Objective read. Head left road forward by 20 ft. again to a Bend at INN CROSS ROADS I.7.C.	/r
			Section 1 & 2 & Carpenters sent to forward billet at PONT du JOUR in evening in Lorries.	
			Sqn. + HQ. also moved to forward billet. - O.C. + 2 Lts BOYD & FJ FERGUSON reconnoitre line & fire positions of enemy rear.	
POND du JOUR #3 C 57 Hill 57/3	26/9/18		Company turned out early to clear up road CHINESE fires - company shelter moved by 17 ARGYLL & SUTHERLAND Hrs Highlanders. - Smith H. Arbuthy in line (Lt. GORDON) & Lt. JEFFRAYS.) - 2 hours pulled & mail. Wet. (Smith, jackson) Rept am. coy. not on trade.	

Army Form C. 2118.

WAR DIARY
or
INTELLIGENCE SUMMARY.
(Erase heading not required.)

400TH (HIGHLAND) FIELD COY. R.E.

Instructions regarding War Diaries and Intelligence Summaries are contained in F. S. Regs., Part II. and the Staff Manual respectively. Title pages will be prepared in manuscript.

Place	Date	Hour	Summary of Events and Information	Remarks and references to Appendices
PONT DU JOUR	27/9/18		Coy returned to billets at abt 6.30 a.m. - CAMBRAI attack - success identified by spasmodic visibility. Both in firework.	—
"	28/9/18		Section 1 worked in relation to 137th Bde. H.Q. + heavy day at extreme hour in 4 relief to 44 scofields. Section 3 on load clearing in ROUSE - PANTON Rd & out to ANZAC & CHINESE Pipes. H.Q. of Section 3 + 4 moved to FAMPOUX. (A.28.a.90.65 - Sheet 57.B.) Section 2 moved to Huts near ECURIE + took over NISSEN Huts at DULHR. Section 2	—
FAMPOUX A.28.a.90.65	29/9/18		Section 1. Cable forward to FAMPOUX, from PONT DU JOUR. Transferred, + FAMPOUX to Huts relieved in ST LAURENT BLANGY (G.18.C.0.4 Sheet 57.B.) Section 1 A. yesterday. Section 3 A. yesterday. Section to supply fillet.	—
"			Section R.S. Delany O.C. ditto assumed of Major L.F.E. Lt. GILLESPIE. W. 409/35. Reinforced from Base.	
"	30/9/18		Section A. yesterday. No special movement in the Coy. 249.477 Lt. SOUTHCOTT J.R. 742.212 Lt. MURRAY J.	—

J. Argel Major R.E.
Lt 400 (H) Field Coy.

Army Form C. 2118.

WAR DIARY
or
INTELLIGENCE SUMMARY.
(Erase heading not required.)

400th (HIGHLAND) FIELD COY. R.E.

Summary of Events and Information

Alterations in Company Strength during September

	Offs.	O.R's
Strength at 31st August	4	206
Increase.		
1 O.R. transferred from 225th Fd Coy.		+1
7 " reinforcements from R.E.B.D.		+7
	4	214
Decrease		
1 O.R. transferred to 135th A.T. Coy. R.E.		-1
9 " struck off after 7 days in hospital		-9
1 " transferred to 529th Field Coy. R.E.		-1
1 " " " Medical Base Depot		-1
1 " " " R.E. Base Depot		-1
Strength at 30th September	4	201

CONFIDENTIAL

War Diary of

400ᵀᴴ (Highland) Field Coy. R.E.

from 1ˢᵀ October 1918 to 31ˢᵀ October 1918

Vol 40

WAR DIARY
or
INTELLIGENCE SUMMARY.

(Erase heading not required.)

400TH (HIGHLAND) FIELD COY. R.E.

Army Form C. 2118.

Place	Date	Hour	Summary of Events and Information	Remarks and references to Appendices
FAMPOUX (A.23.a.90.65)	1/10/18		Relief - I Section & Hd. Qrs in ROUEX. R.M.D. & Coy. H.Q.	1/2
"	2/10/18		Nothing doing. Weather stormy. Lt PROUSE & 2nd class 44 & 5 Sec. carry out to late the work details - Transport for ration lorries & office essentials. Weirnes to ECURIE. 494.443. Spr MIDDLE a trans. pr. to 479 Field Coy. 457.856 " DAVIDSON T. trans. off 16 inf. Pk. Coy. moves & work to ECURIE. A 27 c 7 2	1/2
ECURIE (A 27 c 7 2)	3/10/18		Coy. cleaning & repairing equipment &c. No 3 Section receives hope (Bolero beliefs) fr 103 H. fr. Gen.	1/2
"	4/10/18		Raining again - Capt R. W. MCKENZIE returns from leave.	1/2
"	5/10/18		Raining continues - Issue of No 1 & 2 Return Lists Bn - Also 2 horses killed by enemy. Work = TIMB Corres wirspring to cmdright. 400.067 - 2/4 McILWRAITH trf to 2 Mth C/4c. 400287 Spr MITCHELL W trf 5/4c	1/2
"	6/10/18		Church parade. C. of S. 9.30 a.m. - C. of SCOTLAND 11.45 a.m.	1/2
"	7/10/18		No 1 & 2 Section Gas & Coy stalls - No 3 to PORTUGUAY	1/2

Army Form C. 2118.

WAR DIARY
or
INTELLIGENCE SUMMARY.

(Erase heading not required.)

400TH (HIGHLAND) FIELD Coy. R.E.

Place	Date	Hour	Summary of Events and Information	Remarks and references to Appendices
ECURIE	8/10/18		Coy. moved to new billets in RIENCOURT - QUEANT Rd (V.25 C 7.0)(57.8). Intructed relief of Pontoon & Cyclists marched by road under (2/Lt) McCRONE at 11.00 hr. Arrived 16.20 hr. Balance of Coy. with O.C. proceeded 15.30 to Ecoust /0.W.24 - Buses arrived at 19.50. Detentrained at 22.45 & arrived 23.55 hrs. 2/Lt LAURIE rejoined from leave.	M
V.25 c 7.0	9/10/18		Coy. involved in billets. Inspection Car. 1.T.	M
V.25 c 7.0	10/10/18		Coy moved to BOURLON area. Advance Party under 2/Lt FERGUSON Billeted with O.C. reached BOURLON village (2/Lt) McCRONE with Pioneers Transport, Pack Ponies from Lysorels & Pontoon Wagon. to Neauport left Ecourt & hauled via army, army Column at MOEUVRES. Remainder arrived 16.20. Transport 19.40 Coy. HQ established E 6 C 2.1. Sheet 57.C.	M
E 6 c 2.1	11/10/18		Coy moved 15:15 to learn to bivie at 12:15 - detachment charged en route to S.20 C.15. arrived 23.20.	M
J.20 C.15	12/10/18	0600	Coy moved to RAMILLIES & hauled tile light & heavy in bulk 153 Bgde & THUN ST MARTIN. T.15-d 15.10 steel STR & moved back from Bryces to Pontoons stream at hill bridges	M
J.20 C.15	13/10/18		1 section placed at disposal of 153 Bgde. (no shelter.) 2 sections working on Pontoon Tracks from J.10 F.30.60 to J.10.Y.20 & J.T.6 10.40. Section 1 Bivced by the melle from O/C.	M
J.20 c.15	14/10/18		12.00 from no 3 Reln. Allocated to various work of 153 Bgde. to Beauch of Bridge Tram 2 full Lights. in STATION TRACK. lost testles, stones & found hulls. etc. 1st 00 8 for CORNEL IT Reinforcement to G Depot Coy.	M

Army Form C. 2118.

WAR DIARY
or
INTELLIGENCE SUMMARY.

(Erase heading not required.)

400th (HIGHLAND) FIELD COY. R.E.

Instructions regarding War Diaries and Intelligence Summaries are contained in F. S. Regs., Part II. and the Staff Manual respectively. Title pages will be prepared in manuscript.

Place	Date	Hour	Summary of Events and Information	Remarks and references to Appendices
THUN ST MARTIN	15/10/18		Section worked at Yateley & church of St Aybe.	/k.
"	16/10/18		184003 Spr BRISBANE F church of St Aybe.	/k.
"			Work on Yateley	
"	17/10/18		Section 1 joined section No 2 & 4 & others in STATION ROAD. Patrol work at Pleury-lean. Parties of Section & Pleury-lean to IWN. QUARD	/k
"	18/10/18		Q. Yateley — 77223 Dr ALLEMY A.A. & 450141 SPR HARDING T. shell at village.	/k
"			ISST QUIMBE proceeded to Coof St/k.	
"	19/10/18		Section worked at Yateley — OWR decided for C.H.E. State Between bridges. Locker is & Pont Soct, House Ada 7/3a B.G. commenced 183 Bottom Set of O.C. — O.C. & 2 Box Hd. 1:5.75.1.P. found Hos- Every had commenced return in un-food. 2nd Lieuts. J. Cy & Crew in Coll & Cooper & Lieut St MAND & them had in had IT how to recommend to all River Selle in arrival at FREIR a.w. POIRIER to Pont Husson had was shut a mile from Rue. to Returned to Lieut St MAND & hed his Company before them in the village. Received into the Bot W.R. had worked forward & FREIR a.w. POIRIER to send it COOPER Forward & May at Bot HR with Instruction & Recommend take as soon as further detection.	/k
LIEU ST MAND	20/10/18		Lt. COOPER offic 2 all ranks reconnoitred line west of Upl & O.C. Section & forward to Run & big credit to meline field bridge from Colonel's Copy around from a Volling Crew as us R. & things had for a as &	/k

(A5093) Wt. W12839/M1293 750,000. 1/17. D. D. & L., Ltd. Forms/C.2118/14.

WAR DIARY
or
INTELLIGENCE SUMMARY.

(Erase heading not required.)

400TH (HIGHLAND) FIELD COY. R.E.

Army Form C. 2118.

Place	Date	Hour	Summary of Events and Information	Remarks and references to Appendices
LIEU ST AMAND	20/10/17		Selected another site for a Pilots Bridge - This was erected during the afternoon by N° BOYD & LANDER. No 2 R/A SECTION. Tonight night patrol LIEN ST AMAND by COY. M°CRONE. Billets of Coy went in dawn under 2/Lt FROTE on horse 5/Lt Hamilton Hunter also at PONT de VALENCIENNES. 2/Lt BRENNAN remained in LIEU ST AMAND - BOICHAIN R°. CAPT M°CRONE " MRQR of DOUCHY & Lee 746474 The following reinforcements reported for duty. Sappers - 212619 CATON J. 27736 MARTIN A. 466570 M°GUIRL 461420 BRONSROCK A. 472 OFS TURNER W.A. 463920 DAVIDSON N. 465953 SHARPE J. 466590 NIXON F.	/12
"	21/10/17		Lt BOYD transferred to 404/Field Co. R.E. as 2/C. OC + all officers with L-DOUCHY + took over & Capt in Rest Billets in their lines. Returned to Billet VIEU BILLET &-CEO & HOUSE REPAIRS - an new hut was found at HIBLET & 404 Eth R Engr railway & Builders Of Behrr Nes R VIEU BILLETdown. In rear lines - CARVOYAGE 1530 hours - Billets of Coy found by Col. M°CRONE + 1375 H. Regimental 448861 Sn. GOODWIN A. 466140 GREEN W.H. 258730 LONGSHAW T. at 0100 hr. Some kind of sham attack was likely - all ranks were ordered to the Shelters - This was intercepted & taken to shelters on - as to hostile aircraft - cannot in air positions of Bridge & Railway halts or Hospitals. Enemy aircraft are now chased F & RWD weekly.	/12
DOUCHY	22/10/17			/12

WAR DIARY or INTELLIGENCE SUMMARY

Army Form C. 2118.

400TH (HIGHLAND) FIELD COY. R.E.

Place	Date	Hour	Summary of Events and Information	Remarks and references to Appendices
DOUCHY.	22/10/18		O.C. Wheeler & 3 Recces Conference re/s. attack & Veteran MANQ.	/L
"	23/10/18		NOMNY. Heavy Motor Shewed & Vexp at 10.30 hrs. – Carried on with Head work. Heavy Rain – Harry W. & W. Abstract – live Coke from Commencement 422½ hrs. Actual Labour Hours 34. – (2 relays) CE 22 Coy & inspected bridge. Mar 72/61 – 1224 Manhours – 17 Man Hours per foot run.	/L
"	24/10/18		O.C. COOPER inspected helper demolished in main road in THIANT. Rt. Cooper & No. 1 Section commenced work on Abutment. Central Pier at 1400 hrs. Carried on till 21 hrs. when rebels slackened by shell fire. – 1 relay carried on repairing rainy hole in Bridge in DOUCHY. + every screws or hand rails. 2/L LAURIE & No. 2 Section erected WELDON TRESTLE BRIDGE in R. ECAILLON in SOUTH of THIANT. CPL MATHIESON & 10 men went to Corps in field. Abhhued & help at THIANT. Bridge to be cont. by Div. Bleary at 1100 hrs. as no material could be had through Corps to the demolition by Bridge in PYRAMID DE OSNAIN – THIANT Rd. Hrs 2A Clones & 1800 hrs or 2. RECONITION of No. 4 Section took over work or erected hutts or substructure of bridge relaying at 22.30 hrs.	/L
"	25/10/18		R. COOPER & No. 1/Sect. carried on with superst at 0500 hrs. to Traffic running at 0730 hrs. Actual labour hours 23. – (1 relay) Total time from commencement 442 hrs. – Actual Labour hours under 23. – (1 relay) 328 Manhours or 6·12 Manhours per foot run. CE XXII CORPS inspected helper & was fully satisfied to surfaced heavy track hand cart & cyclist.	/L

Army Form C. 2118.

WAR DIARY
or
INTELLIGENCE SUMMARY.
(Erase heading not required.)

400TH (HIGHLAND) FIELD Coy. R.E.

Instructions regarding War Diaries and Intelligence Summaries are contained in F. S. Regs., Part II. and the Staff Manual respectively. Title pages will be prepared in manuscript.

Place	Date	Hour	Summary of Events and Information	Remarks and references to Appendices
DOUCHY	26/9/18		152 & 153 Bgdes attacked ANNEUX — O.C. 1st LANARK R.E. passed to overlooke the Road-Railway Crossing h.h.w. MARCOING-RAILWAY Rd. & to OVERLOOKING-FINDRE Rd. C. & Capt. 152 Bgde wiped 152 & 3 Bgdes & Lt. FERGUSON who & relieve stopped & 152 Bgde moved forward to THANT. Wire kept repaired for CCE between Cp & THANT & forward cancelled —	W.
"	27/9/18		Men moved to the reserves on Road & Str. herewasted to do the work of THANT-DOUCH R.C. LOWRIE commenced Wiring (Road & traffic) 2nd 28 flanters received heavy Rain in DOUCHY BRIDGE opened — 400 O.R. the BANNERMAN & Hartford & 404 held in Cl.	
"	28/9/18		OC., OC Cottrs Course, & Mens of all relieve held to THANT & out on her Field, work of J6 c 24 & where a Will Rifle Bridge new ... No. 1 Section flored a trucks are stationed note J. 22 c 04 to clear. - Hoisted the maintenance of DOUCHY & THANT heavy bridge and relieves & ASS held to the (40 Str.) Definition between DOUCHY heavy bridge & filled in field works repair.	
"	29/9/18		Cpletion bday at J6 c 24 for mending infantry rifle to OC Cpress - 1 NC 3 O.R. charles (games) disposal to 152 Bgde.	
"	30/9/18		2nd heavy Rain to 9 a.m. 16 c 24 abt 21 week — Return wholes fearops By rifleman Lutn. Mrs Griffith - Wicklo etc. Clothing Report despinated mahurs shiel 17.58.1 BANNERMAN L. 405 3772 RIDDICK J. 139775 — NELSON. J.	

WAR DIARY
or
INTELLIGENCE SUMMARY.
(Erase heading not required.)

Army Form C. 2118.

Place	Date	Hour	Summary of Events and Information	Remarks and references to Appendices
DOMART	31/10/18		Coy marched to PAILLENCOURT 07.35 hr - arrived 11.00 hr - HQ established at N.14.d.88. (Sheet 57A)	

Alteration in Company strength during October.

	O.H.	O.R.
Strength at 30th Sept 1918	4	201
INCREASE		
Reinforcement from Base Depot		+15
" Hospital I.O.R.		+1
	4	214
DECREASE		
By Transfer to M.M.R. I.O.R.		-1
" 404th Field Coy. I.O.R.		-1
" 499th I.O.R.		-1
" 404th O.H.	-1	
Struck off after 7 days in hospital 7.O.R.		-7
Strength at 31st October	6	204

CONFIDENTIAL

War Diary

of

400th (Highland) Field Coy

From 1st November To 30th November 1918

Army Form C. 2118.

WAR DIARY
or
INTELLIGENCE SUMMARY.
(Erase heading not required.)

400TH (HIGHLAND) FIELD COY. R.E.

Place	Date 1918	Hour	Summary of Events and Information	Remarks and references to Appendices
PAILLENCOURT M.19.d.88 (Sheet 51.A)	1/11/18		Orders received from C.R.E. at 04.20 hrs for 10.6 to proceed to TILLOY R.E. PARK. To entrain on arrival. Bridging Officer. O.G. left at 08.45 hrs. Ye turning at 12.45. Immediately orders Coy to move to NEUVILLE ST REMY. Coy detraining in TILLOY R.E. PARK under orders C.R.E. XXII CORPS.	A.
NEUVILLE ST REMY. A.3.a.9.8. (Sheet 51A 1/40,000)	2/11/18		Coy parade 10.00 hrs to proceed to R.E. PARK. to work on pierce Bridge. Coy O.R. now reported as numbered (as per reel) from 31st Oct to that of January, i.e:- SAPPERS: 360,065. MULLERVY J, 155,650. SIBBALD G, 765,970. DAVIDSON H.	B.
Do	3/11/18		Coy parade at 08.30 hrs & continue work on pierce Bridge	B/.
Do	4/11/18		Coy work in yesterday. Order received from C.E. CORPS at 14.40 hrs to have H.E. pier and bridges ready for following day. Fifteen men turned out at 18.00 hrs and worked until midnight	M.
Do	5/11/18		Men turned out from midnight to carry on work. Remainder of Coy paraded 08.30 hrs & carried on work at R.E. PARK.	B/.
Do	6/11/18		Work continued at R.E. PARK.	B/.
Do	7/11/18		Work as yesterday. II. LIEUT. R.G.T. WATSON joined Coy on transfer from 404TH FIELD COY.R.E.	D/.
Do	8/11/18		Work as yesterday. No. 63,924 L/Cpl. COLLYER.A. & No. 359,955. SAPR CLARKE W.R. struck off strength. No. 400,523. CORPL	D/.
Do	9/11/18		Work as 8TH. At 15.30 hrs Coy went to Game seat at FAUBORG ST ROCH (Sheet 51B S.29.Y.5.)	B/.
Do	10/11/18		Work as 9TH Coy played 401. FIELD COY R.E. at football on home ground. Result 2 goals each.	B/.
Do	11/11/18		Work as 10TH Official notification of cessation of hostilities received. No. 400,110 A/CORPL GLASGOW'S injured & off on sick.	B/.
Do	12/11/18		Coy moved at 09.45 hrs to PAILLENCOURT & took over duties of 404TH FIELD COY.R.E.	B/.
PAILLENCOURT M.19.d.4.1 (Sheet 51A 1/40,000)	13/11/18		To-day observed as a holiday (in lieu of 11th instant). No. 400051. SERGT GRIFFEN A & (No. 400,523. CORPL MATHIESON.A. awarded MILITARY MEDALS. 15. R.E. entertaining in 51st Divl CROSS COUNTRY RACE which resulted in the R.E.'s (Divl) obtaining 1st place on points	B/.

(A/3092) Wt. W12839/M1293. 75,000. 1/17. D.D. & L., Ltd. Forms/C.2118/14.

Army Form C. 2118.

WAR DIARY
or
INTELLIGENCE SUMMARY.
(Erase heading not required.)

400th (HIGHLAND) FIELD COY R.E.

Instructions regarding War Diaries and Intelligence Summaries are contained in F. S. Regs., Part II. and the Staff Manual respectively. Title pages will be prepared in manuscript.

Place	Date	Hour	Summary of Events and Information	Remarks and references to Appendices
PAILLENCOURT N.19.d.4.	14/11/18		Coy cleaning Wagons & Equipment	
D°	15/11/18		Cleaning Coy. Equipment. Coy at H.Q's. across country paper chase.	
D°	16/11/18		Work on cleaning billets &c. Rifle musketry at 14.00 hrs. repeated at 15.00 hrs by I.O.M. at THUN LEVEQUE. 402.208 DRIVER DEY. A. attached CL.	
D°	17/11/18		09.30 hrs. Coy. E. Service. 13.00 hrs. Selection Sports for 400, 401, 407 FIELD COYS.	
D°	18/11/18		10.00 hrs. Inspection by G.O.C. DIV. 3. 526, 129. SAPR CLAYSON. H. from R.E. Base &c. reinforcement	
D°	19/11/18		Baths for Coys at HORDAIN, in forenoon. 5 novice water 1701 Coy in afternoon. Recent 701 in	
D°	20/11/18		Work on Billet & village improvements. Work on schemes on. 5 O.R. from 407 Field Coy attached. 400, 014. L/Cpl McDONALD reinforcement from Hospital	
D°	21/11/18		Sections I & II on Physical Service until two short arms. III & IV. work on schemes for improving billets. Ing of harness trees for Drive Sports.	
D°	22/11/18		3 Sections Routemarch. 1 Section Rifle ? K by L/Coporan Ing of two team practice under O. pic. D. our of 701 Coy in afternoon. Practicing schemes on the date of Germany at 17-30 hrs by LIEUT. SIMRDH.	
D°	23/11/18		Sections I & II on Billet improvements Sections III & IV on Physical exercise Ing of war practice in afternoon. Lecture at 17-30 on afternoon. Want to work by REV. W. GILLIESON. LIEUT. C.G.T. COOPER awarded M.C.	
D°	24/11/18		Church parade for Pres by teams at 11.40 hrs. Ing of hour practice in afternoon.	
D°	25/11/18		Coy on Billet improvements & procuring timber.	

Army Form C. 2118.

WAR DIARY
or
INTELLIGENCE SUMMARY.
(Erase heading not required.)

400TH (HIGHLAND) FIELD COY. R.E.

Instructions regarding War Diaries and Intelligence Summaries are contained in F. S. Regs., Part II. and the Staff Manual respectively. Title pages will be prepared in manuscript.

Place	Date	Hour	Summary of Events and Information	Remarks and references to Appendices
PAILLENCOURT M.19.c.4.1. (SHEET 51A) YAPOO	26/11/18.		Lectures I & II on Physical Training & Ceremonial Drill. III & IV on Forest Improvements. Lecture by LIEUT. SIMEON on Book Construction at 19.30 hr. Following reinforcements arrived from Base - Sappers. 480699 HARVEY H.T., 360,065. MULLERY F., 147,130. HAY G. 98,143 NELSON L., 103,040. McKENZIE.G., 397,899. MAYOU.C., 253,230. DRIVER. HOPPER R.W.	
Do.	27/11/18.		09.00 hr O.C's inspection of Coy. Coy Drice. 13.00 hr Preliminary day of Div'l. Sports.	
Do.	28/11/18.		Coy cleaning equipment. Baths at 14.00 hrs. Coy attended lecture Schoolroom by MAJOR F.W. WATT (1/4TH GORDON HIGHRS) on "THE DAILY NEWSPAPER". Instructions recd. from 153RD Infy Brigade regarding Div'l move to new area EAST OF MONS. Capt McCRONE visited Brigade H.Q. during afternoon to get particulars regarding the above party.	
Do.	29/11/18.		CAPT R.W. McCRONE N.C., I MOUNTED N.C.O. & 2 SAPPERS left this morning to proceed to HOLDEING GOEGNIES area (18. HAMUR SHEET 1/100,000) as advance billetting party. Coy. on te march during forenoon. Lecture by CAPT CHRISTIE on "ROBT BURNS" at 401ST Coy H.Q. at 19.30 hrs. Coy boys entertained in the Schoolroom at 18.30 hours	
Do.	30/11/18.		Coy attend Divl Sports at THUN LEVEQUE, commencing at 10.00 hrs.	

(Continued over)

Army Form C. 2118.

WAR DIARY
or
INTELLIGENCE SUMMARY.

(Erase heading not required.)

400TH (HIGHLAND) FIELD COY. R.E.

Summary of Events and Information

Alterations in Comp.ny/Strength during November. 1918.

	Off.	O.R.
Strength at 31-10-18.	6	204
Increase. Reinforcements		+ 10
Transferred	+ 1	
	7	214
Decrease Wounded (Gun.)		- 3. O.R.
Evac.sick.		- 5. O.R. = 8.
Strength on 30th Nov/18.	7	209

30TH November 1918

MAJOR R.E.,
O.C. 400TH (HIGHLAND) FIELD COY. R.E.

CONFIDENTIAL

WAR DIARY
of
400TH (Highland) FIELD COY. R.E.
for
DECEMBER 1918

WAR DIARY or INTELLIGENCE SUMMARY.

Army Form C. 2118.

400TH (HIGHLAND) FIELD COY R.E.

(Erase heading not required.)

Instructions regarding War Diaries and Intelligence Summaries are contained in F.S. Regs., Part II. and the Staff Manual respectively. Title pages will be prepared in manuscript.

Place	Date	Hour	Summary of Events and Information	Remarks and references to Appendices
PAILLENCOURT M19.C.H.1 Sheet 51A 1/40,000	1/12/18	09.30	Company Blanket and iron ration inspection	I/1
		14.30	O.C. and 2/Lt R.G.T. WATSON attended a conference of O.C. Companies and Company Education Officers held at 401st FIELD COY. H.Q. C.R.E. present.	I/2
	2/12/18	09.30	Sections work on cleaning wagons.	
		11.00	Horse and harness inspection by O.C. During the afternoon the Company football team played 'B' Coy M.G. Batt. The game resulted in a win for the latter by 2 goals to 0. Failed to home reinforcement 70.359,955 Spr CLARKE W.R.	I/2
Do	3/12/18	09.00	Sections paraded for inspection. Dress drill order. After inspection they carried on with Company & Ceremonial drill. The following promotions were published in orders 400,100 Sergt CRAIG G. 400,196 Corpl ROBERTSON W.H. 400,113 2/Corpl DUNCAN A.G. 400,520 2/Corpl HAY R. 400,035 2/Corpl FISHER A.C. 400,064 2/Corpl McILWRAITH J. 400,135 L/Cpl GILLESPIE W. 400,032 L/Cpl TAIT A. 400,289 L/Cpl MITCHELL W.	I/3
Do	4/12/18	08.45	Sections worked on Billets and repair to streets in village.	I/3
Do	5/12/18	09.00	Sections worked as yesterday. All Bridging and G.S. wagons turned out to cart material. 25 other ranks attached to Company for notes sources, at their different trades from battalions of the 153rd H'land Brigade.	I/3
Do	6/12/18	09.00	Section IV, N.C.O. joiners, bricklayers and infantry paraded under WILLIAM LAURIE work was commenced on several damaged houses, repairing roofs walls and floors.	I/4
		09.30	Sections I, III & IV work as yesterday. Lt C.G.T. COOPER M.C. & 2/Lt E.M.F. FERGUSSON rejoined from leave	I/2

(A7092) Wt. W1859/M1293. 75,000. 11/17. D.D. & L., Ltd. Forms/C.2118/14.

WAR DIARY
or
INTELLIGENCE SUMMARY.
(Erase heading not required.)

Army Form C. 2118.

400TH (HIGHLAND) FIELD COY. R.E.

Place	Date	Hour	Summary of Events and Information	Remarks and references to Appendices
PAILLENCOURT M.19.c.4.1 Sheet 51A 1/40,000	7/12/18	09.00	Company N.C.O. joiners, bricklayers and masons paraded with Company and carried on work as yesterday.	22
		09.30	Sections paraded and worked on salvage under section officers. An inter-section furanade football competition was run during the afternoon. The following games were played 7/, Sect.III v Sect.I, Sect. IV v Sect. II	21
Do.	8/12/18	08.00	Drummed section and infantry attacked & proceeded to MVV for baths	21
		09.00	Other sections section exercise and a bath. The football tournament was continued. M.G.W. Sect. IV, Sect. II v Sect. I	
Do.	9/12/18	09.00	Work on houses carried on as yesterday	21
		09.30	Sections worked on repairs to streets in village.	
Do.	10/12/18	10.30	O.C. F. LAURIE attended a conference amongst C.R.E. of 401st FIELD COY. M.S., to arrange a programme of inter-Company sports. OFFICERS from each Company.	22
		17.30	Lecture by MEDICAL OFFICER on VENEREAL, in village school. This lecture was followed by a concert. The following N.C.O.s were awarded the MILITARY MEDAL. No. 400,100 SERG. CRAIG G., No.400,261 L/CPL. FISHER W. Work on houses as yesterday.	23
Do.	11/12/18	09.00	Company paraded for route march. Dress drill order. Infantry and Coy N.C.Os carried on as yesterday	15

Army Form C. 2118.

WAR DIARY
or
INTELLIGENCE SUMMARY.
(Erase heading not required.)

400TH (HIGHLAND) FIELD COY. R.E.

Place	Date	Hour	Summary of Events and Information	Remarks and references to Appendices
PAILLENCOURT M.9. C.H.I Sheet 51ᴮ 1/40,000	12/12/18	09.00	Infantry as yesterday. Sections repaired streets at entrance to village. The following N.C.O. and men proceeded to England for demobilization. M/4,348 Sergt Cunningham J. M12,392 Driver Craig G.	/L
	13/12/18		400,530 (C.R.P.) Robertson J. Appointed A/Sergt vice M14,378 Sergt Cunningham J. and posted to Section 2.	/M
		09.00	Infantry and N.C.O.'s as yesterday	/M
		09.00 to 10.00	Sections on Physical Training	/L
		10.30	Company inspection by O.C. Sections then carried on with Company and ceremonial drill.	
		12.30		
		14.00	Harness inspection by C.R.E. The team competition was won by Sectⁿ 4. The G.S. team being second.	/B
			A football match between Sectⁿs I & II, resulted in a draw, 2 goals each	
Do.	14/12/18	08.00	Company Parade for baths at HORDAIN. (M.1.9.a.) Sheet 51ᴮ 1/40,000.	/L
Do.	15/12/18	—	Church parades during forenoon. An inter-section cross country event was run off during the afternoon, which resulted in a win for Section 2.	/L
Do.	16/12/18	09.50		/M
		10.00	Inspection parade. Company and ceremonial drill	
		10.30		
		12.30		

Army Form C. 2118.

WAR DIARY
or
INTELLIGENCE SUMMARY.
(Erase heading not required.)

400TH (HIGHLAND) FIELD COY. R.E.

Instructions regarding War Diaries and Intelligence Summaries are contained in F. S. Regs., Part II. and the Staff Manual respectively. Title pages will be prepared in manuscript.

Place	Date	Hour	Summary of Events and Information	Remarks and references to Appendices
PAILLENCOURT M.19.C.4.I. Sheet 51A 1/40000	16/12/18 (cont'd)	—	No. 459,395 Spr. HUGHES R.T. proceeded to England for demobilization. A shorthand class was commenced. A debate was held in lecture room. Subject; "Is professionalism good for sport?" the affirmative was pronounced winner. Major J.T. ARGENT M.C. R.E. proceeded on leave to England.	£3
Do.	17/12/18		A demolition party of 1 N.C.O. and 4 men proceeded to HORDAIN (M.19.a. Sheet 51A 1/40000) to remove dangerous wall.	Puzzle
Do.	18/12/18	09.00	14 other ranks from units of 153rd INFANTRY BRIGADE attached to Company for trades refresher courses. Work done on damaged buildings. Sections paraded for work on billets and repairs to streets. Football, inter-section league, Section 2, 4 goals Section 3, 3 goals.	
Do.		09.00	Infantry attacked work as yesterday, and a Company N.C.O.'s Section paraded for route march. Route via, WASNES-au-BAC, WAVRECHAIN, BOUCHAIN, HORDAIN & PAILLENCOURT.	Puzzle
Do.	19/12/18	09.00	Cycle inspection parade. A lecture on 'DEMOBILIZATION' was delivered to each section during forenoon. Football, inter section league. H.Q. 4 goals Section 1, 0 goals. Debate "That nationalization of railways is desirable, was won in the affirmative.	Puzzle

WAR DIARY
or
INTELLIGENCE SUMMARY.

(Erase heading not required.)

Army Form C. 2118.

400TH (HIGHLAND) FIELD COY R.E.

Place	Date	Hour	Summary of Events and Information	Remarks and references to Appendices
PAILLENCOURT M.19.C.4.1 Sheet 51.B 1/40,000	20/12/18	09.00	Infantry as yesterday. Lectures as yesterday. 1 Lt. T. DUNSIRE R.E. left for refresher course at RAILWAY WORKSHOPS, AUDRICQ. (3.A. HAZEBROUCK S.A. 1/100,000)	Ruche
	21/12/18	08.00	A Company dance was held in the schoolroom during the evening. Parade for baths. I.M.C.O. and H. men from section to work on repairs to roof of Div. H.Q. Mess, IWUY. (M.35. Sheet 51.A 1/40,000) A whist drive was held in lecture room during the evening.	Ruche
Do.	22/12/18	-	Church parades. An inter Company football match with 401st Field Coy. was played in the afternoon, and resulted in a win for 400th Coy. 3 goals to 2.	Ruche
Do.	23/12/18	09.00	Party work at IWUY as Saturday. Infantry attached returned to units on completion of course. Capt. R.W. McCROFIE M.C. reported from forward area.	Ruche
		09.00	Company parade for Physical Training.	
		10.30	Inspection parade Company & Ceremonial drill.	
		12.30	Football match with 404th Field Coy. ended in a draw, no scoring, the game having been stopped owing to heavy rain. Debate in lecture room Subject: "That the half penny press exerts a harmful influence on the British population" turned down by the negative.	

Army Form C. 2118.

WAR DIARY
or
INTELLIGENCE SUMMARY.
(Erase heading not required.)

400TH (HIGHLAND) FIELD Coy. R.E.

Place	Date	Hour	Summary of Events and Information	Remarks and references to Appendices
PAILLENCOURT M.19.C.H.1. Sheet 51A 1/40,000	24/12/18	—	N.C.O. and fatigue party marched out course for interCompany cross country run. A demolition party reported to S.A.A. Section D.A.C. at NEUVILLE SUR L'ESCAUT (I20. Sheet 51A 1/40,000) to destroy dud shells.	Postde
		09.30	Company parade, fatigue duties. An inter-section tug-of-war competition was won by Head Quarters section.	
		14.30	Inter Company cross-country race, won by No.1st FIELD Coy. R.E.	
		11.30	Elementary French class.	
Do.	25/12/18		Christmas Day, general holiday. A football match was played between H.Q. Section and 1st Section in which ended in a win for the latter 1 goal to 0. The civilians in our billeting area, were invited by the Company to dinner at 17.00 hours. Forty guests were entertained. Lt. G.F. Cooper M.C. presided.	Posted
Do.	26/12/18	10.00	Section paraded for route march. Route taken via ESWARS, THUN - LEVECQUE + PAILLENCOURT. A party of 1 N.C.O. and 5 men proceed to IWUY to destroy dud shells. No. 400,110 Cpl. GLASGOW S. posted to 20TH T.F. DEPOT 3.12.18.	
		18.30	A debate was held in lecture room. Subject "should bachelors be taxed" was won by the negative. Party carried on watch repairs to houses in IWUY.	Posted

Army Form C. 2118.

WAR DIARY
or
INTELLIGENCE SUMMARY.
(Erase heading not required.)

400TH (HIGHLAND) FIELD COY. R.E.

Instructions regarding War Diaries and Intelligence Summaries are contained in F. S. Regs., Part II. and the Staff Manual respectively. Title pages will be prepared in manuscript.

Place	Date	Hour	Summary of Events and Information	Remarks and references to Appendices
PAILLENCOURT M.19.C.H.1. Sheet 51A	27/12/18	—	Repairs to Roads in NUY carried on. Section 3 under 1/Lt E.M.FERGUSSON R.E.(T) worked on destruction of dud shells. A whist drive was held during the evening, in the lecture room.	Roche
Do.	28/12/18	08.00	Company paraded for baths at HORDAIN. Sec. 3 after baths carried on as yesterday. Owing to bad weather the inter-Company Rug.F. was completion had to be cancelled. No. 460,950 Spr. McGUIRE A. evacuated sick and struck off strength.	Roche
Do.	29/12/18	—	Church Parades. The following men posted to 204TH T.F DEPOT No 2208 DR.E.A.	Roche
Do.	30/12/18	—	12 other ranks attached for trades refresher course.. Sections worked on cleaning and repairing wagons. 1/Lieut. A.M.LAURIE proceeded to forward area. The first Divisional Football League match was played during the afternoon between DIV. R.E and 1/8 ROYAL SCOTS. the latter won 2 goals to 0. A debate was held during the evening in the lecture room. Subject:- "Should Co-operative Societies be encouraged" was won by negative.	Roche
Do.	31/12/18	—	Divisional holiday for Hogmanay. The Divisional Cross-country run was started at 10.30 hours. Capt. R.W. McCRONE captained the R.E. team	Roche

(A7092). Wt. W2839/M1293. 75 1/0.0. 1/17. D. D. & L, Ltd. Forms/C.2118/14.

Army Form C. 2118.

WAR DIARY
or
INTELLIGENCE SUMMARY.
(Erase heading not required.)

400TH (HIGHLAND) FIELD COY. R.E.

Instructions regarding War Diaries and Intelligence Summaries are contained in F. S. Regs., Part II. and the Staff Manual respectively. Title pages will be prepared in manuscript.

Place	Date	Hour	Summary of Events and Information	Remarks and references to Appendices

PAILLENCOURT M.19.C.M.1 Sheet 51A 1/40,000			Alterations in Company Strength during Decr. 1918.
			
			           OFF. O.R.
			 Company Strength at 30.11.18 Y 209
			 Increase. Reinforcements, 1.O.R. + 1
			              Y 210
			 Decrease. 3.O.R. demobilged - 3
			     1" evacuated sick - 1
			 Company Strength at 31.12.18 Y 206
			
			 flr Shepstone Capt. R.E.
			 for O.C. 400th Field Coy R.E.	

CONFIDENTIAL

WAR DIARY
of
400TH (Highland) Field Coy. R.E.
for
JANUARY 1919

Army Form C. 2118.

WAR DIARY
or
INTELLIGENCE SUMMARY.
(Erase heading not required.)

400th (HIGHLAND) FIELD COY. R.E.

Place	Date	Hour	Summary of Events and Information	Remarks and references to Appendices
PAILLENCOURT N.19.C.H.I. Sheet 51A 1/40,000	1/1/19	11.00	Sections loaded wagons	m
	2/1/19	09.30	Inspection parade, e/6 mounted section Dress Drill order S.H. other ranks, under 1st Lieut FERGUSSON R.E. (1) proceeded to motor lorry to new area to work on 103rd Inf. Bde. area, fitting up cookhouses own etc. C.O. reported from leave.	m
		09.30	Remainder of Sappers cleaned wagons	m
	3/1/19	09.30	9.H. infantry attached for 2 Wheeler course, carried on with repairs to houses	m
		08.00	Company paraded for baths. Infantry as yesterday	m
	4/1/19		Holiday	m
	5/1/19		Church parades for all ranks.	m
	6/1/19	09.30	Infantry as Friday. Sappers cleaned wagons. Orders received from 153rd Inf. Bde. that move to new area on 8.1.19 is not required. Capt. R.W. McCROHE M.C. visited Bde. H.Q. to obtain particulars of move.	m
	7/1/19	09.30	Infantry attached returned to units. Sappers loaded wagons. 1 mounted N.C.O. Left in advance to billet the transport. Lt. C.G.T. COOPER M.C. R.E.(T) moved off.	m
	8/1/19	06.15	Transport under Lt. C.G.T. COOPER M.C. R.E.(T) moved off. The leading horses of 09.30 hours arrived ONNAING (VALENCIENNES Sheet 2.H.) 14.30 hours. CROIX ST. MARIE (I.18 a.51) was reached at 09.10 150 mm.	m
		09.00	Sappers cleaned out billets. Lorry for baggage reported 16.00 hours	m

Army Form C. 2118.

WAR DIARY
or
INTELLIGENCE SUMMARY.

(Erase heading not required.)

400TH (HIGHLAND) FIELD COY. R.E.

Instructions regarding War Diaries and Intelligence
Summaries are contained in F. S. Regs., Part II.
and the Staff Manual respectively. Title pages
will be prepared in manuscript.

Place	Date	Hour	Summary of Events and Information	Remarks and references to Appendices
PAILLENCOURT T.19.C.H.1 Sheet 51º 1/40,000	9/1/19	08.30	Sappers paraded, full marching order, and proceeded under O.C. to IWUY, and joined Bde. column at embussing point (T.29.C.3.H Sheet 51º) at 09.45 hours. Convoy moved off 09.30 hours, 1 hour halt, travelled via VALENCIENNES, MONS, and arrived at MANAGE, (Sheet H.6 Belgium I.1.C.) 16.10 hours. Sappers billeted and Coy H.Q established at I.C.S.2.	Ph
MANAGE I.C.S.2. Sheet H6 BELGIUM 1/40,000		08.00 09.30	Baggage Coy left PAILLENCOURT and arrived MANAGE 14.30 hours. Transport B/C UNHAINS and arrived JEMAPPES, (VALENCIENNES Sheet 2.R.) 13.50 hours	
	10/1/19	09.00	Parties employed at SENEFFE (Sheet H6 C.1 + J.) and FAMILLEUREUX (Sheet H6 B23.G.) erecting sheds and cookhouses for infantry battalions. Remainder of sappers making batmandah's cleaning out stables etc. Transport B/C JEMAPPES, and arrived MANAGE 16.30 hours.	Ph
	11/1/19	09.00	Sappers work as yesterday, and cleaned wagons	Ph
	12/1/19	09.45 09.30	Church parade for R. C.S.1 Remainder of company paraded for inspection by O.C. Dress drill order.	Ph
	13/1/19	09.00	Sappers paraded. Clean fatigue dress. Men and carpenters carried on making latrine seats, sentry boxes etc. The following went proceeded for demobilisation. 400,223 Dr MCKENZIE J. 458,995 Spr BIGGINS T. 429,426 Spr. EDWARDS F. 486,524 Spr. YOUNG F.W. The company Lieut. J. WYATT Kearn was deputed E Mor of Field Coy R.E.	Ph

(A7093). Wt. W12839/M1293. 75,000. 1/17. D.D. & L., Ltd. Forms/C.2118/14.

Army Form C. 2118.

WAR DIARY
or
INTELLIGENCE SUMMARY.
(Erase heading not required.)

400TH (HIGHLAND) FIELD Coy. R.E.

Instructions regarding War Diaries and Intelligence Summaries are contained in F. S. Regs., Part II. and the Staff Manual respectively. Title pages will be prepared in manuscript.

Place	Date	Hour	Summary of Events and Information	Remarks and references to Appendices
MANAGE	14/1/19	09.00	Work carried on in Section billets and stables. Work at SENEFFE and FAMILLEUREUX completed. The following were demobilised -	JM
I.I.C.5.2. Sheet H6 BELGIUM 1/40,000			402,215 Dr. THOM D.P. HA?,637 Spr. MORRIS E.I. Horses classified by A.D.V.S.	
	15/1/19	09.00	Joiners carried on as before. Remainder as before.	JM
	16/1/19	09.00	Work on yesterday. Horses of certain classes returned to Y.O. The following was posted (a) home establishment :- 244,453 Spr. McCOLL W.	JM
	17/1/19	09.00	Work as yesterday. The following men on leave to U.K. were returned for rollcall. 420,669 Spr. HARVEY M.T. 584699 Spr. MAYOU C. 420,150 Sap. CHISHOLM D. 145,437 Spr. ROEBUCK H.	JM
	18/1/19	10.30	Company paraded for inspection dress - drill order. A football match was attempted between the Coy team and 1/3rd F.d AMBULANCE, but had to be stopped owing to bad weather.	JM
	19/1/19	10.15	Lecture by C.R.E. on "DEMOBILIZATION" and the R.E. WAR MEMORIAL. CAPT. WIMSCROFE M.G.R.(T) and 400,015 Cpl. MITCHELL awarded the Croix de Guerre	JM
		11.00	Church parade.	
	20/1/19	09.00	Joiners and carpenters carried on as before. Remainder of Company on fatigues etc. The following men were demobilized :- 400,136 2/Cpl. McCULLOCH D. 101,149 Dr. CARDWELL A. 98,143 Spr. NELSON L. 420,621 Spr. ARCHER F. 494,125 Spr. GROVE G.	JM

Army Form C. 2118.

WAR DIARY
or
INTELLIGENCE SUMMARY.

(Erase heading not required.)

400TH (HIGHLAND) FIELD COY R.E.

Place	Date	Hour	Summary of Events and Information	Remarks and references to Appendices
MANAGE I.I.C.5.2 Sheet H6 1/40,000.	21/1/19	09.00	Joiners on yesterday Bricklayers and masons worked on chairs to stables. Infantry work on fitting up workshop. The following men proceeded for demobilization:- H20, 550 Spr. PARLOW H. H34, 491 Spr. WILLIAMS T. H65, 392 Spr. RUDDICK J. HH8, 410 Spr. FOYSTER F. G9, 698 Spr. BOOLS J. 519, 064 Spr. RENDLE F.	fm
	22/1/19	09.00	Work as yesterday. The following men proceeded for demobilization 199, 243 Spr. DALE M.F. 388, 294 DYMERCHANT A. 212, 163 Spr. WICKETT F. H00284 L/Cpl. MITCHELL W. The returning officer was demobilized Capt. R.W. McCRONE M.C. R.E.(T)	fm
	23/1/19	09.00	Work as yesterday. The Coy Football team defeated a team from 9th FIELD COY by 2 goals to 1. Match played at MORLANWELZ (O.I.C.S.H.Q.)	fm
	24/1/19	09.00	Work as yesterday. A french class was held from 11.00 to 12.00 A meeting of the Company was held to discuss the question of a 'R.E. MEMORIAL'. It was decided to give a grant from the Company funds for this. 113, 816 Spr. BAINBRIDGE L. evacuated from area and struck of no works. Lists 1 & 2 visited WATERLOO. Lt. C.G.T. COUPER M.C. R.E.(T)	fm
	25/1/19	-	and 15 H, 615 Spr. MARCH H. proceeded for demobilization	fm

(A7092). Wt. W12859/M1293. 75,000. 1/17. D. D. & L., Ltd. Forms/C.2118/14.

Army Form C. 2118.

WAR DIARY
or
INTELLIGENCE SUMMARY.
(Erase heading not required.)

400th (HIGHLAND) FIELD COY R.E.

Instructions regarding War Diaries and Intelligence Summaries are contained in F.S. Regs., Part II. and the Staff Manual respectively. Title pages will be prepared in manuscript.

Place	Date	Hour	Summary of Events and Information	Remarks and references to Appendices
MAMAGE I.I.C.5.2 Sheet 46 1/40 0 G.	26/1/19	—	Church parade. Rest 3 and half of H.Q. dressers invalid WATERLOO.	JP
	27/1/19	09.00	Joiners carried on with latrine seats, sentry boxes and Blackboards. 6 other ranks, joiners, attd from 1/4th BLACK WATCH for repair work.	M
		10.30	Building construction class started. Practice cross country run was held over a 3 miles course. 2nd Lieut. A.M. LAURIE R.E.(T) proceeded on special leave to U.K.	M
	28/1/19	09.00	Work as yesterday. Bunch class 10.30 - 1200 hours. Lecture on "AGRICULTURAL SCIENCE" at 19.30 hours.	M
	29/1/19	09.00	Work as yesterday. Practice cross country run was held over a course of 4 miles.	M
	30/1/19	09.00	Work as yesterday. Building construction class was held from 10.30 hours. Nos. 554,271 Spr. THORNHILL D.C. evacuated from area struck off.	M
	31/1/19	09.00	Work as yesterday	M

Alterations in Company Strength during JANUARY 1919.

	Offrs.	O.R.
Company Strength at 31.12.18.	7	206
Increase	Nil.	
Decrease Demobilized 2 Offs. 27 O.R.	-2	-27
Evacuated sick H.O.R.		-4
Company Strength at 31.1.19	5	175

1/2/19
Major
O.C. 400 (H) Fd Coy RE

CONFIDENTIAL

WAR DIARY

of

400th (HIGHLAND) FIELD COY. R.E.

for

FEBRUARY 1919.

Army Form C. 2118.

WAR DIARY
or
INTELLIGENCE SUMMARY.
(Erase heading not required.)

400TH (HIGHLAND) FIELD COY. R.E.

Place	Date	Hour	Summary of Events and Information	Remarks and references to Appendices
MANAGE T.I.C.S.2 Sheet 46 Belgium.	1/2/19	09.00	Company parade. Clean fatigue dress. Parts employed removing wire from dump at LA CROYERE (M.16 c. Sheet 46) to Bn. H.Q. 4 gunners attached from infantry worked on lathing seats & benches. N°. 422,566 Driver DOW A. returned to U.K. for dispersal. Struck off strength from 11/1/19. N°. 530,352 Spr. LASHBROOK E. posted to 20th T.F. Depot 29/1/19.	✓
	2/2/19	00.00 10.15	Church parade for R.C's. Check parade for all other ranks at 10.15 hours. Church parade for Presbyterians. N°. H66,590 Spr. McGUILL M. posted to 20th T.F. Depot 9.1.19. The following N.C.O's and men proceeded to XXIIIrd Corps Concentration Camp. For dispersal.- H00,254 Spr. MURRISON L., H02,664 Dr. DUNBAR R. H00,113 2/Cpl. DUNCAN A.G., H10,315 Spr. WOOD C.P., H00,292 Spr. LEHANET, H00,523 Cpl. MATHIESON H., H00,520 2/Cpl. HAY R., H00,552 Spr. FERGUSON W., H00,521 Spr. DAVIDSON A., H00,126 Spr. COOPER P.L., H00,057 Sergt. GRIFFETH, H12,724 Spr. PEACOCK D., HH6901 Spr. SAVAGE F., 21394 Spr. WYCHERLEY W.A., 12,365 Sergt. BUSHELL J. H0,262 Spr. STEELE S., H00,218 Spr. SMITH R., H20,431 Spr. M'TURK G., H0010 C.S.M. WEBSTER W.M. H00,193 Spr. REID M., H00,038 Spr. HUNTER J., H139,16 Spr. BROWN W., H00,110 DYMERON H. 02,890 Spr. MICHAEL H. Evacuated to hospital and struck off strength. H00,367 Dr. DOUGLAS A.Y. Major T.T. ARGENT, A.C, R.E. takes over duties of O/C R.E. Section 7. S.H amalgamated owing to reduction of strength, through demobilization.	✓
	3/2/19	09.00	Section paraded clean fatigue dress and worked on improvements to billets, loading stores etc.	✓

Army Form C. 2118.

WAR DIARY
or
INTELLIGENCE SUMMARY.
(Erase heading not required.)

400TH (HIGHLAND) FIELD COY RE

Instructions regarding War Diaries and Intelligence Summaries are contained in F. S. Regs., Part II. and the Staff Manual respectively. Title pages will be prepared in manuscript.

Place	Date	Hour	Summary of Events and Information	Remarks and references to Appendices
MANAGE I.1.C.5.2. Sheet 40 Belgium.	3/2/19 (cont'd)	09.00	Infantry Joiners worked on sentry Boxes, desks & forms. Reinforcement from Hospital 113,8/60 Spr BAINBRIDGE L.	(2)
	4/2/19	09.00	Company paraded and worked as yesterday.	(1)
	5/2/19	09.00	Company proceeded to baths at BESONREUX (H.3.b Sheet 40.) A medical inspection was held on return to Coy. H.Q.	(1)
	6/2/19	09.00	Company paraded. Fatigue times & suppers work on repairs to baths at SENEFFE (C.1.H.d. Sheet 40.) Remainder worked on stores and cleaning up Chateau grounds.	(1)
	7/2/19	09.00	Work as yesterday. 3 Infantry Joiners returned to unit. 1 Lieut T. DUNSIRE RE returned from Pillbox Work Coy.	(1)
	8/2/19		No work. Coy MO. over it Lieut T. DUNSIRE RE recommitted site of new refill dump for A.S.C. at Marche-lez-ECAUSSINES. (B.e.b Sheet 40) 521,241 Spr THORNHILL D.C., 136,120 D'MANN G reinforcement from Hospital. The following N.C.O. and men proceeded for demobilization:— H00,022 L/Cpl TAIT A., H00,221 D'NOBLE D., H00,540 Spr WOODBURN J.	(1)
	9/2/19	10.00	Church Parade for R.C.'s and 10.45 Church Parade for C. of E. A party of 12 ors under H00,100 Sergt CRAIG G proceed to ECAUSSINES to commence work on refill dump. 2 Sappers worked on erection of bath plant at GODARVILLE (I.16.b Sheet 40). 2 Sappers employed erecting Field Oven at La CROYERE. Remainder of Coy. on Fatigues.	(1)
	10/2/19			(2)

A5834 Wt W4973/M687 750,000 8/16 D.D. & L. Ltd. Forms/C.2118/13.

Army Form C. 2118.

WAR DIARY
or
INTELLIGENCE SUMMARY.
(Erase heading not required.)

400TH (HIGHLAND) FIELD COY R.E.

Place	Date	Hour	Summary of Events and Information	Remarks and references to Appendices
MANAGE I.C.52. Sheet 46 Belgium	11/2/19	09.00	Work on yesterday. N° 43035 L/Cpl. REAY J. returned on U.K. for shipyard, which proceeded from 15/1/19.	
	12/2/19	09.00	Work as yesterday.	
	13/2/19	09.00	Work as yesterday. The following men proceeded U.K. for shipyard:- 143360 Spr. WATT R., 108199 Spr. LEWIS A., 212,080 Spr. BRADLEY P.R. Evacuated to hospital and struck off for seven days, 143531 Spr. HEWITT T.	
	14/2/19	09.00	Work as yesterday. Remainder of Infantry attached returned to units on completion of course. Works on Docks at GODARVILLE postponed until further notice.	
	15/2/19		'No work carried out. N° H00,213 D/ WEBSTER J. appointed A/L Cpl. was H00,022 A/Cpl. TAIT A. demobilised. The following N.C.O.s and men proceeded to XXIIIrd Corps Concentration Camp for disposal:- H00,100 Sergt. CRAIG G., H00,015 Cpl. MITCHELL A., H00,135 Cpl. GILLESPIE W., H00,172 2/Cpl. PARK J., 454,254 L/Cpl. JOHNSTON R., H00,069 L/Cpl. THOMSON F., H00,064 D/ ALLAN D., 80,025 Spr. BREWSTER G., H00,235 Spr. BROWN T., 212,019 Spr. CATON J., H20,061 D/ COOPER J., H00,054 Spr. DONOHUE R., H02,641 D/ GREIG J., H00,080 D/ GRIEVE A., H00,099 Spr. GIBSON W., 300,395 Spr. HAMPSON T., H02,601 Spr. KEITH A., H08,198 Spr. LAIRD J., 143,422 Spr. MARTIN G., H00,117 D/ McKAY R., 103,340 Spr. McKENZIE G., 140,986 Spr. McLENNAN J., H00,199 Spr. McLEOD A.B., 23,483 Spr. OSBORNE G., H00,17 Spr. OSBORNE J., 219,883 D/ PAGE A.T., 32H,H89 Spr. POTTER G., H00,238 Spr. ROSS M., H0H,410 Spr. SHEPPARD R., H00,244 Spr. WILSON J., 145,805 Spr. PACEY W.	

Army Form C. 2118.

WAR DIARY
or
INTELLIGENCE SUMMARY.
(Erase heading not required.)

400th (HIGHLAND) FIELD COY R.E.

Instructions regarding War Diaries and Intelligence Summaries are contained in F. S. Regs., Part II. and the Staff Manual respectively. Title pages will be prepared in manuscript.

Place	Date	Hour	Summary of Events and Information	Remarks and references to Appendices
MANAGE. I.1.e.5.2.	15/2/19 (cont'd)	—	1 Lt. T. DUNSIRE R.E. and 1 Lt. R.G.T. WATSON R.E., detailed for duty as Draft Conducting Officers, left for XXII Corps Concentration Camp.	B
	16/2/19 10.00		Church Parade for R.C.'s. No other services.	B
Sheer-to. Belgium.	17/2/19 09.00		Field day at LA CROYERE completed. Company work on improvements to stables and cleaning and dressing around. 11 Zappers attacked to Mounted Section to make up strength. Horses demobilised	B
	18/2/19 09.00		Work as yesterday. Party of fifteen paraded for Races at MONS.	B
	19/2/19 09.00		Work as yesterday. Party paraded for Boxing Finals at MONS.	B
	20/2/19 09.30		Bank at BESONRIEUX. Bridge over canal at C.26.a.7. reported dangerous where it had been mined & charges withdrawn. Two sappers on duty proceed. LIEUT A.M. LAURIE. R.E.(T) rejoined from leave.	B
	21/2/19 09.00		Coy Parade, Clean fatigue, work on stables, horses, grooming with ashes. Horses paraded & 22 selected for sale by A.D.V.S. 51st (H) Div." The following N.C.O's & men proceeded to XXII Corps Concentration Camp for dispersal :— 400,527. Cpl. ANDERSON A., 400,261. L/Cpl. FISHER W., 414524. Sp. CULLEN M, 400,326 Spr. GORDON J., 400,069. Dvr. HAMILTON G., 400,334. Dvr. LENNON J., 136,780. Dvr. MANN G., 81,149. Spr. MURPHY J., 400,514. Dvr & McKELLAR G., 541675. Spr. PEALL W.R. 400,061. Dvr & PATON J., 249,677. Spr. SOUTHCOTT J., 400,030. Dvr. URE J., 400,140. Dvr. WRIGHT G., 5484-12. Spr. WARWICK J., 472,630. Sapr. HAY.G.	B
	22/2/19	—	No Work.	B

Army Form C. 2118.

WAR DIARY
or
INTELLIGENCE SUMMARY.

(Erase heading not required.)   400TH (HIGHLAND) FIELD Coy. R.E.

Place	Date	Hour	Summary of Events and Information	Remarks and references to Appendices
MANAGE I.I.C.5.2. Sheet 46. BELGIUM.	23/2/19	09.30	Sappers detailed to proceed with horses for sale.	
	24/2/19		Twenty one horses & one mule sold by Auction at LA LOUVIERE (H.27.2.4). Two Sappers employed on repairs to Bath at SENEFFE. All tools, carts & bridging stores removed to Chateau BOUGARD (I.1.C.4.2.) & placed under cover.	
	25/2/19	09.00	12 Sappers & Infantry work on approach to bridge over GANAL MANAGE-SENEFFE ROAD.	
	26/2/19	06.00	Party marched to Corps race meeting MONS. Remainder work on fatigues &c. No.155,443 Spr ATTWOOD J. proceeded to XVII Corps Concentration Camp for dispersal.	
	27/2/19	09.00	Men employed cleaning & oiling wagons & dismantling huts at GODARVILLE. No.493,453, SAPR HEWITT T. (Agonea)(Reinforcement from Hospital)	
	28/2/19	09.00	Baths at SENEFFE dismantled. Remainder work as yesterday.	

ALTERATIONS IN COMPANY STRENGTH DURING FEBY. 1919.

Coy. Strength on 31.1.19.   5. Off.   195. O.R.
Increase:- From Hospital   5. "
                                   ―――――――――――
                                   5. "   180   "
Decrease:- Demobilized   O.R. 1.
            Evac Sick   3.
                                  ――――   4   "
                                   ―――――――――――
Coy. Strength on 28/2/1919.   5. Off   176. O.R.

28-2-19.   M Grant
                                            MAJOR. R.E.
                                  O.C. 400TH (HIGHLAND) FIELD Coy. R.E.

CONFIDENTIAL.

WAR DIARY

OF

400TH (HIGHLAND) FIELD COY. R.E.

FOR

MARCH 1919.

Army Form C. 2118.

WAR DIARY
or
INTELLIGENCE SUMMARY.
(Erase heading not required.)

400th (HIGHLAND) FIELD COY. R.E.

Place	Date	Hour	Summary of Events and Information	Remarks and references to Appendices
MANAGE I.C.52 Sheet 46	1/3/19	09.00	Inspection Parade by O.C., dress Drill Order	
Belgium	2/3/19	11.00	Church Parade for C. of E. Orders received from C.R.E. to reconnoitre canals in the 153 Bde Area	
	3/3/19	09.00	MAJOR J.T. ARGENT M.C. R.E. with 2/Lt E.M.F. FERGUSSON R.E.(T) and a party of men left 09.00 hrs to reconnoitre BRUSSELS-CHARLEROI CANAL. They started from D.5.05.08 and worked to D.6.25.20 (Sheet BRUSSELS 6 1/100,000) taking width and average depth of water, details of banks & locks for possible prepared area which could be flooded. Remainder of Coy work on clearing wagons and repairs to stables	
	4/3/19	07.00	O.C. and same party carried on with reconnaissance on side of canal. They started from LUTTRE E.6.48.05 (BRUSSELS Sheet 6 1/100,000) and worked back to D.6.25.20 thus finishing the reconnaissance. Remainder carried on as yesterday. H.C.412.599 DRIVER FULTON J. evacuated from area sick, and struck off strength	
	5/3/19	09.00	Company Parade safe/pers carried on with erection of ballast cleaning wagons. Sappers MAJOR J.T. ARGENT M.C. R.E. & II Lt E.M.F. FERGUSSON R.E.(T) left for ANTWERP on 3 days leave	
	6/3/19	09.00	Work on yesterday	

WAR DIARY
or
INTELLIGENCE SUMMARY.
(Erase heading not required.)

Army Form C. 2118.

400TH (HIGHLAND) FIELD COY R.E.

Place	Date	Hour	Summary of Events and Information	Remarks and references to Appendices
MAHAGE Hut 52	1/3/19	09.00	Work party yesterday	/B
(Hut 46 Brussels)	8/3/19	09.00	Check parade. O.C. & 2/Lt FERGUSSON R.E.(T) returned from ANTWERP. 3 mules transferred to Army of Occupation. 2 light draught horses evacuated to mobile.	/B
	9/3/19		Orders received to send 14 L.D. horses for sale in 10th inst. Sappers detailed to accompany horses / parade for instructions	/B
	10/3/19		14.L.D. horses sold by Auction. Remainder of company work on cleaning wagon harness & checking stores. 2/Lt T DUNSIRE R.E. rejoined from Divl Conducting duty	/B
	11/3/19	09.00	Sappers now released from care of horses work on cleaning & disinfecting harness, cleaning wagons & tools. 2/Lt R.G.T. WATSON R.E. reported from Sch of Engineering duty. LIEUT A.M LAURIE R.E.(T) left for 3 day leave to ANTWERP. 400,026 L/Cpl BROWN J & 551,044 SAPR SIMONS A returned UK hospital under A.F. Z.10 & struck off strength	/B
	12/3/19	09.00	Work as yesterday	/B
	13/3/19	09.00	Work party as yesterday	/B

Army Form C. 2118.

WAR DIARY
or
INTELLIGENCE SUMMARY.
(Erase heading not required.)

400th (Highland) FIELD Coy R.E.

Instructions regarding War Diaries and Intelligence Summaries are contained in F. S. Regs., Part II. and the Staff Manual respectively. Title pages will be prepared in manuscript.

Place	Date	Hour	Summary of Events and Information	Remarks and references to Appendices
MANAGE I.16.62 (Sheet 46.) (Belgium)	14/3/19	09.00	Work as yesterday. Interviewed for precautions under A.O. XIV of £21/1/19 to proceed to 64th FIELD Coy R.E. Army of Rhine on 16th instant. Kit inspection.	
	15/3/19	09.00	worked at 14.00 hours LIEUT A. M. LAURIE rejoined from leave Check Parade. Stores moved from N.Q. Stables to CHATEAU BOUZARD I.C.31.	
	16/3/19	11.00	Message received from CRE that MAJOR J.T. ARGENT, LIEUT A. M. LAURIE, RET. & 2nd LIEUT R.G.T. WATSON, R.E. will be the three officers in readiness to proceed on posting to the 209th FIELD Coy R.E. (34th DIV)	
		19.30	The following men proceeded to join the 64th FIELD Coy R.E. Army of Rhine:- SAPPERS No 244,316 MASLEN A, 466,420 BARNBROOK A. 466,598 NIXON F. 446,861 GOODWIN A. 215830 LONGWORTH J. 526,129 CLAYSON H. 412812 MURRAY J. 213,497 HASTINGS F. 160431 GRIFFITH G. 400581 WRIGHT R. 265,512 BENNETT A. 167970 OAKLEY C.K. 398754. DAVIES J.R. 409298 McINTOSH G. 230989 HESSELTINE T. 186,648 GUILLEMARD E. 446,966 HEAD C.J. 255,230. DRIV HOPPER W. 526,264 DRIV PARKER H.	
	17/3/19	09.00	Men carrying cleaning harness &c. No 465,970 SAP. DAVIDSON H. posted to No 20 T.F. DEPOT.	

Army Form C. 2118.

WAR DIARY
or
INTELLIGENCE SUMMARY.
(Erase heading not required.)

400TH (HIGHLAND) FIELD COY. R.E.

Instructions regarding War Diaries and Intelligence Summaries are contained in F. S. Regs., Part II. and the Staff Manual respectively. Title pages will be prepared in manuscript.

Place	Date	Hour	Summary of Events and Information	Remarks and references to Appendices
MANAGE I L 52 (Sheet 46) (Belgium)	18/3/19	09.00	Work as usual. The following appointments to promoted made (Authority E.R & Regt Order No. 264 dt 14/3/19):- 400,268 2/Cpl BURROWS W. to be A/Cpl, 400,014 L/Cpl McDONALD J. to be A/Cpl, 400,191 L/Cpl McLUCKIE R. to be A/2/Cpl, 454,690 L/Cpl GREEN J.K. to be A/2/Cpl, 63,727 L/Cpl COLLYER A.T. to be A/2/Cpl, 400,213 A/L/Cpl WEBSTER J. to be A/2/Cpl. At (Authority E.R & Regt Order No. 268 dt 16/3/19):- 554,271 SAPPER THORNHILL D.C., 472,083 SAPPER TURNER W.H., 184,034 SAPPER CROFT T. to be A/L/Cpls (Paid)	✓
	19/3/19	09.00	Work as yesterday. LIEUT K.N. MORHAM R.E.(T) reported on posting from 401ST FIELD COY R.E. to take over the duties of O.C. Coy from the 20th instant. The following men proceeded to XXII Corps Boxing Championships for Dispersal:- SAPPERS:- 400,082 RAMSAY R., 69,595 BENTLEY R., 550,860 OLIVER R.L., 504,524 MASLEN C., 496,590 BARTLEY H., 471,730 WARD F.C., 400,184 MURPHY R. DRIVERS:- 400,060 GROAT J., 400,144 STEWART D., 400,306 O'DONNELL A., 400,308 STRACHAN R., 526,184 PETTITT S.	✓
	20/3/19	09.00	Work as usual. Orders received from C.R.E. for MAJOR J.T. ARGENT M.C.R.E. LIEUT A.M. LAURIE R.E.(T), 2/LIEUT R.G.T. WATSON R.E. to proceed to 209TH FIELD COY R.E. by train leaving MONS 04.00 hrs on 21st for COLOGNE.	✓
		18.30	MAJOR J.T. ARGENT M.C.R.E., LIEUT A.M. LAURIE R.E.(T) & 2/LIEUT R.G.T. WATSON R.E.	

Army Form C. 2118.

WAR DIARY
or
INTELLIGENCE SUMMARY.

(Erase heading not required.)

400TH (HIGHLAND) FIELD COY R.E.

Place	Date	Hour	Summary of Events and Information	Remarks and references to Appendices
MANAGE Lic 52 (cold) (Sheet 46) BELGIUM	20/3/19		left MANAGE in box car for MONS en route to join 209th FIELD COY R.E.	W.J.M.
	21/3/19	09.00	N° 360.065. SAPR MULLERY F. posted to 209th FIELD COY R.E. N° 400,127. L/Cpl/S/Sgt McNEILL C. proceeded to XXII CORPS CONCENTN CAMP for Dispersal	W.J.M.
	22/3/19	09.00	Work as usual. N° 300,966. SAPR CHAPMAN A.R. posted to 64TH FIELD COY R.E.	W.J.M.
		20.00	Warning orders & details of proposed move of Coy recd on 26th instant for Port of Embarkation received from C.R.E.	
	23/3/19		No work	W.J.M.
	24/3/19	09.00	Work on pack King of wagons	W.J.M.
	25/3/19	09.00	Work on packing wagons. Remainder of Coy horses (14) handed over to Machine Gun Battalion for Army of Occupation	W.J.M.
	26/3/19	09.00	Work on loading wagons & on to one also erection of latrines at MANAGE STN. 2/Lieut J.R. McEWAN R.E. posted from 401st Field Coy to 400th Field Coy to complete Cadre Establishment. N° 299494. SAPR ROGERS H. posted to 64TH FIELD COY. R.E. Army of Occupation	W.J.M.
	27/3/19	09.00	Work as yesterday	W.J.M.

WAR DIARY
or
INTELLIGENCE SUMMARY.

Army Form C. 2118.

400TH (Highland) Field Coy R.E

Place	Date	Hour	Summary of Events and Information	Remarks and references to Appendices
MANAGE	28/3/19	09.00	Work as yesterday.	K.W.M.
I.C.5.2.	29/3/19		As above.	K.W.M.
(Sheet 46)	30/3/19		No. 412599 Dvr. FULTON T reported (reinforcement from Base Depot)	K.W.M.
BELGIUM	31/3/19	09.00	Work on packing up & checking stores	K.W.M.
			ALTERATIONS IN COMPANY STRENGTH DURING MARCH 1919	
			STRENGTH ON 28-2-19:— — — — — — — — 5 Offs/2 146. O.Rks	
			INCREASE:- Posted from 401 Field Coy RE 2 " " "	
			TOTAL:— — → 7 " " 146	
			DECREASE:- DEMOBILISED 1 Off 95 O.Rks	
			Posted to 209TH Field Co RE 3 " 1 " "	
			" " 64TH " " " — " 21 " "	
			To HOSPITAL (off STRENGTH) — " 1 " "	
			4 " 118	
			STRENGTH of Coy on 31/3/19:— — — —→ 3 Offs/2 58 O.Rks	
			[signature] K.M. Mackern LIEUT. R.E.	
			O.C., 400TH (HIGHLAND) FIELD COY R.E	

51st Div.

CONFIDENTIAL.

WAR DIARY

of

400TH (HIGHLAND) FIELD COY R.E.

From

1/4/19 to 10/4/19 INCLUSIVE.

Army Form C. 2118.

WAR DIARY
OR
INTELLIGENCE SUMMARY.
(Erase heading not required.)

400TH (HIGHLAND) FIELD Coy. R.E.

Place	Date	Hour	Summary of Events and Information	Remarks and references to Appendices
MANAGE 1.1.c.5.2. (Sheet 46) BELGIUM	1/4/19	09.00	Work on cleaning wagons & packing harness. Forecast of entraining arrangements for 63rd div, 51st & 52nd Divisions received from C.R.E. with orders for the destination "GAILES" to be painted on all wagons.	
	2/4/19	09.00	Coy work as yesterday	L.N.Lb
	3/4/19	09.00	Coy work as yesterday	L.N.Lb
	4/4/19	09.00	Coy work as yesterday	L.N.Lb
	5/4/19	09.00	Coy work as yesterday. O.C. 9. 2nd LIEUT McEWAN visited COURRIERE - L.3 - VILLE (B.10.a) to value a German Dynamo left by the Germans. Report sent to C.R.E. Phone message received from C.R.E. at 18.15 hours that Coy will entrain on 7th instant at 09.30 hours at MANAGE STATION	L.N.Lb
	6/4/19	09.00	Coy paraded 09.00 hours and every available man proceeded to LA LOUVIERE (H.4) for bath and change of clothes.	L.N.Lb
	7/4/19	09.00	Two horses were sent from H.Q. Train A.S.C. to shift wagons to loading bank in Station. By 15.00 hrs all wagons were entrained. Coy paraded 19.30 hours and marched to station. The train moved off at 19.45 hours	L.N.Lb
	8/4/19	03.00	The troops on train were ent [?] tea with tea at 09.00 with breakfast	L.N.Lb

Army Form C. 2118.

WAR DIARY
or
INTELLIGENCE SUMMARY.
(Erase heading not required.)

400th (HIGHLAND) FIELD COY R.E.

Place	Date	Hour	Summary of Events and Information	Remarks and references to Appendices
DUNKIRK	8/4/19	12.15	Arrived DUNKIRK and detrained at 13.15 hrs. Coy marched to Reception Camp where they had dinner & tea. Fixed up for the night.	K.M.M.
Do	9/4/19	09.00	A party went off to the Docks to unload from & man-handle their gear into position for loading on the boat. The party marched back to Camp & the whole Coy paraded in full marching order and proceeded to the Embarkation Camp about 4 Kilos distant, where they passed the night. During the day the O.C. Lieut. K.H. MORHAM R.E.(T) proceeded to WIMEREUX, BOULOGNE to clear Imprest Account & 2/Lieut. J.R. McEWAN was left in command of the Coy	E.M.M.
Do	10/4/19	15.45	Coy paraded and marched to the Docks. At 16.50 hrs they embarked on S.S. KOURSK which carried ladies of 1 Field Coy, 2 Field Ambulance, 1 Signal Coy & 3 Infy Battns. all of the 51st (H.) Divn. The boat pulled out at 19.30 hours. During the day No. 400,367 DVR. DOUGLAS.A. rejoined from Hospital, having proceeded from MANAGE on 8th.	A.M.M.

Army Form C. 2118.

WAR DIARY
or
INTELLIGENCE SUMMARY.
(Erase heading not required.)

400TH (HIGHLAND) FIELD COY. R.E.

ALTERATIONS IN COY STRENGTH FROM 1/4/19 to 10/4/19.

COY STRENGTH at 31/3/19   3 Offrs.   58. O. Ranks

INCREASE:- Reinforcement from Hospital —   1   "
                                         ___   ___
                                         3   59

DECREASE:- To Army of Occupation   1   "
           Demobilised (from leave) —   1   "
                                        ___   ___
STRENGTH on 10/4/19   2   " 58 "

K. W. Morham. LIEUT R.E. (T)
O.C. 400TH (HIGHLAND) FIELD COY R.E.

www.ingramcontent.com/pod-product-compliance
Lightning Source LLC
Chambersburg PA
CBHW080842010526
44114CB00017B/2358